THE GEOGRAPHER'S WAY 2

Geography for the Junior Certificate

Tony Dunne

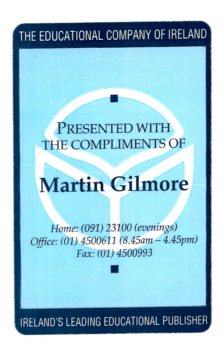

The Educational Company of Ireland

First published 1995
The Educational Company of Ireland
Ballymount Road
Walkinstown
Dublin 12

A trading unit of Smurfit Services Limited
© 1995 Tony Dunne

Design and Layout: Peanntrónaic Teo.
Cover design: Design Image
Illustrations and maps: Daghda
Colour Reproduction: Impress Communications Group Ltd.
Printed in the Republic of Ireland by Smurfit Web Press

Acknowledgements
In particular I wish to thank Tom Marmion for his encouragement at the initial stages of this project and for his very active involvement in the planning, writing and development of this book.

I also wish to thank the following:
Margaret Dunne for her constant support, encouragement and word processing.
Anthony Murray, Editor, The Educational Company, for his patience and hard work.
The students, staff and management of Holy Child, Community School, Sallynoggin, and in particular my colleagues in the Geography Department for their comments and advice.
Seamus Cannon, Director, Tom Mac Mahon, Lil Lynch and Evelyn Logan, all of The Blackrock Teachers' Centre for their advice and support especially with computers.
Colm Regan, Head of Education, and Anne Kinsella, librarian, Trócaire for their assistance in sourcing information.
Elaine Kelly Conroy, St David's Secondary School, Greystones and Sr. Jacinta Prunty, University College Dublin, for commenting on an early draft of Book One.

The publishers would like to acknowledge the assistance of the following in the preparation of this book.
Royal Netherlands Embassy; Aerocamera-Bart Hofmeester; Irish Life; Bord Na Móna; Shannon Development Photo Library; Tara Mines; Telegraph Colour Library; Science Photo Library; Oxford Scientific Films; Dorothy Harrison, Trócaire; Inter Nationes, Bonn; Steve Treacy; Dr. Peter Foss, Irish Peatland Conservation Council; Tony Hurst Associates; The Ordnance Survey.

0 1 2 3 4 5 6 7 8 9

CONTENTS

1	Building the Crust: Internal Forces	5
2	External Forces 1: Mass Movement	21
3	External Forces 2: The work of Rivers	33
4	External Forces 3: The work of Moving Ice	48
5	External Forces 4: The work of the Sea	67
6	Variations in Temperature	87
7	Pressure and Wind	100
8	Climate	115
9	Vegetation	130
10	Settlements	143
11	The Growth of Towns	160
12	The Structure of Towns	169
13	Population Growth	179
14	Population: Density and Distribution	194
15	Population Structure	207
16	Primary Industries	217
17	Energy	233
18	Local Farm Study	247
19	The Location of Manufacturing Industry	259
20	Industrialisation	272
21	Tourism	286
22	Inequality	303
23	Inequality and Development 1	318
24	Inequality and Development 2	334
25	Map and Photograph Section	348
	Index	368

PREFACE

The Geographer's Way aims to lead students through the Junior Certificate Geography Syllabus in a fresh, active way. It is designed to provide a path through the concepts, knowledge and skills required by the course while introducing the settings, attitudes, vocabulary and correlated ideas in a sequence which is manageable and interesting. Great care has been taken to chose photographs and maps of suitable size to illustrate the work and to provide a basis for study and activity. Encouraging an appreciation of the environment is central to the approach, as is the development of an awareness of the issues of poverty and inequality in the world.

Book Two builds on the foundation laid in Book One. Though more content-based, it continues the same active approach to the subject. Taken together, the two books of the series cover all aspects of the Junior Certificate Syllabus and provide ample material to prepare for the Junior Certificate examination. The following features are integral to the approach:

- Emphasis on students' involvement in their own learning.
- Ideas, concepts and skills introduced in a way which makes them relevant.
- The work is graded in difficulty. Each stage is designed and written for the target age group. Language levels, concepts and skills are developed accordingly.
- Signposts make clear the ideas and skills covered in each chapter.
- Plenty of activities of great variety are provided after each section. It is not intended that all the activities should be done. The teacher has a wide choice from which to select classwork and homework.
- Revision exercises throughout allow the teacher to gauge and review progress before going to a new topic. The revision sections also provide excellent material for exam preparation.
- The work is built on the study of photographs and maps. As soon as possible the 1:50,000 O.S. maps are introduced. The 1:25,000 and 'Town Plan' scales are also studied.
- Topics and exercises for Higher Level are included. These are clearly indicated by a bar in the margin like the one opposite.
- Key words are printed in bold like **this**. All words in bold are included in the revision exercises. The index provides a rapid reference to most of these words.
- Peters Equal Area Projection Maps of the world are used extensively.

1 Building the Crust: Internal Forces

IN THIS CHAPTER YOU WILL LEARN

- How internal forces shape the Earth's crust.
- The internal structure of the Earth.
- Crustal plates and their constructive and destructive boundaries.
- The Theory of Plate Tectonics.
- How to test an hypothesis.

SHAPING THE CRUST

The upper surface of the crust forms the natural landscape. The crust is not smooth. It is shaped into physical features. These include mountains, valleys and coastlines. Sometimes bare rock appears at the surface. These landforms usually have a rugged appearance. Often there is a thin layer of debris, called **regolith** covering the crust. This is made by weathering and erosion. Sand, scree and soil are three kinds of regolith. Regolith helps to shape the natural landscape by covering rock which is bare. It is easy to shape features formed in the debris because the materials are loose. For instance, wind changes the shape of a sand dune. To change the shape of rock in the crust immense amounts of energy are needed. Yet reshaping of the crust is occurring all the time. It happens in many ways, for example a volcanic eruption, an earthquake, a flood or a rockfall.

Forces inside and outside the Earth cause these changes in the crust. The **internal forces** usually tend to build up the crust, creating folds, ridges and mountains. The **external forces** work in the opposite direction, wearing down features made by the internal forces. Usually we are not aware of these forces as they work very slowly. But they can work quickly, even suddenly, as in the case of eruptions and earthquakes. We will study the internal forces first. Before doing so we must examine the strucure of the Earth.

THE GEOGRAPHER'S WAY 2

THE STRUCTURE OF THE EARTH

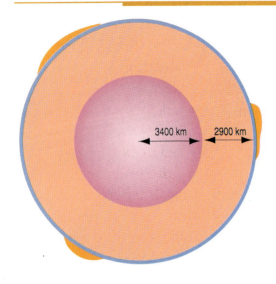

Fig 1.1

The Earth consists of a number of layers around a core. The **core** is very heavy and extremely hot. Surrounding the core there is a layer of hot, almost liquid, rock called the **mantle**. This layer is about 2900 kilometres thick. Above the mantle there is the **crust**. In comparison with the mantle, the crust is very thin, like the skin on an apple. Study figure 1.1 which shows the main layers of the Earth.

Scientists know less about the inside of the Earth than they do about Outer Space because they have only penetrated a few miles into it. The tremendous heat and pressure of the interior are the main obstacles. Recently progress has been made in finding out about the crust. Our new knowledge of what is happening in the crust and upper mantle helps us understand how many of our landforms are made.

We have learned three important things about the crust.
Firstly, the crust has two layers. One of these is made of basalt. This heavy, dense rock forms the deeper layer and extends right round the Earth. Granite, a much lighter rock, lies above the basalt layer. Examine figure 1.2 which shows this. Note how the granite forms huge masses

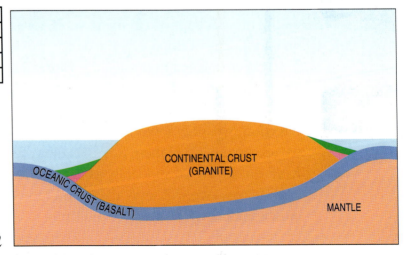

Fig 1.2

BUILDING THE CRUST: INTERNAL FORCES

lying above the basalt. These granite masses are the continents and they actually float on top of the basalt. This means that the continental masses can move around just as a heavy log moves in water. The diagram shows how the basalt forms the floors of the oceans and extends as a continuous layer beneath the continental masses. Usually layers of sedimentary rock cover the basalt on the floor of the ocean near the continents. These sediments are carried down to the sea by rivers and build up over time. They are shown in figure 1.2. Because basalt forms the ocean floors it is sometimes called **oceanic crust**. Granite which forms the continents is called **continental crust**.

Secondly, we now know that the earth's crust is broken up into large pieces called **plates**. There are seven large plates and a number of smaller ones. The main plates are shown on the map in figure 1.3. Notice how a plate may consist of both continental and oceanic crust. Or a plate may be made only of oceanic crust; in this case it forms the ocean floor.

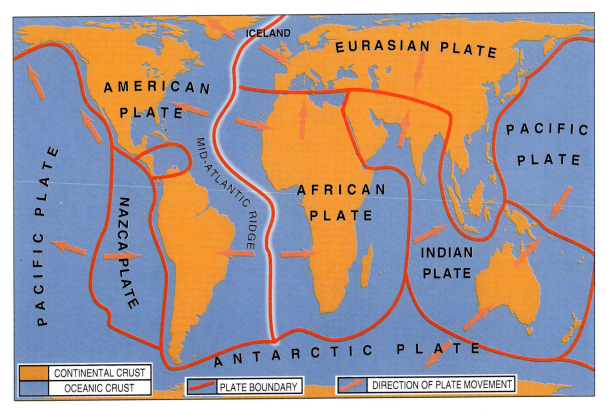

Fig 1.3

Thirdly, the plates move around. This movement is usually slow, as little as 1 cm per year but it can be as much as 9 cms a year. The movement of the plates is caused by their being carried by great currents in the mantle which flow slowly beneath the crust. These

THE GEOGRAPHER'S WAY 2

massive flows of almost liquid rock are the internal forces which help to shape our landscape. Differences of heat and pressure are believed to cause the mantle currents. The directions in which the various plates move are shown in figure 1.3.

ACTIVITY 1

1. Copy the diagram in figure 1.1 into your copy.
   (a) Identify the different layers of the internal structure of the Earth with neat labels.
   (b) Show the thickness of each layer using a suitable method.
   (c) Calculate the diameter of the Earth at the Equator given that the ocean and crust is about 12km thick and the continental crust is about 35km thick.

2. Study the map in figure 1.3 then do the following with the help of an atlas.
   (a) Name the seven large plates shown on the map.
   (b) Name the plate on which each of the following countries lie:
       Brazil, Mali, Australia, USA, Ireland, Argentina
   (c) What continents lie on the Eurasian plate?

3. Name a plate which has only one continent on it.

4. Name two plates which have two continents on them.

5. Which plate is made up almost totally of oceanic crust?

6. Name two regions where plates are colliding and two regions where plates are separating.

CONSTRUCTIVE PLATE BOUNDARIES

Study of the plates in figure 1.3 shows that all have edges or **boundaries**. Most of the changes caused by internal forces happen at these boundaries. From figure 1.3 you can also tell how the plates move in different directions. Putting these two ideas together helps us to understand what is happening in the crust.

There are two types of plate boundary. One is where plates are moving towards one another. The other is where plates are moving apart. Figure 1.4 shows what happens when plates move apart. Examine this and refer to it as you read on. The plates A and B are

BUILDING THE CRUST: INTERNAL FORCES

being pulled away from each other by mantle movements at C and D. As the plates are carried apart cracks occur in the crust. These cracks are called **faults**. **Volcanic eruptions** occur when very hot liquid rock called **molten magma** pushes up through faults. When it pours out on the surface magma is known as **lava**. The lava builds up on the ocean floor and cools to become basalt. The basalt forms a ridge along the crack. This is called a **mid-oceanic ridge**. At these ridges new oceanic crust is being formed and is added to the boundaries of the plates. For example in figure 1.4 plate A is being added to at E and plate B is being added to at F. Because new rock is being added to the plates at these

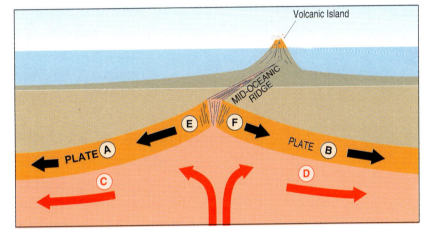

Fig 1.4

boundaries, they are called **constructive boundaries**. Constructive plate boundaries are found where plates are being pulled apart.

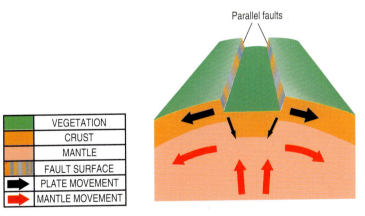

Fig 1.5

Sometimes at constructive plate boundaries faults occur parallel to each other. Then the crust between them can sink down to form a valley. Figure 1.5 shows this. Such valleys are called **rift valleys**. Large rift valleys are found in East Africa, Scotland and on the Rhine river in Germany. Find these rift valleys in your atlas.

The Atlantic Ocean was formed by the American plate moving away from the Eurasian and African plates. A mid-oceanic ridge formed at the boundaries of these plates. This plate movement is still happening, so the Atlantic is slowly widening. Find the Mid-Atlantic

Ridge on the map in figure 1.3. Using the map, work out where other mid-oceanic ridges are likely to be found. Remember to check the directions of plate movement.

Sometimes after many eruptions the mid-oceanic ridge builds up enough to rise above sea-level. Then an island is formed as shown in figure 1.4. Such islands are called **volcanic islands** because they are formed from lava flowing from a fault in the crust. Iceland is a volcanic island made in this way. Notice from figure 1.3 how Iceland lies right on the Mid-Atlantic Ridge. There have been many volcanic eruptions on the island. In 1783 there was a tremendous eruption at a place called Laki. A **fissure** or crack opened up in the crustal rock. It was 35 kms long. The lava flow killed one-fifth of the people in Iceland and covered huge areas of fertile farmland, ruining it. The cooling lava formed a basalt plateau. A **plateau** is a flat-topped upland or mountain. In Ireland the Antrim Plateau was formed by a number of lava-flows like the one at Laki.

Icelanders suffer from volcanic activity but they also benefit. Where there are active volcanoes the ground water is often heated by the rock it touches, so hot springs are common. There are over 800 hot springs in Iceland. These are of great value. Hot water is piped to the homes of Icelanders providing heating and domestic hotwater. Steam from **geysers**, the Icelandic word for a hot spring, is used to generate electricity. Energy of this kind from inside the Earth is called **geothermal** energy. *Geo* means Earth and *thermal* means heat.

ACTIVITY 2

1. Explain what a 'plate' is. Where are plate boundaries found? Why are plate boundaries important?
2. Using diagrams explain how each of the following are formed:
   mid-oceanic ridge, volcanic island, rift valley
3. Explain how Icelanders have suffered and benefited from the volcanic activity on their dangerous island.
4. Research one of the following major eruptions. Your school or local library will help you.
   Mt. St. Helens in 1980, Krakatoa in 1883, Mt. Pélee in 1902.

BUILDING THE CRUST: INTERNAL FORCES

DESTRUCTIVE PLATE BOUNDARIES

Constructive boundaries happen where plates are moving apart. **Destructive boundaries** are found where plates are colliding or moving against each other. Figure 1.6 shows what happens.

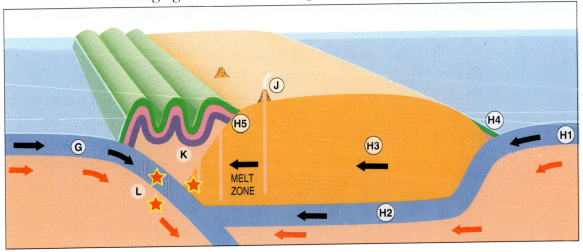

Fig 1.6

Plate G is composed completely of oceanic crust but plate H is different. It has oceanic crust at H1 but continental crust at H3. Notice how the lighter continental crust rock (granite) is floating on the heavier oceanic rock (basalt). Plate H also has layers of sedimentary rocks which have built up on its edges at H4 and H5. These are the sedimentary rocks, referred to on page 7, which formed from sands and clays brought to the sea by rivers.

A number of things happen as the plates collide. We will take these step-by-step.

First, the sedimentary rocks at H5 are put under great pressure. They become like plastic and gradually fold up into mountains. Mountains made in this way are called **fold mountains**. They often form long ridges. Sometimes the pressure is so great that metamorphic rocks are formed: sandstone becomes quartzite; limestone becomes marble and so on.

Second, the heavy oceanic crust of plate G slides down below the lighter continental crust of plate H. As plate G slides down, it bends and eventually cracks. Faults occur at point L. The sudden cracking of the rocks causes shock waves to pass through the crust. These shock waves cause it to shake. This shaking and jerking of the crust is an **earthquake**.

A strong earthquake can shake buildings, dams and bridges to pieces unless they have been specially built to withstand shock. Nowadays earthquake disasters are made worse because powerlines, pipelines and sewers are damaged by the earth tremors. The fires, flooding and disease which follow can do more damage than the earthquake. Shock waves also cause huge waves in the sea known as **tidal waves** or '**tsunamis**'. These cause great loss of life in low-lying coastal areas.

Third, as plate G sinks deeper into the crust it gets hotter till it melts. Then it becomes molten magma. Some of this burns its way to the surface through the rocks to erupt in a volcano. See J in figure 1.6. Other magma forces its way beneath the fold mountains at K. There it bakes the underside of the rocks and changes them into metamorphic rocks. Gradually the magma cools deep inside the folded crust and forms the granite and similar rocks in a **batholith**. These rocks which cool slowly have large crystals. Slow cooling of igneous rocks produces large crystals; fast cooling produces rocks with tiny crystals and a smooth texture. Now you know why granites have large crystals and a rough texture: and why basalts have tiny crystals and a smooth texture. It all depends on where and how fast they cooled down.

From figure 1.6 it is clear that plates are being destroyed when they collide and slide one beneath the other. They are being melted down to make new mantle material. This is the reason why the edge of a plate where this is happening is known as a destructive plate boundary.

ACTIVITY 3

1. Explain why some plate boundaries are 'destructive' ones.
2. Using two simple diagrams explain the difference between a constructive plate boundary and a destructive one.
3. Explain how fold mountains are formed when plates collide.
4. What kind of rock is often found where folding took place?
5. Explain why volcanoes are found where plates are in collision.
6. Explain how some earthquakes happen. Why are earthquakes common at places near plate boundaries?
7. Using an atlas and the map in figure 1.3 identify which plates collided to form the following fold mountain ranges:

    The Alps,   The Atlas,   The Rockies,   The Himalayas,   The Andes

BUILDING THE CRUST: INTERNAL FORCES

TESTING A HYPOTHESIS

One important way in which we learn is to suggest an idea and then test it to see if it is true. We give the name **hypothesis** to the idea or theory to be tried out. Hypothesis testing is a useful skill. We will use it to find out more about volcanoes and earthquakes.

We make the following statement an hypothesis:

"Volcanoes and earthquakes only occur at or near plate boundaries."

To find whether this hypothesis is true or false, we test it against the facts.

The locations of five major volcanoes and five major earthquakes are given. Plot the location of each volcano and each earthquake on the map in figure 1.7. using the latitude and longitude references as a guide.

VOLCANOES		
Cotopaxi	1° S	78° W
Krakatoa	6° S	105° E
Etna	38° N	15° E
Fuji	35° N	138° E
Mt Pélee	15° N	61° W

EARTHQUAKES		
Valparaiso	33° S	72° W
Anchorage	61° N	150° W
Lisbon	39° N	9° W
North Assam	27° N	91° E
Tokyo	36° N	140° E

Fig 1.7

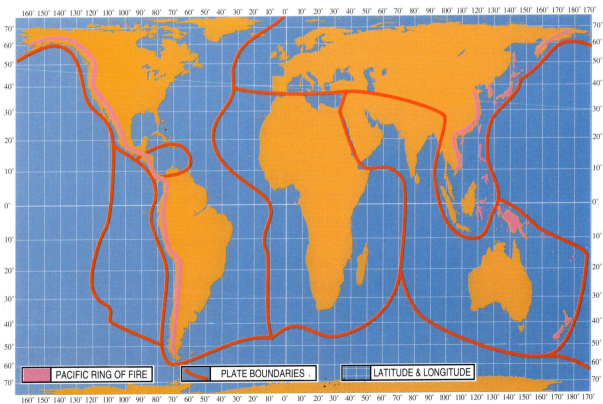

PACIFIC RING OF FIRE — PLATE BOUNDARIES — LATITUDE & LONGITUDE

THE GEOGRAPHER'S WAY 2

When you have plotted the location of the volcanoes and earthquakes on the map, examine their distribution. Find out whether the distribution is related to the location of plate boundaries. Using this information decide whether the hypothesis is true, partly true or false. State your conclusion and explain how you reached it.

PLATE TECTONICS

For many years people have known that volcanoes, earthquakes and fold mountains tended to occur together. Around the edges of the Pacific Ocean there is a zone where there are many fold mountains: for instance, the Andes in Latin America, the Rockies in North America. Volcanoes and earthquakes often happened in this zone. Because of this the zone was given the name **Pacific Ring of Fire**. Famous volcanoes in the 'Ring' include Cotopaxi in Latin America, Mount St. Helens in North America, and Mount Fuji in Japan. Terrible earthquakes have occurred in the zone: at Valparaiso in Latin America, Anchorage in North America and at Tokyo and, very recently, in Kobe in Japan.

Although people realised there was some connection, they did not know what the link was between the folding of mountains, volcanoes and earthquakes. With our knowledge about the crust we can now understand what is happening and realise that they are all the results of movements of mantle material deep inside the Earth. The theory which explains the workings of the crust and mantle is called **Plate Tectonics**. Plates are the large pieces into which the crust is split up. 'Tectonics' means 'knowing how to build'. Plate Tectonics will some day allow scientists to predict when earthquakes and volcanic eruptions are going to happen. In this way millions of lives will be saved and property protected from destruction.

What a contrast this makes with the superstition of the past. One of the most destructive earthquakes in Europe happened in Lisbon on All Saints' Day, 1755. The earthquake destroyed most of the city, including its churches which were full of people because it was a Holy Day. Thirty thousand people were killed, many by falling buildings. A tsunami 9m high washed in over the lower parts of the city drowning many who had rushed to the shore for safety. Fires raging in the ruins killed many more. Because the disaster happened on a Holy Day, the earthquake was taken as a sign from God to warn people to lead better lives. Today we realise that the Lisbon earthquake was due to

BUILDING THE CRUST: INTERNAL FORCES

movement along a fault. This fault was caused by the African Plate colliding with the Eurasian Plate. Look back at the map in figure 1.7 and mark in the location of Lisbon.

ACTIVITY 4

This is an activity to improve your tracing and map drawing skills, so pay particular attention to this aspect of your work.
1. Trace a large map of the world which shows the Pacific Ocean clearly and in one piece, preferably at the centre of the map.
2. Using the map in figure 1.3 draw in the plates of the Pacific region. Identify each with its name. Show the direction of movement of each plate with an arrow.
3. Draw in the Pacific Ring of Fire.
4. Find the places referred to in the 'Hypothesis' section on page 13. Plot these onto your map, using suitable symbols to show volcanoes and earthquakes. (Don't forget your legend.)
5. Draw in the ranges of fold mountains which are found close to the Pacific Ocean.

Suggestion: Keep this map carefully, mounting it on cardboard. Use it to plot the location of any 'tectonic' happening (earthquake or volcano) which is in the news.

MT. VESUVIUS

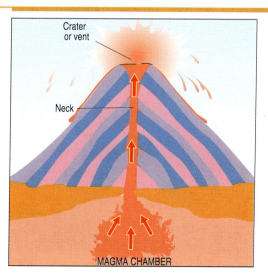

Fig 1.8

Volcanoes can be destructive. They can also benefit people. Mount Vesuvius is an example of this. Mount Vesuvius is an Italian volcano located near the city of Naples. It is a **cone-shaped** volcano. It has this shape because the material it erupts comes out through a **vent** or hole in the crust as shown in figure 1.8. **Crater** is another name for vent. The lava

15

from this volcano is thick so it doesn't flow far from the vent. The lava also contains gases which cause the eruptions to be very explosive. In figure 1.8 you can see that the cone is built up of many layers of ash, cinders and basalt. The ash and cinder layers were formed when the eruptions were explosive. The basalt layers formed when lava poured out of the crater down the mountain. Volcanoes made of layers of ash and basalt are called **composite** volcanoes.

A volcano which has erupted recently is called an **active** volcano. A volcano which has not erupted for a long time but still may be active is known as a **dormant** volcano. Mt. Vesuvius is an active volcano. It erupted in 1944 but its most famous eruption occurred in 79 AD. This was a very violent eruption which blew away the top of the cone. The nearby Roman town of Pompeii was covered in ash. Two thousand people were trapped and smothered by the gases and ash which fell on the town.

Today the area around the volcano is heavily populated. The volcanic ash weathers into a fertile soil, so the land is excellent for arable farming. This is one way people benefit from Mt. Vesuvius. In other parts of the world, the slopes of volcanoes are heavily populated for the same reason. Large numbers of tourists are attracted to the area to see the famous volcano. They also visit the excavated site of Pompeii to find out what life was like two thousand years ago in a Roman town. So eruptions can be of value to people in different ways. They can help people to make a living.

ACTIVITY 5

Fig 1.9

Kilauea volcano, Hawaii

BUILDING THE CRUST: INTERNAL FORCES

1. Draw a picture of a cone-shaped volcano erupting. Use the following words to label it: lava, ash, layers, vent, crater, cinders, gases.
2. Explain how a composite volcanic cone develops.
3. Examine the photograph of Kilauea volcano, Hawaii in figure 1.9, then answer the following questions:
   (a) What type of photograph is it?
   (b) What evidence is there in the photograph to suggest that it is an active volcano?
   (c) Locate Hawaii in your atlas, then plot its location on the map of the Pacific you traced for activity 4 above. Explain why this is an unusual location for a volcano.

PLATE TECTONICS AND IRELAND

Fig 1.10

Ireland is positioned on the Eurasian Plate, well away from a plate boundary. There is little risk of our having volcanoes or earthquakes. We are just being carried along with the rest of our plate and the internal forces at work beneath us have little effect on our part of the crust. This was not always the case. In the distant past Ireland was much closer to plate boundaries. It experienced volcanic eruptions, earthquakes and the folding of mountain ranges.

The map in figure 1.10 shows some of the evidence that Ireland was once shaped violently by internal forces.

Fold mountains The mountains of Counties Cork, Kerry and Waterford are our most recently folded mountains. They are made of sedimentary rocks such as Old Red Sandstone and limestone. More than 200 million years ago these rocks were lying on the edge of one plate when another plate moved against it

17

causing them to fold up into mountain ranges. As the plates were moving mainly from the South, the ridges and valleys ran from West to East. The mountains of Munster still have this pattern today.

Other fold mountains are shown on the map. These are the result of older plate movements. They are in Connacht, Leinster and Ulster. The ridges of these foldings run in a North-east to South-west direction. These very ancient foldings also played a part in shaping Ireland.

Volcanoes The largest volcano in Ireland formed the Antrim Plateau about 60 million years ago. A series of fissure eruptions like those in Iceland built the basalt plateau over millions of years. It covers most of County Antrim and parts of Counties Derry, Tyrone and Armagh. Antrim was then close to the boundary of the Eurasian Plate. The Antrim volcano is now extinct. **Extinct** means it does not erupt any more. Other extinct volcanoes in Ireland are Lambay Island, Vinegar Hill and Slieve Gullion. Find these in your atlas.

Earthquakes Earthquakes have happened in many parts of Ireland. The evidence is found in fault-lines which cross the crustal rocks. At the faults the crust cracked and moved when under pressure. Figure 1.11 shows a quartz vein displaced by a fault. An earthquake caused a fault to form running from A to B. The fault moved in the direction shown by the arrow and the quartz vein was broken and displaced.

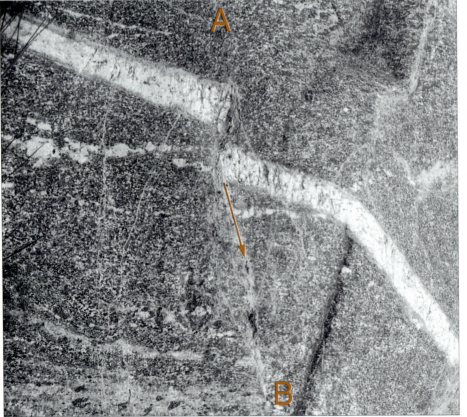

Fig 1.11

2 External Forces 1: Mass Movement

IN THIS CHAPTER YOU WILL LEARN

- The relationship between weathering, erosion and denudation.
- The role of gravity in shaping the crust.
- Rapid, medium and slow mass movements.
- How to do a fieldstudy on local slopes.

EXTERNAL FORCES 1: MASS MOVEMENT

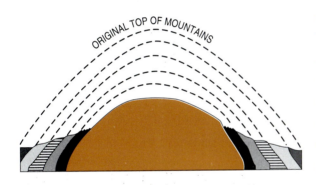

Fig 2.1

Figure 2.1 shows a cross section of the Wicklow Mountains. In it the mountains appear as they do today. The cross section shows that the Wicklow Mountains are made mainly of granite. There are also metamorphic and sedimentary rocks on the eastern and western sides of the granite core. This arrangement of the rocks with granite at the surface and other rocks at the sides raises a question. In Chapter 1 you learned how granite forms deep inside the Earth's crust. How is it that it appears at the surface in the Wicklow Mountains?

The Wicklow granite was not always at the surface. It formed deep inside the mountains which were folded up nearly 400 million years ago. The dotted lines show the mountains as they must have appeared just after they were formed. Then they were possibly 7000 metres high, or even more. Notice that the granite at that time was beneath the sedimentary and metamorphic rocks. Today the granite is exposed because the rocks which covered it have been removed. Weathering and erosion caused them to be stripped away. **Weathering** which you studied in Book 1 is the breaking up and rotting of rock material.

Erosion is the breaking up, carrying away and dropping of debris. The 'carrying away' is called **transport**; the 'dropping' of material is called **deposition**. Rivers, moving ice, wind and waves are the main causes of erosion. We call these the **agents of erosion**. Working together, weathering and erosion wear away the land surface and bring it down to a lower level. Eventually all the debris is moved to the seabed where it is deposited. Sometimes the movement of material can take millions of years. We use the word **denudation** to describe the lowering of the land surface by weathering and erosion.

The forces of denudation are operating all the time. Usually their work is very gradual and slow but given enough time they can make enormous changes in the appearance of the surface of the Earth. Because they work from outside the crust, they are called **external forces**. It is these external forces which stripped away or denuded the sedimentary and metamorphic rocks which once covered the Wicklow granite.

The landscape we see in Wicklow now is the result of two opposing sets of forces. The internal forces caused the movement of plates which built the fold mountains and formed their granite core. The external forces of denudation wore down the fold mountains to their present shape and height.

Before learning more about the agents of erosion which play such an important part in denudation, we must examine the work of gravity in the landscape.

ACTIVITY 1

1. List the external forces which shape the crust of the earth.

2. What is denudation?

3. Copy the flow chart in figure 2.2 into your exercise book. Use the following words to fill in the boxes:
   crust, external forces, landscape, internal forces

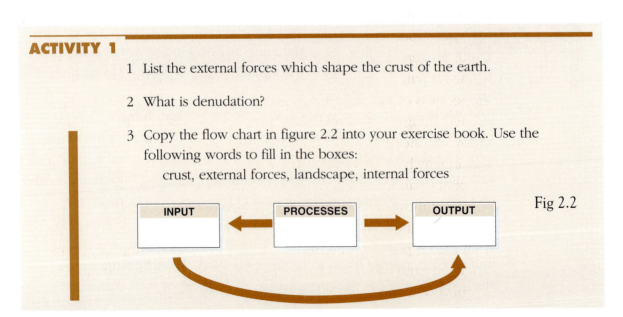

Fig 2.2

EXTERNAL FORCES 1: MASS MOVEMENT

4   Match the letters in column X with the number of its pair in column Y.

X		Y	
A	external forces	1	agent of erosion
B	river	2	breaking up of rock
C	internal force	3	denudation
D	weathering	4	debris
E	sand	5	folding

A	
B	
C	
D	
E	

5   With the help of a diagram explain how the Wicklow landscape was shaped by internal and external forces.

GRAVITY

Gravity is the force which causes objects to fall. They fall because they are attracted to the Earth. This 'pull' of the Earth has an enormous influence on our lives and on the world around us. It is this force which keeps us on the surface of the Earth instead of flying off into space. The crust of the Earth is greatly affected by gravity. As soon as debris becomes loose, it has a natural tendency to fall down or move lower unless something stops it. Rubbing against things, or **friction**, is the usual reason why debris does not move lower. But if there is a steep slope, or if the surface is slippy, friction does not have the power to hold debris in place, so it moves down.

The movement of debris downslope is called **mass movement**. The word 'mass' is used because debris usually moves down as a mass or large amount together. On steep slopes, downward movement is rapid; on gentle slopes there may be little or no movement at all. If the surface is flat, debris may remain where it is for a long time. The slipperiness of the surface can make a great difference. On a slippy surface, things move down even very gentle slopes. If the surface is slippy and steep, the movement can be very rapid. Water is the main way in which rocks and debris are made slippy, therefore it plays an important part in causing mass movement.

Mass movement is an important factor in shaping the landscape. Movement caused by gravity is at work all the time removing debris from higher places and bringing it down to lower ones. It lowers the mountains and hills and fills up the valleys. It also helps shift vast amounts of material to the floors of seas and oceans.

THE GEOGRAPHER'S WAY 2

ACTIVITY 2

1. Examine the O.S. map on page 56. Find each of the following points and tick whether there is likely to be fast or slow mass movement happening at it.

GRID REFERENCES	FAST	SLOW
1 L 812 659		
2 L 815 674		
3 L 845 670		
4 L 847 661		
5 L 796 660		

RAPID MASS MOVEMENT

Rapid movement of debris occurs suddenly and can cause great damage. It usually happens on steep slopes or rock faces where the pull of gravity is most effective. We will examine two kinds of mass movement by studying photographs.

ACTIVITY 3

Examine the photograph in Figure 2.3, then do the following:
1. Using evidence from the photograph identify the type of rock in the photograph.
2. Locate three pieces of evidence in the photograph which show that rapid mass movement occurs in the area shown.
3. Suggest two ways the mass movements shown in the photograph can affect people.

Fig 2.3

EXTERNAL FORCES 1: MASS MOVEMENT

Cliff Falls The cliffs shown in figure 2.3 are cut in Old Red Sandstone and other sedimentary rocks. The large blocks in the foreground and middleground have fallen off the cliff. These are examples of **rock falls**. They were caused by the sea cutting in under the beds of rock so there was nothing to hold them in place. Gravity then caused them to collapse. The sign warns people to stay clear of the cliffs.

Landslides Another type of rapid mass movement is a landslide. A **landslide** happens when rock and debris slides down a slope. Landslides happen on steep slopes after heavy rain or an earthquake. Rain water seeps into the ground and makes it heavy and slippery. The increased weight and slippiness means gravity becomes more effective causing the material to slide. Shaking caused by earthquakes may loosen rocks and debris so that gravity can pull them downslope.

People can also help to cause landslides. An example of this is the landslide which happened in 1881 at Elm in Switzerland. Examine the diagram of the Elm area.

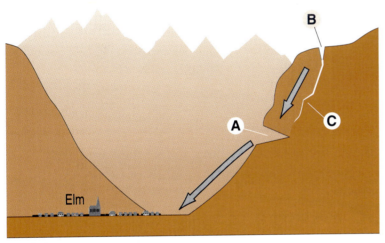

Fig 2.4

The village of Elm was on the floor of a steep U-shaped valley. Rock was quarried half way up one of the valley sides at A as shown in the picture. Gradually the block of rock above the quarry became undermined. A fissure opened up in the ridge above the quarry at B. Rainwater seeped down through the fissure into the rock making the surfaces in the crack slippy. The block of rock at C suddenly slid down the valley side and into the quarry. There it was deflected out across the valley. The landslide lasted less than a minute but it destroyed the village of Elm and 115 people were killed. People quarrying rock certainly helped cause this landslide.

Rapid mass movements are easy to identify as they leave a scar in the landscape. The material which has moved is often found in a mound at the bottom of the scar. The scar and the mound may become covered over with vegetation as time passes.

THE GEOGRAPHER'S WAY 2

ACTIVITY 4

Fig 2.5

Examine the photograph in Figure 2.5. It shows the site of a landslide.
1 Using evidence from the photograph give two causes of the landslide.
2 Explain two ways in which human activities were effected by the landslide.
3 Suggest ways to make this slope more stable.

SLOW MASS MOVEMENT

Slow mass movements are not eye-catching, in fact they are barely noticeable. They don't leave scars or great mounds of debris after them so they can be difficult to detect.

Fig 2.6 A

Soil creep is the commonest kind of slow mass movement. It is a gradual, slow movement of debris downslope and can happen on very gentle slopes. Although it is slow it moves more material downslope than any other type of mass movement. To detect soil creep you must be able to identify the clues it leaves behind. Some of these clues are shown in the photographs in figure 2.6.

Figure 2.6 A shows a tree affected by soil creep. Notice how the bottom of the tree trunk is curved. The curve is caused by the tree trying to keep itself upright as the soil creeps downslope.

EXTERNAL FORCES 1: MASS MOVEMENT

Fig 2.6 B

Fig 2.6 C

Figure 2.6 B shows a series of steps on the side of a hill. These are called **terracettes**. They look as if they were caused by animals walking across the slope but they are caused by soil creep.

Figure 2.6 C shows how soil creeping down the slope has built up against the upslope side of the wall. On the downslope side the soil moves away. The wall often bulges downslope due to the build up of soil.

MEDIUM MASS MOVEMENT

Fig 2.7

These kinds of mass movement are not as fast as landslides nor as slow as soil creep.

Mudflows are mass movements which happen when debris gets very wet after heavy rain. The debris becomes like a porridge which can flow. The photograph Figure 2.7 shows a mudflow. Notice how wet the mudflow is and how it is flowing over the stones in the foreground.

27

THE GEOGRAPHER'S WAY 2

Fig 2.8

Bogbursts are similar to mudflows. They occur after heavy rain when the peat layer becomes saturated. Peat can hold an enormous amount of water but if there is too much the weight becomes too great and the mass starts to move downslope. A thick porridge of peat and water flows across the surface sweeping away anything in its path. The most serious bogburst in Ireland happened near Killarney in the late 19th century when a number of people were killed. The photograph in figure 2.8 shows the effects of a bogburst.

ACTIVITY 5

1. Which of the following statements is correct?
   (a) Landslides, mudflows and soil creep are all examples of rapid mass movement.
   (b) Mudflows and bogbursts are only caused by earthquakes.
   (c) Rapid mass movements leave scars in the landscape.
   (d) Soil creep occurs only on steep slopes.

2. Examine the photograph in figure 2.9 then answer the following:
   (a) Describe the relief of the area.
   (b) Give two reasons why mass movements are likely to happen in the area.
   (c) Using evidence from the photograph name two types of mass movement which have occurred in this area.

Fig 2.9

EXTERNAL FORCES 1: MASS MOVEMENT

THE IMPORTANCE OF MASS MOVEMENT

Mass movement plays a very important part in the lowering of the landscape. It is usually not spectacular in the way it works but it is happening all the time. Its results become evident over a long period. Slowly and steadily debris is moved down slopes to the floors of valleys where it is picked up by rivers. These transport the debris to the sea where it is deposited.

Mass movement also affects people's lives. Rapid movement can cause great damage to property and sometimes loss of life. It influences the siting of buildings and roads. For example, houses should not be built where there is a danger of landslides, rockfalls or mudflows. In mountain areas where slopes are steep and rainfall heavy, people choose the sites for settlements carefully so that they will be safe.

Modern roads and railways are kept as level as possible so traffic can move quickly and safely. To achieve this **cuttings** are made through hills. The sides of deep cuttings shouldn't be too steep. If the slopes are great, mass movement happens. The photograph in figure 2.10 shows a landslide in a road cutting. These are dangerous as they can cause serious traffic accidents. They often occur after very heavy rainstorms. To prevent them vegetation is planted on the slopes so that the roots hold the soil together. Engineers take care to make sure the drainage system is good so that excess water is carried away and not allowed soak into the regolith.

Fig 2.10

ACTIVITY 6

Fig 2.11

Examine the photograph in figure 2.11 of a road cutting then do the following:
1. What type of mass movement do you think affected this slope?
2. What do you think is the purpose of the lines of stones which have been built into the slope?
3. Will the action taken stop mass movement on this slope? Explain your answer.

REVISION

Rewrite the following text into your copy filling in the blank spaces using words from the box

> gravity   mudflow   transport   soil creep   rockfall   agents of erosion
> cuttings   external forces   bogburst   weathering   terracettes
> erosion   landslide   mass movement   denudation
> friction   deposition

_____ is the breaking up and rotting of rock. The breaking up, carrying away and dropping of debris is _____. The carrying away of debris is _____. The dropping of debris is _____. This work is carried out by rivers, moving ice, wind and waves which are known as _____ _____ _____. The lowering of the land surface by weathering and erosion is called _____. Weathering and erosion are _____ _____ which shape the outside of the Earth's crust. _____ is the force which makes things fall. When things move they are slowed down by rubbing against other things. This is called _____. Debris moving downslope is called _____ _____. A sudden movement of rock downslope is a _____. Another rapid movement is a _____. The slow movement of soil is called _____ _____. _____ are a sign that soil is moving downslope. A porridge of mud moving downslope is a _____. A bog may also move downslope. This is called a _____. To keep modern roads as level as possible engineers construct _____ for them to pass through.

EXTERNAL FORCES 1: MASS MOVEMENT

LOCAL SLOPES FIELD STUDY

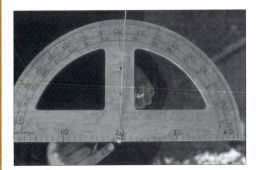

Fig 2.12

Fig 2.13

Fig 2.14

The aim of this fieldstudy is to test the following hypothesis:
"Terracettes only occur on slopes with an angle greater than 30°". The equipment you will need is the following:

a large protractor

a piece of string with a weight on one end. This is called a **plumb line.**

a thumb tack

a clipboard and pencil

Making a Clinometer

The protractor and plumbline are used to make a clinometer. A **clinometer** is an instrument for measuring slopes. Attach the plumbline to the protractor at the central point as shown in figure 2.12. Make sure the plumbline is free to swing from side to side.

Using a Clinometer

To use a clinometer you need two people of roughly the same height. One person holds the clinometer and the second person moves 10 metres down the slope.

The person holding the clinometer should hold it to his/her eye as shown in figure 2.13. This person looks down the slope to the second person and makes sure the edge of the protractor is in line with the other person's eyes. The dotted line in figure 2.13 shows the line of sight. The plumb is let free. When the plumb comes to rest the angle at which it has come to rest is noted.

The photograph in figure 2.14 shows a reading on a clinometer. Reading from 0° the plumbline crosses the scale at 40°. Subtract 40° from 90° and you get the angle of slope. In this case the slope is 50°.

THE GEOGRAPHER'S WAY 2

Fig 2.15A

Fig 2.15B

Fig 2.15C

Examine the photographs in figure 2.15 then match the letters on the photographs with the angles of slope they show.

Slope	Letter
20°	
45°	
70°	

Fieldwork

Identify slopes which have terracettes on them. Measure the angle of the slope at each of the sites you identify. Record them on a table like the one in figure 2.16. The larger the number of slopes measured the better.

1 LOCATION	2 ANGLE	3 SLOPE (90 MINUS VALUE IN COLUMN 2)
1		
2		
3		
4		
		TOTAL SLOPES

Fig 2.16

Processing of results

Add up the slopes in Column 3. Divide this total by the number of slopes. The answer will give you the average slope in degrees. Compare the average slope with the slope given in the hyphothesis. After you have compared the two slopes you can then decide whether the hypothesis is true, partly true or false.

Report

Write a report on your field study under these headings:

TITLE   AIMS   EQUIPMENT NEEDED   FIELDWORK
PROCESSING OF INFORMATION   RESULTS   CONCLUSIONS

3 External Forces 2: The work of Rivers

IN THIS CHAPTER YOU WILL LEARN

- How rivers break down rock.
- Ways of looking at rivers: Long profiles and cross sections.
- How features are formed in the upper middle and lower courses of rivers.
- How rivers help to lower the landscape.
- The importance of rivers to people.

A **river** is a channel in which run-off flows. The **channel** consists of the river's bed and banks. Rivers are the main way water drains from the land. They are one of the most important external forces which shape the Earth's crust. To do this shaping a river needs energy. The energy it has depends on two things. Firstly, its energy depends on the slope of the river. The steeper the slope the faster the river flows. The faster it flows the more energy it has. Secondly, a river's energy depends on the amount or **volume** of water in it. The greater the volume of water, the more energy it has. Large volume rivers flowing down steep slopes have enormous power. The river Colorado in the United States has cut a trench a mile deep at the Grand Canyon. Every hour this river carries an average of 28,900 tonnes of debris to the Pacific.

Normally a river does not fill its channel. It flows well below the top of the banks. But after heavy precipitation when run off increases, river volume may grow to fill the channel. When the channel is full the river is at **bank-full** stage. If there is any further increase in volume, then it floods. Water spills over the banks and spreads beyond the channel. Rivers do most of their shaping of the land when bank-full or in flood. At low water they do little to change the landscape.

ACTIVITY 1

1. Using an atlas find the Colorado river. Name two large lakes on the river and two dams.
2. Examine the photographs in figure 3.1 The photographs show a section of the Slaney river at different times in 1994.

THE GEOGRAPHER'S WAY 2

Fig 3.1A

Fig 3.1B

(a) In which of the photographs is the river bank-full? Give evidence from the photographs to support your answer.
(b) Contrast the weather, season, vegetation and river level in both of the photographs.

2 Examine figure 3.2 showing the village of Lynmouth, England, when the River Lyn burst its banks after an extraordinary storm.

Fig 3.2

'Lynmouth 1952'

(a) Describe the photograph, giving details of its type and date.

34

EXTERNAL FORCES 2: THE WORK OF RIVERS

(b) Identify and give the location of three pieces of evidence to show how powerful the river was when in flood.
(c) Give three likely effects this flood had on the lives of the people in Lynmouth.
(d) Draw a sketch of the main features in the photograph and indicate where you think the original river channel was.

EROSION BY RIVERS

A river is a good example of an agent of erosion because it shows clearly the three essential elements of erosion:
(a) Destruction of rock, thus making debris.
(b) Movement of this debris by the agent of erosion.
(c) Deposition of the debris in a new place.

Rivers shape the land in these three ways. They cut into the rock and regolith. They pick up pieces of debris and transport them downstream. The material transported is called the river's **load**. Rivers deposit their load when they run out of energy to carry it. Usually the load drops out gradually: heavy debris first, lighter material later.

HOW RIVERS BREAK DOWN ROCK

Rivers cut into the crust like a saw cutting into wood. They do this in two main ways, by abrasion and by solution.

Abrasion means scraping. If a river has enough energy, it picks up sand, pebbles, even rocks from its bed and banks and carries them along as its load. The load bumps along the channel rubbing and scraping. This wears the channel, lowering the river bed and cutting back the banks. It is the load which gives the river the 'teeth' to cut like a saw.

River water like rainwater can dissolve certain minerals. This dissolving is called **solution**. It eats into the rock along the channel, lowering the river bed and widening the channel.

WAYS OF LOOKING AT RIVERS

To see how and where a river does its work, we must be able to observe it. There are two ways in which we can observe a river. The first one is to see it 'in profile'. The word **profile** means how a thing appears from the side. This view shows how a river appears from its source to where it ends. This is called the 'long profile of a river'. The second way is to see it as a cross-section view at some point in its course. The diagrams figures 3.3A and 3.3B show these two views.

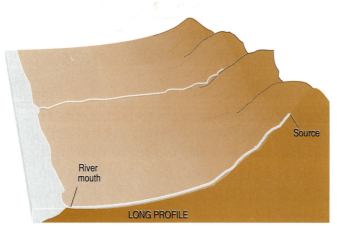

Fig 3.3 A

Fig 3.3 B

THE LONG PROFILE OF THE RIVER LIFFEY

A **long profile** of a river is really a line graph which shows how the height of a river changes along its course. The diagram in figure 3.4 shows the long profile of the River Liffey from source to mouth. The source is just over 500m up in the Wicklow Mountains. For the first 10km it flows down steep slopes. In this part the Liffey makes half its total descent to sea level. This is its upper course. After 10km the slope becomes gentler; this part continues for about 30km. This is the middle course. After about 40km from its source, the Liffey descends by an almost flat slope to the sea. It only falls about 100m in the last 57km, its lower course.

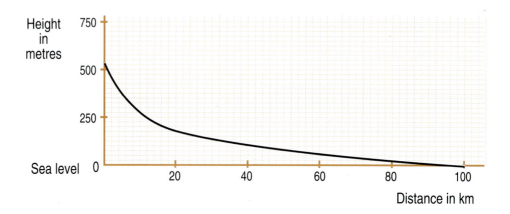

Fig 3.4

EXTERNAL FORCES 2: THE WORK OF RIVERS

ACTIVITY 2

Fig 3.5

Location on the river	Height above sea level
Source	750m
15km from source	200m
25km from source	100m
115km from source	0m

1. Using the information in the table in figure 3.5, draw the long profile for this river. To do this, copy the axes of the long profile shown in figure 3.6 which allow 1000m on the height axis and 120km on the distance axis.
2. Is the long profile you have drawn roughly the same as the long profile of the River Liffey? Try to divide the profile you have drawn into the three different stages where the river's gradient changes.
3. (a) What are the three essential elements of erosion?
   (b) Explain the processes of abrasion and solution.

Fig 3.6

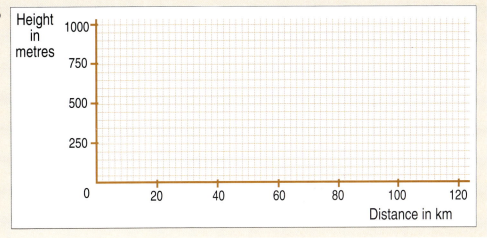

RIVER COURSE FEATURES

From what you have already learned about rivers in Book One you know that they have stages: an upper, middle and lower course. By studying the long profiles of two rivers you have now learned to decide where the different stages begin and end. You also learned about the typical features found at each stage of the river's course. Knowing how weathering and river erosion work, we can now find out how these features are made.

UPPER COURSE FEATURES

Narrow V Valleys   In mountains and uplands rivers flow quickly down steep slopes. These give them energy to erode. Study figure 3.7 as you read. The river itself can only cut down where its channel is. So working on its own, a river can erode a valley only as wide as its channel. As it cuts down, the river exposes its valley's sides. These are steadily worn back by weathering. The debris produced slips down the slopes, falls into the river and is carried away. The sides at the top have been exposed for longer, so they are worn back more. The sides near the valley floor have been exposed for a shorter time, so they have only been cut back a little. This produces the V shape typical of upper course river valleys. If a valley is very deep and narrow it may be a **gorge**.

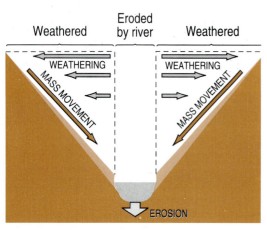

Fig 3.7

Interlocking Spurs   Spurs are caused by the downcutting river winding its way around obstacles in its path, such as small ridges. The inside of each bend becomes a spur. As the river twists its way down the valley, the spurs interlock with one another as they grow.

Fig 3.8

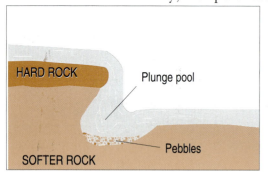

Waterfalls   These are caused by rocks in the bed of the river being of different hardness. If a river flows from a resistant rock onto a weaker one, the weaker one will be eroded more as shown in figure 3.8. As the difference in height grows, the water falls from one level to another. Abrasion causes the development of a **plunge pool** under the fall.

MIDDLE COURSE FEATURES

At this stage the river flows down gentler slopes and should have less energy but this is often not so. Tributaries will have joined the main river increasing its volume and energy. Rivers in the middle stage often have more energy to do work than in the upper course.

EXTERNAL FORCES 2: THE WORK OF RIVERS

Wider Valley The river widens its channel by eroding its banks more than its bed. This happens because the bed now has a thick covering of debris which protects it from abrasion. The banks are not protected in this way so they continue to be eroded. The wider channel helps to widen the valley floor. The valley sides become worn back and less steep due to weathering and mass movement of debris. The hills between the river valleys are also lowered by weathering and mass movement. These changes are shown in figure 3.9.

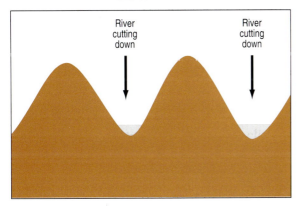

Fig 3.9 A

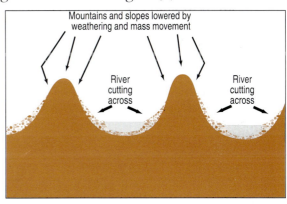

Fig 3.9 B

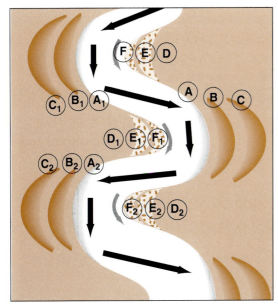

Fig 3.10

Meanders These are large bends which develop in the river's course. They cut across the valley floor because of the way the water flows. The diagram in figure 3.10 shows a series of meanders. The arrows indicate the path followed by the water: their thickness shows their speed and energy. Study how the water strikes the outside bank, eroding it. The diagram shows how this bank is shifted from A to B to C. Next, study how the water flows faster on the outside of the bend and slows down on the inside. This causes the river to cut more strongly into the outer bank. On the inside there is less energy, so the river drops some of its load here. The inside of the bend grows from D to E to F. In this way meanders grow steadily, the bends getting more and more curved.

As meanders cut across they form a plain around the river. This is fairly flat and close to the level of the river, so it is easily flooded at times of high water. It is called a **flood plain** because of this. Meanders also help to cause flooding by slowing up the flow of water in flood time.

Bluffs These features of river valleys are made by meanders cutting into the valley sides. Bluffs often form lines of low steep slopes along the edges of the valley floor. See page 260 Book One.

ACTIVITY 3

Fig 3.11

1. Examine the photograph in figure 3.11. Decide whether it shows the upper or middle course of a river. Give three pieces of evidence from the photograph to support your answer.
2. Refer to the photograph in figure 3.1A page 34. Using the method you have been taught, locate each of the following features:

| meander | flood plain | bluff line | submerged fence | field | flood settlement |

Fig 3.12

3. Using evidence from the photograph in figure 3.12 explain the location of the settlement in the photograph.

EXTERNAL FORCES 2: THE WORK OF RIVERS

LOWER COURSE FEATURES

Fig 3.13

The long profile of a river shows how it passes gradually from the middle to the lower stage. The photograph in figure 3.13 shows the typical landscape of the lower course. Notice how the countryside is low and fairly flat. The river has reduced the landscape to an extensive floodplain. This is made mainly of regolith which has been deposited by the river. The river winds its way across this plain in enormous meanders. Three features are commonly found in the lower course landscape: ox-bow lakes, levees and deltas.

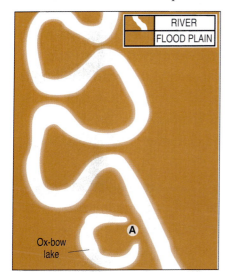

Fig 3.14

Ox-bow lakes Examine diagram 3.14. This shows large meander curves. In time of flood the swollen river may cut through the neck of the meander as shown at A. This causes the meander to become cut off from the main river channel. A separate curved lake forms as a result. This is known as an **'ox-bow'** lake. After a time these lakes dry up because no water flows into them any more. The traces of numbers of ox-bow lakes can be found along the banks of many lower course rivers.

Levees When a river bursts its banks, it deposits most of its load close to the edges of its channel. After a number of floods, these deposits build up, raising the level of the banks. These raised banks are **levees**. They are shown in figure 3.15A. After a long time levees grow to a stage where the river

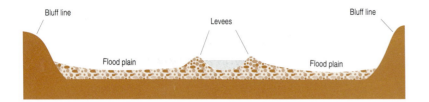

Fig 3.15A

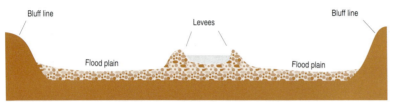

Fig 3.15B

Fig 3.16

actually flows at a level above the surroundingflood plain. This is shown in figure 3.15B. This can be dangerous because if the river breaks through its levee, it will pour out and flood a very wide area.

The photograph in figure 3.16. shows a levee on an Irish river. In this case people built the levees to protect the buildings in the middle-ground from being flooded. Gorse was planted on the levees to make them look better and to discourage children from going too close the river bank.

Deltas Most rivers reach the sea in their lower course. The sea water slows the river's flow and its load is gradually dropped. If there are no strong currents or tides to wash the deposits away, they can build up to form new land at the river's mouth. When this happens a delta is formed. Not all rivers end in the sea. Many rivers empty into lakes. A river entering a lake may build a lake delta. See page 262 Book One.

HOW RIVERS HELP LOWER THE LANDSCAPE

Given enough time rivers can help to wear away an entire landmass till it is reduced to a level plain close to sea level. To see how this happens, it is important to understand how the three shaping forces of weathering, mass movement and erosion interact. In this study we will use the other view of a river, the cross-section view. Follow the diagrams in figure 3.17 carefully as you read.

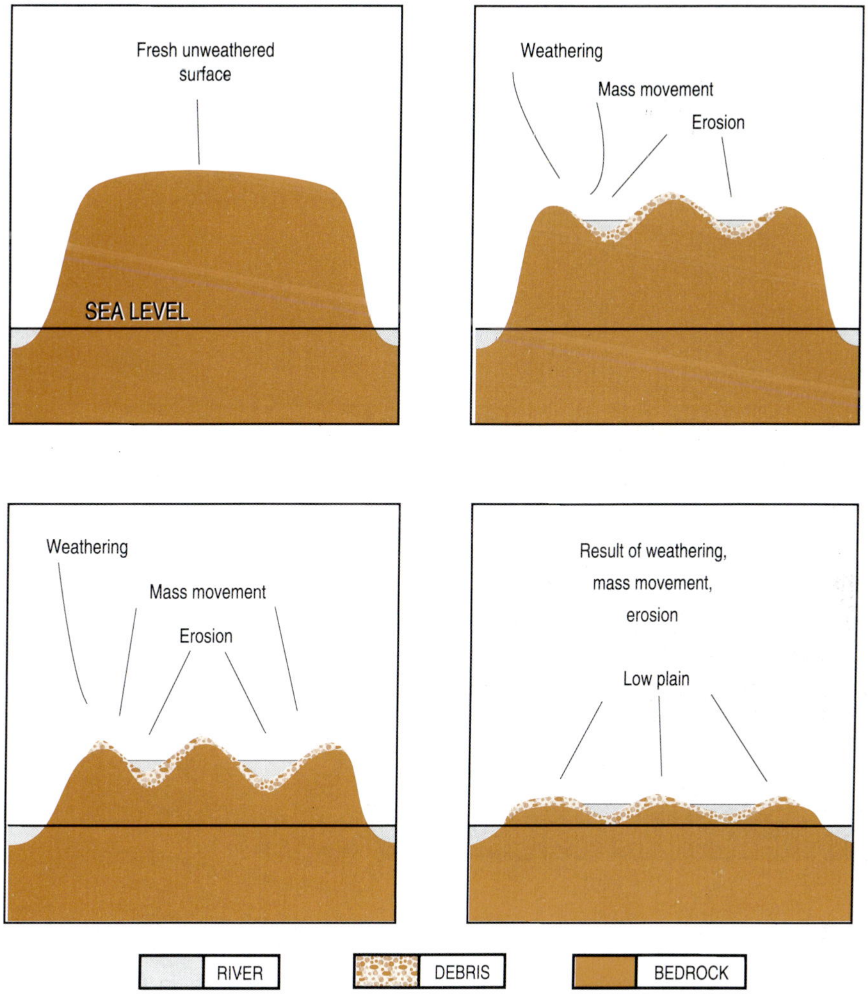

EXTERNAL FORCES 2: THE WORK OF RIVERS

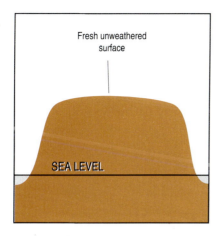

Fig 3.17A — Fresh unweathered surface, SEA LEVEL

Fig 3.17B — Weathering, Mass movement, Erosion

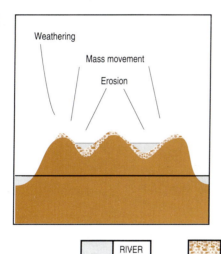

Fig 3.17C — Weathering, Mass movement, Erosion

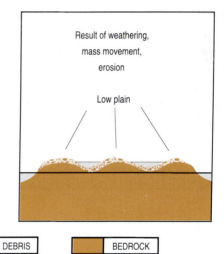

Fig 3.17D — Result of weathering, mass movement, erosion; Low plain

RIVER | DEBRIS | BEDROCK

Imagine that a piece of crust has been uplifted by recent plate movement to make new land. The diagram in figure 3.17A shows this. The fresh surface begins to be weathered and a layer of regolith forms. This is shown in figure 3.17B. Two rivers start to flow across the landscape cutting channels in the surface. These channels form river valleys and make slopes. Mass movement shifts debris down these slopes. When the debris reaches the river, it is carried off as part of the river's load. This speeds up erosion by the river. See figure 3.17C. Weathering, mass movement and erosion by streams steadily wear back the slopes and lower the hills between the river valleys till an almost flat plain results. This is shown in figure 3.17D. Reducing mountains to a low plain like this takes an enormous length of time to happen.

THE GEOGRAPHER'S WAY 2

ACTIVITY 4

1. Examine the photograph in figure 3.18 then do the following:
(a) What type of photograph is it?
(b) What views does it give of the landscape?
(c) Does it show part of the middle or lower course of a river? Use evidence from the photograph to support your answer.
(d) Explain two effects this river has on the lives of people in the area. To **explain** means to make something as clear as possible.
2. Using diagrams explain how rivers help to lower the landscape.

Fig 3.18

FEATURES OF THE RIVER LIFFEY

Fig 3.19

Having studied the work of rivers, we can now return to the River Liffey to see what we can find as we follow its course.

The photograph in figure 3.19 was taken along the upper course close to the source. Notice its steep valley, the small waterfall, and how the spurs interlock as the little river twists its way down the slope. The height is about 370m. Mountains about 600m high surround the valley.

EXTERNAL FORCES 2: THE WORK OF RIVERS

Fig 3.20

The photograph in figure 3.20 was taken 15km downstream from the last one. The height is about 200m. See how the valley has widened. Meanders, a flood plain and bluff lines have developed. The river is still surrounded by hills but these are much lower, about 300m high.

The photograph in figure 3.21 was taken at the mouth of the Liffey. Here there is a wide plain almost at sea level which stretches out on either side of the river. At the mouth there are deposits of mud and sand which the sea has been strong enough to wash away to form beaches in Dublin Bay. Only a few hills remain near the river.

Fig 3.21

ACTIVITY 5

Using an atlas locate a major river in your area. Measure its length from source to mouth. Note its height at the source and at various distances from the source. Using this information draw a long profile of the river and divide it into upper, middle and lower courses.

RIVERS AND PEOPLE

Rivers are natural resources, though they can be destructive when in flood. From earliest times people have been attracted to settle by rivers because they provide so many basic needs: water, food, a means of transport and travel, defence. The first settlers in Ireland lived by rivers, and later the Vikings chose riverside sites for their towns. Today, rivers still provide water, food and means of transport. With the increase in leisure time, rivers are a resource for recreation: fishing, sailing, swimming and so on.

For centuries rivers have been used to power mills. The energy of falling water is now used to generate **hydro-electricity**, or **HEP**. In countries with dry climates or dry seasons, rivers provide water to irrigate crops. To **irrigate** means to water crops.

The Nile   This huge river rises in the damp cool highlands of East Africa. It flows 6,400km to reach the Mediterranean Sea in Egypt. For hundreds of kilometres the Nile flows across the Sahara Desert, a region where little rain falls. The map in figure 3.22 shows north-east Africa with the Nile, the Sahara and the Mediterranean. It also shows the distribution of population in the region. Identify the areas where the population densities are high and where they are low.

The densities are high close to the Nile and low away from it. The reasons for this are that the Nile floods regularly creating a flood plain with very fertile soil. It also provides water for irrigation. The only land which can be farmed is close to the river, so people have settled here for thousands of years. The river was so important in the lives of the people of ancient Egypt that they worshipped it as a god. The Nile made possible the growth of one of the great civilisations, the Kingdom of the Pharoahs.

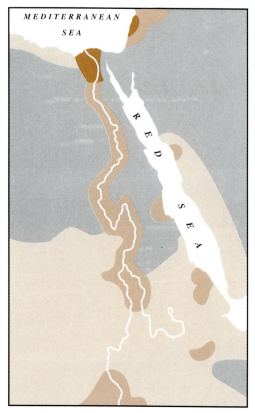

Fig 3.22

Persons per square kilometre
- OVER 50
- 10 – 50
- 1 – 10
- UNDER 1

Recently the Nile has been dammed at Aswan forming an enormous reservoir, called Lake Nasser. This is a multi-purpose project. This means it has a number of purposes. The main purposes are to provide HEP, water for irrigation and for drinking. It has been successful in doing this but it has also caused problems. Firstly, the reservoir has flooded a very large area of farmland. Secondly, the river deposits its load in the reservoir, so below the dam the river can pick up more load and start eroding again. Thirdly, because so much water is being taken from the Nile, the volume of water reaching its mouth is lessened. This means less load is being deposited in the delta. The delta is getting smaller because the amount of material being eroded by the sea is now greater than the amount the Nile deposits. This loss of land is serious as it is very fertile and supports a high population density.

EXTERNAL FORCES 2: THE WORK OF RIVERS

The fishing industry at the delta has also been affected badly. As less water enters the sea, less nutrients are being washed from the land to the sea. These nutrients are food for the plants the fish live on. So there are fewer fish to catch.

Interfering with the Nile by damming it has had good and bad effects. This happens with most natural forces. If we interfere with them in one place and try to control them, we often make problems in other places. It is important to try to find out what all the effects of our interference will be. In this way we can avoid making mistakes.

ACTIVITY 6

Explain some of the ways people interfere with rivers and what the effects of human interference can be.

REVISION

Rewrite the following text into your copy using words from the box to fill in the blank spaces.

irrigation	channel	plunge pool	bank-full	gorge	river
load	spur	flood plain	explain	levees	volume	profile
HEP	abrasion	ox-bow lake	hydro-electricity	long profile

A _____ is water flowing across the landscape in a _____. The amount of water is its _____. When a river's channel is full it is said to be _____ _____. The debris carried by a river is its _____. The scraping action of a river is _____. A _____ is what something looks like from the side. A side view of a river from source to mouth is called its _____ _____. A deep steep-sided river valley is a _____. A piece of land jutting out is a _____. The deep water below a waterfall is a _____ _____. The _____ _____ is the flat land on either side of a river channel which floods when the river level rises. A meander which has been cut off from a river may form an _____ _____. Deposition on the banks of rivers builds up _____. Electricity produced by the power of falling water is called _____ or _____. Watering crops is called _____. To _____ is to make something clear.

4 External Forces 3: The work of Moving Ice

IN THIS CHAPTER YOU WILL LEARN

- Ice Ages, glacier types and how glaciers erode.
- Erosional features produced by mountain and lowland glaciers.
- Depositional features produced by melting ice.
- How glaciers affect people.
- How to identify glacial features on OS maps.

Where the climate is very cold ice is a powerful force shaping the landscape. Figure 4.1 shows a place where ice is at work. It is a region of high mountains where the upper slopes are so cold that the climate is polar. Notice the jagged rocks and peaks. From this you can tell that freeze/thaw weathering is active. This is one way ice shapes the landscape. Now see how much bare rock there is at the peaks and steeper places. Snow and ice cannot lodge here. They fall to the gentler slopes and hollows below and gather there. This is where the work of moving ice begins.

GLACIER ICE

When snow falls and not all of it melts before the next snowfall, it begins to gather. If more falls than melts, the build-up goes on. Gradually the upper layers compress the bottom ones changing them into solid ice. It takes about 10 cm of snow to make 1 cm of ice. Refer to figure 4.1. The white areas have snow on top but underneath there is a mass of ice. This may be hundreds of metres thick and very heavy.

Ice flows if there is enough of it. It is affected by gravity and can flow slowly downhill. It also spreads out under its own weight. In figure 4.1 see how the ice mass is flowing like a great river. The direction of flow is from the background to the foreground. A flow of ice like this is called a **glacier**. Glaciers are powerful agents of erosion.

A landscape is said to be **glaciated** when glaciers helped to shape it. There are two main kinds of glaciation: **mountain** glaciation, and **lowland** or **continental** glaciation. In the mountain type, glaciers form in **snowfields** in the mountains and flow down valleys towards the lowlands. On their way, they erode powerfully, reshaping the landscape. When the glaciers reach the lowlands they melt if it is warm enough. Otherwise the ice spreads out covering the lowlands. In the second type a lowland region is covered by massive bodies of ice called **ice sheets**. Greenland and Antarctica are covered by ice sheets, like the one shown in figure 4.2. It is called continental because it can cover a continent as in Antarctica today. Here the ice is thousands of metres deep. During the Ice Age, Ireland was affected by both types of glaciation.

Fig 4.1

Fig 4.2

You have to use your imagination to realise what Ireland was like during an ice age. In mountain areas such as Kerry and Donegal the scene was like that in figure 4.1. In the lowlands, great ice sheets covered the countryside. Here and there snowy summits showed through the ice sheets. It probably looked like the scene in figure 4.2.

THE GEOGRAPHER'S WAY 2

The Ice Age began about two million years ago. Over a long period the climate began to change. It became much colder and then warmed again. This happened several times. The last cold period ended only about 11,000 years ago. Since then Ireland has had a climate like that at present.

When a cold period began, the temperatures gradually changed from temperate to polar in Ireland and Northern Europe. Most precipitation fell as snow. The colder summers did not have the warmth to melt all the snow that fell so ice accumulated. It gathered first in upland areas forming snowfields and glaciers. The ice flowed to the lowlands where it was no longer warm enough for melting to happen. Ice sheets began to form fed by glaciers. This movement of ice away from where it gathers is known as an **ice advance**. Not only did ice advance from the Irish mountains. Ice around the North Pole also advanced, covering Norway, Scotland and parts of Ireland. These huge ice sheets spread across land and sea building to depths of thousands of metres. When a warmer period came, more ice melted than gathered. The ice began to shrink back or **retreat**. We are now in a period of ice retreat. Even in the highest areas of the Alps, glaciers are melting quickly and becoming smaller.

ACTIVITY 1

1. Describe what happened at the start of an Ice age.
2. Explain how glaciers advance and retreat.
3. Examine the map in figure 4.3 which shows how much of Europe was covered by ice when the Ice Age was at its peak. With the help of an atlas do the following:

Fig 4.3

Tick the correct answers in the boxes provided.
(a) All of Europe was covered by ice. ☐
(b) All of Norway was covered by ice. ☐
(c) Most of Britain was covered by ice. ☐
(d) France was only affected by ice from the Alps and the Pyrenees. ☐
(e) Only part of Ireland was covered by ice at this time. ☐
(f) Italy was not affected by the ice. ☐

GLACIATED AREA
LIMIT OF ICE
PRESENT COASTLINE
LAND
SEA

EXTERNAL FORCES 3: THE WORK OF MOVING ICE

HOW ICE ERODES

As an ice mass advances it builds into itself loose material which it picks up. This is its load. The bottom and sides of the ice mass become embedded with rock which scrapes the surface underneath. The scrape marks made in the surface by the moving ice are called striae. **Striae** are shown in the photograph in figure 4.4. These can tell a lot about how and where the ice flowed long after it has melted. The scraping action is called **abrasion**, just as it is with rivers. Freeze/thaw weathering, usually very active near ice masses, adds jagged debris to the load making it more abrasive. Ice is very heavy so a mass of moving ice armed with rock teeth has enormous power to abrade.

Moving ice also plucks debris from the surface under it. It does this by sticking to it and pulling it away as it moves. The plucked material is added to the load. When rock is layered or cracked, plucking often leaves large hollows behind called **rock basins**. These become lakes when the ice melts.

Fig 4.4

ACTIVITY 2

1 Explain how glaciers erode the landscape.

2 In the boxes provided match each letter in column X with the number of its pair in column Y.

X	Y
A ice moving forward	1 striae
B scraping by ice	2 ice advance
C ice moving back	3 rock basin
D climate becomes colder	4 Ice Age
E scrapes on rock	5 retreating
F hole left by plucking	6 abrasion

A	
B	
C	
D	
E	
F	

51

THE GEOGRAPHER'S WAY 2

FEATURES OF MOUNTAIN GLACIATION

These are found in upland areas. Features made by mountain glaciers are usually easy to recognise. Examine the photograph in figure 4.5 carefully. Using what you learned about glacial features in Book One, see how many you can identify.

Fig 4.5

Corries and Arêtes Corries formed by ice gathering in mountain hollows. Under its own weight the ice began to move, abrading and plucking as it travelled downslope. The scraping action deepened the hollow while the plucking formed the steep backwall and sides. Once they started to form, corries grew steadily larger. Irish glaciers usually had their beginning in corries. The enlarged hollow became the collecting ground for the ice that fed the glacier. Some Irish corries like Coomshingaun in the Comeragh Mountains are huge. This one has sheer cliffs over 300m high.

Sometimes two corries formed side by side. As the hollows grew, they joined to make one larger feature. If the land between the corries was eroded till only a narrow

Fig 4.6

EXTERNAL FORCES 3: THE WORK OF MOVING ICE

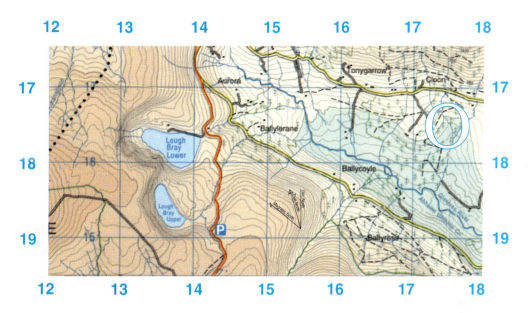

Fig 4.7

ridge remained separating them, an **arête** was made. Figure 4.6 shows two corries. The yellow line shows the arête. Both corries have tarns but only one of them is visible. The O.S. extract figure 4.7 shows how these corries and the other glacial features appear on a map.

ACTIVITY 3

Examine the photograph in figure 4.6 and the O.S. extract in figure 4.7 then do the following.

1. (a) Name the tarns and give a grid reference for each. ☐
   (b) Give a grid reference for the arête. ☐
2. Tick the correct statement below.
   (a) Lough Bray Upper is larger than Lough Bray Lower. ☐
   (b) A national primary road passes the eastern end of Lough Bray Lower. ☐
   (c) Both corries face eastwards. ☐
   (d) Lough Bray Upper has a settlement on its shores. ☐
3. In which direction do you think the ice moved from these corries? Give a reason for your answer.
4. What direction was the photograph in figure 4.6 taken from?

THE GEOGRAPHER'S WAY 2

U-SHAPED VALLEYS AND THEIR FEATURES

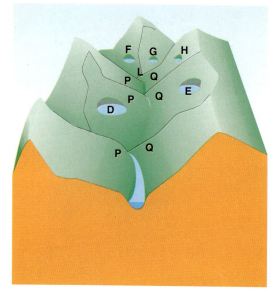

Fig 4.8A

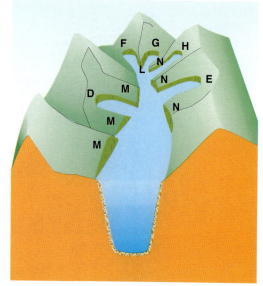

Fig 4.8B

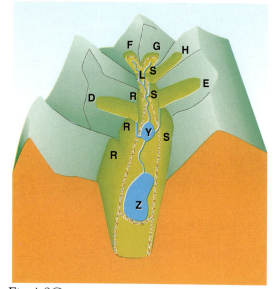

Fig 4.8C

	BEDROCK
	GLACIAL DEPOSITS
	ALPS
	GLACIAL DEPOSITS
	RIVERS
	LAKES

The **U-shaped valley** is the most typical feature of mountain glaciation. To study it we will use a series of diagrams showing a mountain landscape before, during and after glaciation. Figure 4.8 A shows the area as ice advances. The corries D, E, F, G, and H fill with ice. They become the sources of a number of glaciers. As the ice flows from the corries it follows the courses of V valleys cut by rivers before the Ice Age. The glaciers coming from corries F, G and H join up at L to form the main glacier. The other smaller glaciers D and E join the main glacier as **tributary glaciers** and increase its size and weight.

As it moves down its valley, each glacier reshapes it. This is best seen in the main glacier. It eats deeply into the floor of the main valley and cuts back the valley sides. It can do this because it is so massive. Valley glaciers can be hundreds of metres deep, so their weight and size make them powerful eroders. Even the tributary glaciers are large enough to deepen and widen their valleys. This is seen in Figure 4.8B.

Figure 4.8 C shows the landscape after the ice has melted. Now other features typical of mountain glaciation become visible.

U-Shaped Valleys Each glacier has cut a U-valley with steep sides and a flat floor. The old V-shaped outline of the river valleys has gone.

Trough-Ends A trough-end is a step in the valley floor where the valley suddenly becomes deeper. This happened at L in the diagram where the three glaciers met. The step is caused by the increased weight and power of the ice as the glaciers united.

Hanging Valleys The increased erosive power of the main glacier has left the valleys of the tributary glaciers perched high above the floor of the main valley. They are said to 'hang' on the side of the main U-valley. The glaciers in these valleys were much smaller than the main ice flow and so eroded shallower valleys. After the Ice Age when rivers returned, there were often waterfalls where streams from 'hanging' valleys dropped down to the floor of the main valley.

Truncated Spurs Truncated means 'cut off' or shortened. Glaciers are so massive that they cannot twist around spurs as rivers do. They plough their way through them, straightening out the valley as they go. The truncated remains of the spurs at P and Q in figure 4.8 A are shown at R and S in figure 4.8 C.

Ribbon Lakes These are long narrow lakes found in glaciated valleys. Sometimes they are rock basins caused by plucking which fill with water after the Ice Age. The lake at Y in Figure 4.8 C is a rock basin lake but the lake at Z is dammed by glacial deposits. (Ribbon lakes may also be made as a result of deposition. See page 60.)

Alps In the mountains the ice can flow away downhill. It does not cover the entire landscape. So ice does not reshape everything. Traces of the old V valleys remain above the level reached by the valley glaciers. This is shown at M and N in figure 4.8 C. These upper slopes of the original valley are called **alps**. The Alpine Mountains get their name from the **change of slope** where the 'alp' ends and the glaciated trough begins. The meadows on the alps provide summer grazing for cattle in the mountains of Switzerland, France and Austria. The 'alp' was so important in the way of life of the people there that it gave the mountains their name.

ACTIVITY 4

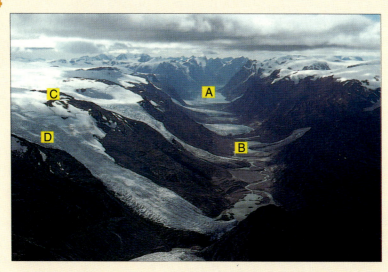

Fig 4.9

1. Examine the photograph in figure 4.9 carefully and identify the glacial features marked A, B, C, D on the photograph.

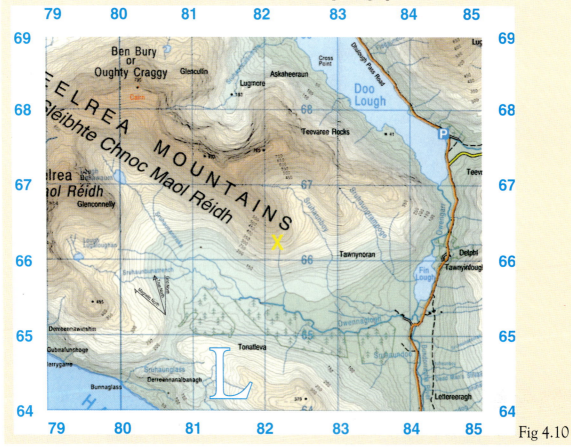

Fig 4.10

EXTERNAL FORCES 3: THE WORK OF MOVING ICE

2 The OS map in figure 4.10 shows an area which was glaciated. The yellow X on the map marks a truncated spur. Examine the map carefully. On it there is at least one example of each of the following:
U-shaped valley, hanging valley, corrie, tarn, arête, truncated spur, ribbon lake. Identify these features then do the following:
(a) Using grid references give the location of three corries and two truncated spurs.
(b) Name two rivers which flow on the floors of a U-shaped valleys.
(c) Name two rivers which flow from hanging valleys.
(d) Name a river which flows down a trough end.
(e) What type of lake is Doo lough?

3 In which direction or directions do you think the ice moved in the area shown on the map. Give a reason for your answer.

ICE AS AN AGENT OF EROSION

Moving ice is an example of an agent of erosion. First, it breaks up and destroys rock and regolith. Second, it transports the debris it makes and brings it to another place. Third, it deposits its load when it can carry it no further. The features we have studied so far have been made by erosion and transportation. These are found mainly in mountain areas because here ice had most energy to erode and carry material. But in the lowlands ice still had enough energy to do some eroding and transporting. We will look at this before going on to study deposition, the main work of lowland ice.

LOWLAND ICE

The ice sheets which spread across Northern Europe were huge. Figure 4.11 shows a cross-section of an ice sheet. The ice was thickest at the centre. This was where most of the accumulation happened. The weight of ice caused it to advance outwards from the centre. This movement and the enormous weight gave the ice

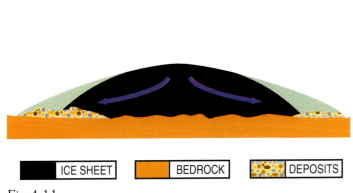

Fig 4.11

energy to erode. The underlying rock and regolith were scraped, worn down, plucked and rounded as the ice passed over.

Knob and Lochan Scenery. This is a typical landscape left behind by eroding icesheets. Here the lowland ice shaped the harder rock into knobs and rock hillocks. The rock hillocks are called **roches moutonnées**. They have a typical shape: one smooth gently sloping side with the opposite side steep and rough. The softer rock was gouged into rock basins which later formed small lakes. Finland with its hundreds of lakes provides an example of this landscape. Knob and lochan scenery is found south of Clifden, Co. Galway. Here a large icesheet scraped the local granite into a wilderness of little lakes and rocky hillocks.

REVISION 1

Rewrite the following text using the words in the box to fill in the blank spaces.

> mountain glaciation   alps   Ice Age   retreating   tarn   striae
> U-shaped valleys   corries   truncated spurs   glaciers
> ice sheets   hanging valleys   ribbon lake
> arête   rock basins   glaciated   continental glaciation
> trough end   plucking   tributary   advancing
> roches moutounées   builds up   knob and lochan

When temperatures fall ice _____ _____ in the mountains. The ice forms armchair shaped hollows called _____. Rivers of ice called _____ flow downslope. The shaping of mountainous regions by ice is called _____ _____. The shaping of lowlands by huge _____ _____ is called _____ _____. The period when ice shaped the Irish landscape is called the _____ _____. During this period ice was _____ from the mountains and from the North Pole. When ice was melting back we say it was _____. The landscapes formed by ice are called _____ ones. Scraping by glaciers causes _____. Glaciers erode by pulling or _____ lumps of rock from the underlying rocks. This leaves large holes called _____ _____ in the landscape. A _____ is a lake in a corrie. A sharp ridge between two corries is an _____. Glaciers change V-shaped valleys into _____ _____. Along these valleys smaller glaciers called _____ glaciers cut shallower valleys which we call _____ _____. The remains of the V-shaped valley are called

EXTERNAL FORCES 3: THE WORK OF MOVING ICE

_____. At the head of the valley there may be a step called a _____ _____. Interlocking spurs are eroded away leaving _____ _____. A long narrow lake on the floor of a glaciated valley is called a _____ _____. A landscape almost stripped bare of soil and severely eroded into hollows and small hills is called _____ _____ _____ relief. The hills are called _____. They have one gently sloping ice smoothed side and the other is steep and jagged.

DEPOSITION

Fig 4.12

Fig 4.13

Debris deposited by glaciers and ice sheets also shapes the landscape. Deposition features are usually lowland ones because it is here that the ice eventually loses its energy and melts. Deposition happens in two ways. First, the material the ice can no longer carry is dropped or dumped where it is. This material is called **till**. Till is a jumbled-up mixture of clay, sand, gravel and boulders. Examine the photograph in figure 4.12 which shows how mixed till is. Second, meltwater streams flowing through and from the ice pick up debris, transport it and deposit it just as a river does. These are called **outwash deposits** because they are washed out of the ice as it melts. Outwash deposits are different to till because the debris is sorted into layers of coarse and fine material. Compare the outwash deposit in figure 4.13 with the till in figure 4.12. These deposits of till and outwash material provide the raw material out of which soil is made. Soil is our most valuable natural resource.

The lowland ice sheets carried a great load of debris. Part of this came from erosion by the ice sheet itself. Much also came from the mountain glaciers which flowed down to join the lowland ice. When the ice began to melt, most of the load was dropped as an uneven carpet of till, known as **moraine**.

Fig 4.14

Fig 4.15

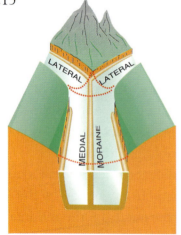

| ICE |
| ALPS |
| MORAINES |
| BEDROCK |
| ORIGINAL SLOPE |

Moraines The photograph in figure 4.14 shows a retreating glacier. There are mounds of deposited till along the sides and at the front or **snout** of the glacier. These mounds are called **moraines** and are made of debris which the ice carried. The moraine along the side of the glacier is called **lateral moraine**. Lateral means 'on the side of'. The arc-shaped moraine along the snout of the glacier is called **terminal** or **end** moraine. Terminal moraine often forms a ridge across the valley as the ice melts. This can act as a dam when rivers begin to flow again, making a **moraine-dammed lake**. (See also ribbon lake, page 55.) Lake Como in Italy is an example of a large moraine-dammed lake.

When a glacier is retreating, the rate at which it melts varies. If the weather is warmer for a few summers, the ice retreats quickly covering the floor of the valley with a thin and fairly even layer of till called **ground moraine**. If the weather is colder for a while, the ice retreat may slow down or stop. Then large deposits of moraine build up leaving mounds and even small hills of till at the snout. A terminal moraine which looks like a range of low hills is found near Blackwater, Co. Wexford. When one glacier joins another as a tributary, two of their lateral moraines join to become a **medial** or middle moraine as shown in figure 4.15. There will be a medial moraine in the main glacier for every tributary that joins it. Medial moraines leave mounds and hummocks of till on the valley floor as the ice retreats.

Outwash plains Examine figure 4.14 again. **Meltwater streams** are flowing from the snout of the glacier. These carry a heavy load of debris out of the melting ice. Beyond the snout, they begin to behave like rivers. They deposit the heaviest material quickly but carry the fine debris further. This explains why outwash deposits are sorted and layered. Outwash streams often meander across the valley floor. This makes the surface of the

EXTERNAL FORCES 3: THE WORK OF MOVING ICE

deposits they leave fairly smooth and flat. They are called **outwash plains** for this reason. The Curragh, Co. Kildare is an example of an outwash plain. Because outwash plains are made of sand and gravel, the soil is very permeable. It drains quickly and makes good land for the training and racing of horses. It is usually not very good agricultural land.

ACTIVITY 5

1. Describe till and outwash deposits.
2. Using diagrams explain how three different moraines are formed.

Fig 4.16A

Fig 4.16B

Fig 4.16C

3. Examine carefully the photographs in figure 4.16, then match the following descriptions with the photographs using the boxes.
   - [ ] a U-shaped valley with a ribbon lake on its floor and a lateral moraine with a road on top of it.
   - [ ] a corrie lake or tarn.
   - [ ] a medial moraine where two U-shaped valleys meet.

There are two lowland deposition features in Ireland left by ice which must be mentioned because the Irish names for them have become their geographical names. These are **drumlins** and **eskers**. Ireland has some of the best examples of these features.

Drumlins Figure 4.11 shows that the icesheet became thinner towards the edges. Here it had less weight and power. Erosion gradually stopped and the ice began to drop its load. But it still had enough energy to make it advance and shape the moraine as it moved over it. This formed small hills of till called drumlins. In Irish this word means 'little hill'. Figure 4.17 shows a drumlin. Notice its typical shape: a long gentle slope and a short steep one. Drumlins are often found together in large numbers called **drumlin swarms** or **belts**. A swarm of drumlins stretches across Ireland from Clew Bay, Co. Mayo to Strangford Lough, Co. Down. The O.S. map in figure 4.18 shows part of Clew Bay. The small hills with summits about 30m are drumlins. Some of them have become islands because sea level rose with the melting of the icesheets after the Ice Age. Counties Cavan and Monaghan are noted for their drumlins.

Fig 4.17

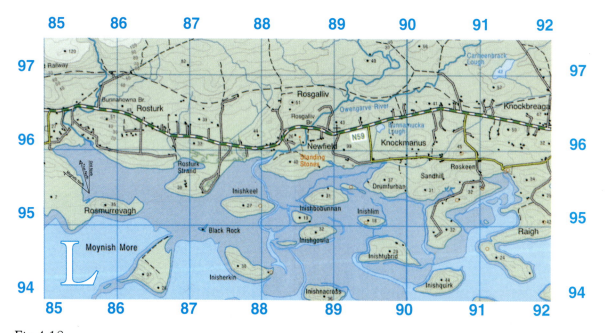

Fig 4.18

EXTERNAL FORCES 3: THE WORK OF MOVING ICE

Eskers An esker is a long narrow ridge of outwash sand and gravel, usually about 15 to 30m high. They can extend for many kilometres. The Esker Riada stretches from Dublin nearly to Galway. The eskers are deposits laid down on the beds of meltwater streams which flowed under the icesheets. When the ice melted, the deposits were left as ridges winding across the lowlands. They made routeways to cross the flat boggy land of the Central Lowlands and were used by the Celts as roads in ancient Ireland. Because they are made of sand and gravel, their soil is poor, supporting only short grasses. Therefore they stand out as brightly-coloured green hills against the darker colours of the surrounding countryside. Eskers were often known as '**greenhills**'; there is a suburb of south-west Dublin called 'Greenhills'. The photograph in figure 4.19 shows the Greenhills Road which follows an esker. The modern road still runs along the top of it. The name 'esker' is also common in place names.

Fig 4.19

ACTIVITY 6

1. Using a diagram show how drumlins were formed in an ice sheet.
2. Describe knob and lochan relief and explain how it came about.
3. Examine figure 4.20, then match the letters in the diagram with the features below.
   esker ☐, outwash plain ☐, knob and lochan relief ☐, drumlin belt ☐, terminal moraine ☐.

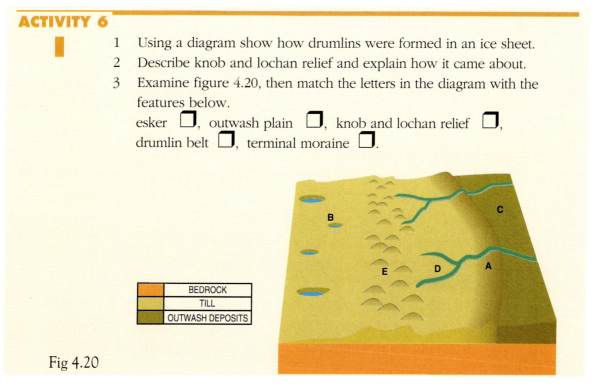

Fig 4.20

THE GEOGRAPHER'S WAY 2

IDENTIFYING GLACIAL FEATURES

Glaciation features are found in all Irish mountains. They are mainly erosion features but you can find plenty of deposition features because the ice eventually melted in the mountains too. Erosion features are easy to identify in the landscape and on O.S. maps because they are usually big. Deposition features like moraines and outwash plains are not so easy to recognise because they are often small and may be covered with vegetation. On maps they may be too small or too low to show up as contour patterns. But most Irish lowlands will show evidence of glacial deposition if they are examined carefully.

PEOPLE AND THE ICE AGES

Soils The influence of glaciation on our soils is by far its most important effect. The parent material of nearly all Irish soils is glacial deposit of some kind. Outwash deposits produce light, sandy, soils which need frequent manuring and watering. Till deposits are often clayey and make heavy, poor-draining soils. The drumlin belt has soils like this, so farmers here concentrate on pastoral rather than arable farming. The drumlin belt is an important milk-producing area. Other till deposits have less clay and are less heavy. These make fertile, well-drained brown earths which suit arable farming. From these examples it is clear that the pattern of Irish farming is strongly influenced by glaciation. On the other hand, where ice scraped the rock bare of soil, we have almost a desert, as in parts of the Burren, Co. Clare.

Scenery The features of glacial erosion make our mountain scenery dramatic. Famous beauty spots like the Gap of Dunloe, Co. Kerry, Kylemore Lough, Co. Mayo, Derryveagh National Park, Co. Donegal and Glendalough, Co. Wicklow owe much of their beauty to the glaciers which shaped them. Such lovely scenery attracts tourists from home and abroad and is a valuable natural resource.

Power resources Corries and hanging valleys are used as collecting grounds and reservoirs for HEP stations. Norway, Sweden, Switzerland, Italy and France have many power stations located in their glaciated mountains. Industries which need a lot of electricity locate in the mountain valleys bringing valuable employment to the area.

EXTERNAL FORCES 3: THE WORK OF MOVING ICE

Communications Glacial features can help or hinder communications. Many mountain routes follow glaciated valleys up to cols or gaps. The famous Alpine routes like the St Gotthard and the Mont Cenis are examples. But if a U-valley ends in a steep troughend, it can make transport difficult. There are many examples of this in the Alps and Pyrenees. Road and rail tunnels often begin where a trough-end is a serious obstacle on a route.

ACTIVITY 7

Fig 4.21

1. Explain how glaciation has affected the area in the photograph in figure 4.21.
2. Explain how the Ice Age affects our life today. In your answer refer to advantages and disadvantages.
3. What effect had glaciation on your area? The soil study in Book One and your local library may provide you with some helpful information.

THE GEOGRAPHER'S WAY 2

REVISION 2

Rewrite the following text using the words in the box to fill in the blank spaces.

> terminal   till   outwash   end moraine   belts
> moraines   drumlins   medial moraines   lateral moraines
> outwash plain   ground moraine   snout   esker   meltwater streams
> drumlin swarms   greenhills   moraine-dammed lakes

The front of a glacier is its _____. Unsorted glacial debris is _____. If it is spread thinly across the landscape it is called _____ _____. Sorted glacial deposits are called _____ deposits. They are sorted by _____ _____. Mounds of unsorted material are called _____. If these are at the side of a glacier they are _____ _____ but if they are down the middle they are _____ _____. A mound across the snout of a glacier is a _____ or _____ _____. Lakes dammed by these mounds are called _____ _____ _____. A flat area of sorted deposits beyond a terminal moraine is an _____ _____. Small hills of unsorted debris rich in clay and shaped by the ice are _____. These small hills occur in groups called _____ _____ or _____. A long narrow hill of sand and gravel is an _____. They are also called _____.

5 External Forces 4: The work of the Sea

IN THIS CHAPTER YOU WILL LEARN

- The relationship between wind and wave energy.
- How waves erode, transport and deposit material.
- How waves shape coastal features.
- How people interfere with coastal processes and the results of this.
- How to identify coastal features on OS maps.

The sea is an important agent of erosion but its action is limited to the coast. Like other erosion agents the sea acts in three ways. It attacks the rocks of the coast and breaks them up. It transports the debris it makes to other places. It deposits the debris when it can carry it no further. In these ways the sea reshapes coasts all the time. How much the sea does depends on its energy. We will examine how the sea gets its energy and how it does its work.

The sea gets most of its energy from wind blowing across it. Wind makes **waves** in the water and it is these which act on the coast, eroding it in some places and building it up in others. The size and power of waves depends on the wind; the stronger the wind, the more powerful the waves will be. The strength of waves also depends on the fetch. The **fetch** means the distance that wind blows over open sea. If there is a long fetch, the wind will be stronger and the waves will have plenty of time and space to grow big.

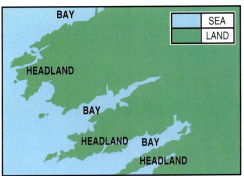

Fig 5.1

The west coast of Ireland provides an example of how fetch influences the energy of the sea and its power to shape a coastline. The west coast is very different to the east coast. The west coast is jagged and indented. **Indented** means 'eaten into'. It has many headlands and bays. **Headlands** jut into the sea; the **bays** are hollowed out where the sea has cut inland. Examine figure 5.1 which shows these features.

An indented coast is usually a sign of powerful marine erosion. The east coast is only slightly indented and is more straight and smooth. Wave erosion is not so powerful there.

THE GEOGRAPHER'S WAY 2

The west coast is the most eroded of the Irish coasts for several reasons. First, the prevailing south-westerly wind blows onshore here. An **onshore** wind is one which blows from the sea to the land. The south-west winds blow waves against the coast so that they strike it with full force. Second, the fetch of waves on the west coast is very great. The wind has blown across the Atlantic Ocean for thousands of kilometres. This allows the wind to make very large waves. Third, storms with gale-force winds are common in the North Atlantic. A coast which is often affected by storms and powerful waves is called a **high energy coast**. The west coast is an example of a high energy coast. The east coast is much less exposed to storms and big waves. Here the prevailing wind is off-shore. **Offshore winds** blow from land to sea. On this coast the fetch is much shorter, about 100 kilometres. Therefore the east coast is an example of a **low energy** coast. This is why this coast is smoother and less indented.

ACTIVITY 1

Examine the map of Ireland in figure 5.2, then with an atlas do the following:

1. Name the bays from B1 to B 17 which are shown.
2. Name the headlands from H1 to H9.
3. Match the bays and headlands in column A with its pair in column Y.

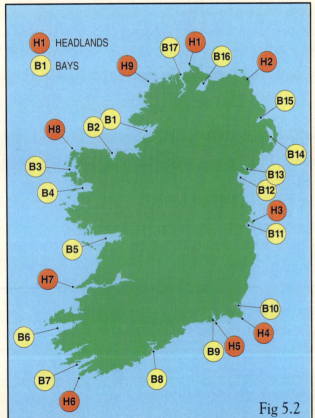

Fig 5.2

	X		Y
A	Carlingford lough	1	West coast
B	Donegal Bay	2	West coast
C	Waterford Harbour	3	North coast
D	Galway Bay	4	East coast
E	Lough Foyle	5	West coast
F	Clew bay	6	South coast

A		D	
B		E	
C		F	

EXTERNAL FORCES 4: THE WORK OF THE SEA

HOW THE SEA ERODES

Fig 5.3

The photograph in figure 5.3 shows powerful waves crashing against the coast near Doolin, Co. Clare. The cliffs in the middleground are 30 metres high. The spray is being blown over the top of the cliffs. This gives some idea of the force of the wind and waves. Waves like these can destroy rocks. They pound the rock and break it up by sheer force. The waves hurl stones, gravel and sand against the rockface wearing it away. This is abrasion. The waves also trap air in cracks in the rock. As a wave crashes down the air is compressed. When the wave moves back, the pressure is suddenly released. These repeated changes of pressure shatter rock. Solution, or dissolving of minerals, by sea water also plays a part in wearing away the coast.

Fig 5.4

In the middleground of the photograph in figure 5.3 there are large breakers. **Breakers** are waves which topple over as they near the shore. There are two kinds of breakers. **Plunging breakers** like the ones in the photograph are made by high waves. The falling mass of water in these has great energy and can be very destructive. When there is a storm most of the waves are plunging ones. **Spilling breakers** like the ones, in figure 5.4, are made by low waves. Because they spill over rather than plunge, they do not erode the coast. Instead they carry material onto the shore by washing up sand and gravel. Most of the time a coast is affected by spilling waves because there is calm weather more often than storms. It is the erosion which happens during storms which causes most of the reshaping of the coastline.

THE GEOGRAPHER'S WAY 2

WAVE ATTACK

Fig 5.5

Fig 5.6

Wave erosion is most effective where rock is weak. Often the point of weakness is a bed of softer rock or where there is a fault. Figure 5.5 shows a cliff with a cave at its base. The cave has been eroded where there is a fault. You can see the fault as a white line running up the cliff from bottom to top. If the weakness is a bed of less resistant rock, a bay may form. Figure 5.6 shows Killiney Bay. This bay formed because the coast here is made of glacial deposits which are much weaker than solid rock. At either end of the bay there is a headland; Bray Head to the south made of quartzite and Sorrento Point to the north made of granite. These have eroded much more slowly than the weak beds where the bay has formed.

Fig 5.7

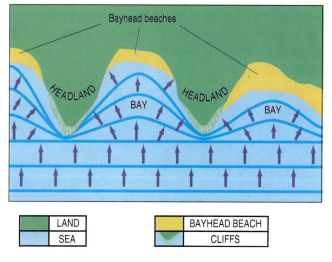

Waves approaching a coast often swing round to meet it in rows which run parallel to the shoreline. This bending of waves is called **wave refraction**. Around headlands the waves sweep in on either side. This is shown by the arrows in the diagram in figure 5.7. In bays the opposite happens. The wave spreads out as it moves into a bay and so its energy is decreased. In this way wave refraction increases wave energy at headlands and reduces it in bays. This

EXTERNAL FORCES 4: THE WORK OF THE SEA

Fig 5.8

is why erosion is the main activity around headlands and deposition becomes more important in bays. This explains why beaches form in bays, and headlands are nearly always rocky features as shown in figure 5.8. Beaches formed in this way are called **bay head beaches**.

ACTIVITY 2

1. In the boxes provided match each letter in column X with the number of its pair in column Y;

X		Y	
A	wind blowing from land to sea	1	fetch
B	type of sea erosion	2	breaker
C	line of weakness	3	onshore
D	wind blowing from sea to land	4	abrasion
E	when a wave falls over	5	offshore
F	distance wind blows across sea	6	fault

A	
B	
C	
D	
E	
F	

2. Cross out the incorrect words in these statements.
    (a) The sea erodes by plucking/abrasion.
    (b) The fetch of the waves is larger/smaller on the east coast than on the west coast of Ireland.
    (c) Coastal erosion forms corries/bays.
    (d) Most coastal erosion is carried out by solution/wave action.
3. Using an annotated sketch map explain why the west coast of Ireland is more indented than the east coast.
4. Explain how the sea erodes the land.

71

THE GEOGRAPHER'S WAY 2

EROSION FEATURES

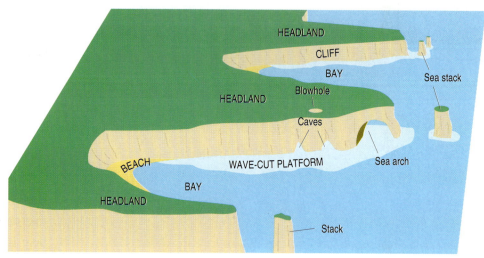

Fig 5.9

Because headlands take the full energy of waves, they are good places to observe erosion features. Figure 5.9 shows a number of these: cliffs, wave-cut platforms, caves, sea-arches, sea-stacks and blowholes.

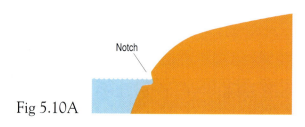

Fig 5.10A

Fig 5.10B

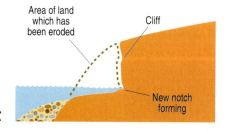

Fig 5.10C

Cliffs Figure 5.10 shows how these form. Waves erode a **notch** or hole at a point of weakness, As time passes the notch gets bigger and the rock above it is left unsupported. The rock collapses and a cliff begins to form. The fallen debris at first protects the base of the cliff but it is pounded by the waves till it is broken up to a size which the waves can shift. Then the wave attack begins again cutting a new notch. And so the erosion continues.

72

EXTERNAL FORCES 4: THE WORK OF THE SEA

Fig 5.11

Wave-cut platform When a cliff is cut back like this, it is said to be **retreating**. Where the cliff once was, there is now only the base or platform on which it stood. This is called a **wave-cut platform**. Figure 5.11 shows a retreating cliff with a wave-cut platform in the foreground. In the middleground look for a cliff with a fresh notch at its base. A large boulder has fallen from the notch.

Caves, sea-arches and stacks Caves are eroded at points of weakness in rock. Once it begins to form a cave can grow rapidly due to wave action and abrasion. **Compression** of the trapped air as waves roll in also helps to shatter the rock of the walls and roof. If caving occurs along a line of weakness which runs right through a headland, then caves can form at each side. These may join to form a sea-arch. With time, the roof of the arch collapses leaving an isolated sea-stack. Figure 5.12A shows a sea-arch, 5.12B shows a sea-stack.

Fig 5.12A

Fig 5.12B

Blowholes These are features which form where rocks are bedded and jointed i.e. sedimentary. Air compressed in a cave by waves forces its way to the surface through cracks which widen gradually. The escaping air makes a 'whooshing' sound as it comes out the blowhole.

THE GEOGRAPHER'S WAY 2

If the waves are powerful, water as well as air gushes up like a fountain. Blowholes rapidly shatter the cliffs in which they develop. Figure 5.13 shows a blowhole.

Fig 5.13

ACTIVITY 3

1 Using diagrams explain how a cliff forms.
2 Draw a diagram of a headland. On the diagram show the following features: cliffs, caves, sea-arch, sea-stack and blowhole.

Fig 5.14

3. Examine figure 5.14 then do the following:
   (a) Identify and locate four different coastal features.
   (b) Explain how this coast is being eroded. In your answer refer to three features.

REVISION 1

Rewrite the following text into your copy using words from the box to fill in the blank spaces.

> waves   headlands   cave   plunging breakers   sea-arch
> wave-cut platform   notch   breakers   towards
> high energy   fetch   bays   sea-stack   low energy   spilling waves
> compression   indented   retreating   wave refraction
> blowhole   bayhead beaches

Most of the work of the sea is carried out by _____. The distance the wind blows across the sea is the _____. An _____ coast is eaten into by the sea. It has _____ where the land juts out into the sea and it has _____ where the sea has cut inland. Onshore winds blow _____ the shore. Coasts which frequently get strong winds and powerful waves are called _____ _____ coastlines. Coasts which are seldom affected by powerful waves are called _____ _____ coasts. When waves topple over they are known as _____. High waves crash down with great force and are called _____ _____. _____ _____ topple gently onto the coast and add material to it. _____ _____ is the bending of waves around headlands and into bays. This causes _____ _____ _____ to form in bays. A hole cut by waves at the bottom of a cliff is a _____. When cliffs are eroded backwards they are said to be _____. A flat rock surface is left where the cliffs were; it is called a _____ _____. When the sea erodes along a line of weakness a hole called a _____ forms. If the sea erodes through a headland a _____ forms. When the roof of a sea-arch collapses a _____ is left. When waves trap air in holes in the rock the _____ of the air by the wave causes erosion. The compression of air in a cave causes a _____ to form _____.

COASTAL TRANSPORTATION

The material eroded from the coast is worn down by wave action. The rock is broken up into boulders and stones. These are then ground down to become pebbles, shingle and sand. **Shingle** is the name given to the water-worn pebbles found on the shore. When the debris size is reduced, the material can be lifted and carried by waves. It becomes part of the load of the sea. When waves are strong, this load can be quite heavy, large stones being tossed and tumbled about. Spilling waves move sand and shingle.

Coastal debris is moved in several ways, but mainly by wave action. Currents and tidal-flows can also shift large amounts of fine debris. Because transport by waves happens as an endless sequence of lifting and re-depositing material, it is best to study marine transportation under the heading of deposition.

DEPOSITION

When a wave breaks, water runs up the shore. This movement up the shore is called **swash**. The movement of water back to the sea is **backwash**. If the swash is stronger than the backwash, more material is carried up the shore than is washed back, so a deposit of sand and shingle is left behind. This deposit builds to become a **beach**. If a beach already exists, the swash can add to it. With spilling waves the swash is greater than the backwash, so this kind of wave makes beaches. This explains why spilling waves are called **constructive waves**. Plunging waves, the kind experienced in storms, have stronger backwash so they tend to wash materials away from the shore. They are **destructive waves**. A sequence of storms, or even one bad storm, can wash away a beach which it has taken years to build.

BEACHES

A **beach** is a build-up of debris, usually sand and shingle, deposited by waves. Beaches form where the waves are mainly constructive ones and where wave energy is low. For this reason beaches are found on low-energy coasts and along the shores of bays or where there is shelter from the full force of wind and waves.

EXTERNAL FORCES 4: THE WORK OF THE SEA

Beaches are changing all the time, particularly in Ireland where the direction and strength of wind and waves often vary. If you live near a beach, you could study how a beach changes over time by keeping a diary. Because there are more storms in winter than summer, winter is a good time to carry out regular surveying. Why not use a camera to collect photographic evidence of the changes that occur?

ACTIVITY 4

Fig 5.15A

Fig 5.15B

The photographs in figure 5.15 were taken a few days apart. Examine them carefully, then do the following.
1. How has the beach changed from the time photograph A was taken to the time photograph B was taken.
2. What were the causes of these changes?

Sand dunes These features are found beyond the point that tides usually reach. **Sand dunes** are hills of sand piled up by the wind as it blows inshore. A special grass called **marram grass** is planted on dunes to prevent the sand from moving inland and covering fields and buildings. This grass which has long roots and spiny leaves fixes the sand and keeps it in place. The photograph in figure 5.16 shows marram grass growing on a sand dune. Many beaches in Ireland are backed by sand dunes which are a valued feature of many holiday resorts.

Fig 5.16

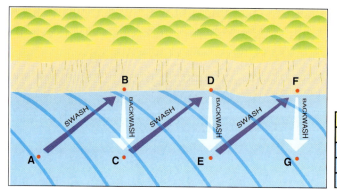

Fig 5.17

Longshore drift This plays an important part in beach formation and change. It causes the movement of sand and shingle along the shore parallel to it. It happens when the swash of the waves carries material up the beach at an **oblique angle**, that is, an angle of less than 90°. The backwash then runs straight back to the sea. If you follow the movement of the swash and backwash in figure 5.17 and the movement of the particle from A to B, C, D, E, F and G you will see how the debris travels along following a zig-zag pattern. Longshore drift can shift sand and shingle along a coast quite quickly. It often has the effect of smoothing the outline of a coast. It can also wash away a beach if steps are not taken to prevent erosion. Sea defences called **groynes** are used to slow down erosion by longshore drift. See page 83 which explains how groynes are used at Rosslare Strand to protect the beach.

Spits When material carried by longshore drift reaches a bay, the movement continues and a spit begins to build across the gap. A **spit** is a narrow bank of sand and shingle which grows across the mouth of a bay or out towards the sea. This is shown in figure 5.18. Longshore drift carries material from A to the mouth of the bay at B. Here the water is deeper, so the material sinks. With time the deposit at B builds

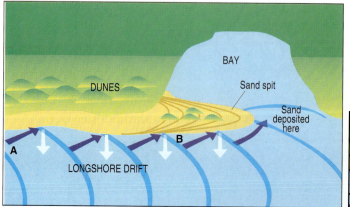

Fig 5.18

EXTERNAL FORCES 4: THE WORK OF THE SEA

Fig 5.19

up and rises above sea level forming a spit. This continues to extend as drift provides more material.

Beaches and sand dunes develop as the spit grows longer. Tramore beach in County Waterford shown in figure 5.19 is a good example of a spit.

Bars and lagoons A **bar** is a bank of mud, sand or shingle which forms in the mouth of a bay or estuary. It is often caused by a spit growing right across an opening in the coastline. Figure 5.20 shows a **baymouth bar**. A baymouth bar may trap an area of sea water behind it like a lake. This is called a **lagoon**.

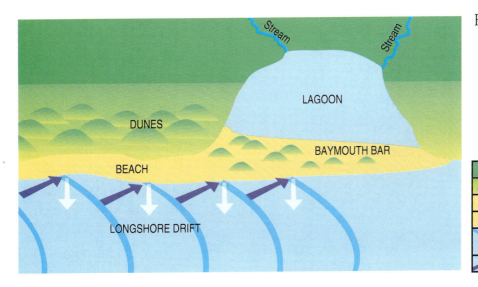

Fig 5.20

79

THE GEOGRAPHER'S WAY 2

Tombolo A **tombolo** is a special kind of bar which grows in the shelter of an island off the coast. When fully grown a tombolo joins the island to the mainland. Howth Head on the northern side of Dublin Bay is joined to the mainland by a tombolo at Sutton Cross.

ACTIVITY 5

Fig 5.21

1. Using a diagram explain how longshore drift happens.
2. Explain with the help of a diagram how a sand spit forms.
3. Examine the photograph in figure 5.21.
   (a) What evidence is there in the photograph for wave refraction?
   (b) Explain why longshore drift is likely to be taking place on the beach.
   (c) Is the longshore drift likely to be towards or away from the camera? Give a reason for your answer.

MARINE EROSION AND PEOPLE

Fig 5.22

Erosion by the sea can affect people's lives badly in two main ways. First, it can destroy valuable land. This may be farmland, residential land or land used for recreation such as beaches, golf courses and so on. Second, it can deposit material where it is not wanted. It may form bars and spits at the mouths of ports making danger for shipping, or build sand dunes which swallow up farmland.

EXTERNAL FORCES 4: THE WORK OF THE SEA

If a coast is made of resistant rock, marine erosion is slow and any problems it causes can be foreseen. Difficulties are rare, provided people are sensible in deciding how to use the land. If the coast is made of weaker materials such as glacial or beach deposits, then erosion can be a serious problem. The photograph in figure 5.22 shows a coastline made of glacial deposits. The cliffs are eroding rapidly, in some places at the rate of 0.5 metres per year. The wall in the right foreground was built over a 100 years ago to protect the base of the cliffs from wave attack. It was important to protect the cliff because a railway line ran along the coast at this point. The engineers thought they could control the sea, but the sea proved more powerful.

Fig 5.23

The wall did not protect the coast and later on the railway had to be moved inland away from the retreating cliffs.

To-day we are not so sure we can control the sea by building walls. Sea-walls have to be very strong to withstand the waves of high energy coasts where erosion is most common. This kind of engineering is very expensive. New approaches are now being used. One idea is to build defences which absorb the power of the waves rather than stand up to them. Examples are shown in the photograph, figure 5.23. The large boulders are known as **rock armour**. The wire cages full of small boulders located behind the rock armour are called **gabions**. They each do the same job. When waves strike, their force is broken up as the water enters the cracks in them. A second approach is to keep adding material to the beach. The waves use up energy lifting and moving this extra load, leaving little for erosion. These modern ways of dealing with wave energy are still expensive.

In Britain where there is a serious problem of erosion along the North Sea coast, the government has decided not to try to defend the coast except where large numbers of houses are at risk. It is estimated that the cost of protection is far greater than the value of the land and property being protected. So the idea is to let marine erosion take its course except in special cases. Instead, compensation will be paid to people who suffer loss.

THE GEOGRAPHER'S WAY 2

A STUDY IN CONFLICT OF INTEREST

Fig 5.24

Fig 5.25

We have an illustration at Rosslare of how sea defences at one place can cause difficulties at another on the same coast. The map, figure 5.24, shows the area. There are two settlements called Rosslare. One is Rosslare Harbour; this is Ireland's main ferryport linking to Europe. The other, a couple of miles away, is Rosslare Strand. This is a holiday resort on a long sandy spit which reaches out into Wexford harbour. The material for this spit was eroded from the cliffs of glacial deposits to the south-east of Rosslare Harbour.

Recently the harbour was improved and long sea-walls were built. As the longshore drift was from SE to NW, these new sea walls caused the longshore drift to drop much of its load. The photograph in figure 5.25 was taken from point X on the map. It shows the cliffs in the left foreground. The deposits caused by the new sea wall are shown in the middle ground. These are made of sand which used to supply beach material to the spit at Rosslare Strand; this supply has now been cut off. The result is that the beach at Rosslare Strand is being eroded.

EXTERNAL FORCES 4: THE WORK OF THE SEA

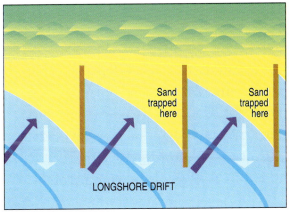

Fig 5.26

The beach is a valuable holiday attraction; if it is destroyed the resort will be less popular. Land with hotels, a golf course and houses on it is also being eroded. In this way improvements to the harbour at Rosslare have created serious problems up the coast at Rosslare beach, an important natural resource.

Groynes To preserve the beach at Rosslare, **groynes** have been built. These are walls built out into the sea at right angles to the beach. They trap the drifting material as shown in the figure 5.26.

Marine erosion also helps people. It provides many valuable natural resources. Bays and coves eroded by the sea provide harbours which have been used by sailors and fishermen since earliest times. Headlands make natural fortifications to protect land from attack. Headland forts were among the places settled when the first people came to Ireland. The part played by marine deposition has also been important to people. Much of the land of the western part of the Netherlands is built on huge banks of sand and mud deposited by the sea. Sandbanks make excellent fishing grounds for certain kinds of fish. You have already learned about the many marine features which make our coasts such interesting places to visit and spend holidays.

Fig 5.27

ACTIVITY 6

Figure 5.27 shows groynes on the beach at Rosslare strand. Examine it carefully then do the following:
1. Is the longshore drift moving towards or away from the camera? Give a reason for your answer.
2. Are the groynes preserving the beach? Use evidence from the photograph to support your answer.

83

THE GEOGRAPHER'S WAY 2

COASTAL FEATURES ON MAPS

The O.S. extract figure 5.28 shows features of coastal deposition. The yellow represents a beach; Tramore Strand stretches from Manar to Carrickfadda. This beach is a sand spit. The 10m contour shows that there are sand dunes on the spit. Clooney Lough is a lagoon cut off from the sea by the growing sand spit. Inishkeel Island is nearly a tombolo. At low tide it is joined to the mainland by a growing spit.

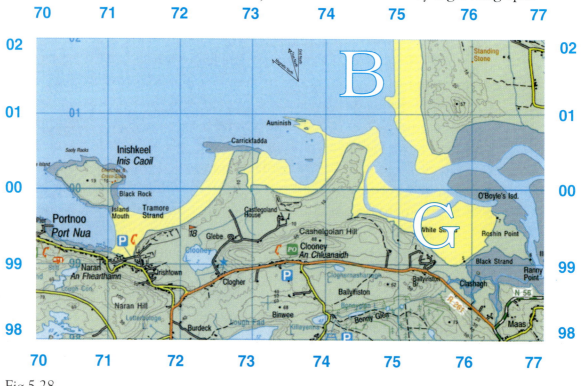

Fig 5.28

The O.S. extract figure 5.29 shows an indented piece of coast. In the south-east corner contours are packed very close together along the coast. This contour pattern represents cliffs. Along these cliffs there are sea-stacks around Rossarell Point. They are at the tip of the red arrow on the map. Gloster rock is another example of a stack. There are many headlands and bays. The largest bay is at 'The Doon'. Trabane beach is a 'bayhead' beach which has been deposited in the shelter of this bay.

EXTERNAL FORCES 4: THE WORK OF THE SEA

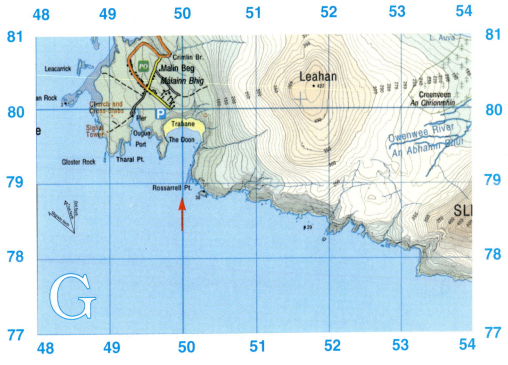

Fig 5.29

REVISION 2

Rewrite the following text into your copy using words from the box to fill in the blank spaces.

gabions	lagoon	shingle beach	swash	rock armour
groynes	oblique angle	tombolo	backwash	spit
marram grass	sand dunes	longshore drift		baymouth bar

A stony beach is called a _____ _____. When a wave breaks the rush of water up the beach is the _____. The _____ is the water returning down the beach. Mounds of sand next to beaches are _____ _____. They are held in place by _____ _____. The current which carries material along the beach is known as _____ _____. For this current to flow waves must strike the beach at an _____ _____. To stop material drifting along a beach walls called _____ are built out into the sea. A deposit of sand and shingle which builds out into a bay is a _____ _____. If the deposit builds out right across a bay and blocks its mouth it is a _____. The area of sea trapped behind such a deposit is a _____. If a spit joins an island to the mainland it is called a _____. Large boulders put on the coast to absorb the energy of the waves are called _____ _____. _____ are wire baskets filled with small boulders.

THE GEOGRAPHER'S WAY 2

ACTIVITY 7

Examine the O.S. map in figure 5.30 then match the features in column X with the grid references in column Y.

X		Y	
1	beach	A	B 650 178
2	island	B	B 673 176
3	bay	C	B 633 150
4	stack	D	B 652 196
5	cliff	E	B 666 140

A	
B	
C	
D	
E	

2. Use evidence from the map to support your answer.
   (a) Which side of the island has a high energy coastline?
   (b) Why is most of the settlement on the eastern side of the island? Use evidence from the map to support your answer.

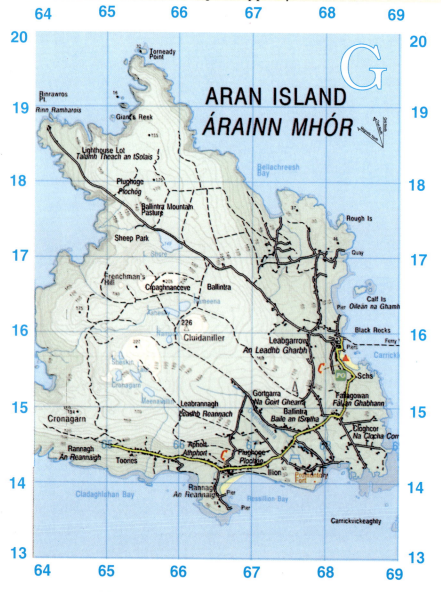

Fig 5.30

6 Variations in Temperature

IN THIS CHAPTER YOU WILL LEARN

- How the sun heats the Earth.
- The factors which influence temperatures and cause them to vary.
- The causes of day and night.
- The causes of the seasons.

Living things depend on energy from the sun. Plants use sunlight to make their food. Other forms of life, including people, depend on the food produced by plants. The external forces which shape the surface of the Earth are also powered by the sun's energy. For example, rivers get energy by descending slopes. But it is the sun's energy which first lifts water into the atmosphere from which it falls as rain. The rain water feeds rivers which in turn shape the land by erosion. Without the sun, life could not survive on Earth. There would be no energy to power natural forces, such as the weather, erosion and the processes of weathering.

HOW THE SUN HEATS THE EARTH

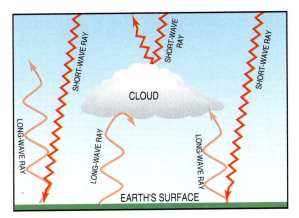

Fig 6.1

The sun is a **star** which sends out rays of heat and light. The sun's rays are **shortwave** ones. These pass through the Earth's atmosphere without heating it. Some of them do not reach the Earth's surface because they are reflected by clouds back into space as shown in figure 6.1. Study this diagram. The rays which reach the surface of the Earth are absorbed by the ground and heat it. The heated ground then gives out **longwave** radiation. This heats the atmosphere because the water vapour and carbon dioxide in it absorb longwave rays which heat them. In this way the atmosphere is mainly heated from below.

THE GEOGRAPHER'S WAY 2

ACTIVITY 1

1. Cross out the incorrect words in the following sentences:

> The radiation given off by the sun is longwave /shortwave radiation.
> The radiation given off by the earth is shortwave/longwave radiation.
> The gases which absorb longwave rays are oxygen, carbon dioxide, water vapour and nitrogen.

2. Explain with the aid of a diagram how the sun's rays heat the Earth's atmosphere.

DIFFERENCE IN TEMPERATURES

The amount of sun's energy reaching the Earth's surface varies from place to place. This variation is important in deciding the kinds of climate in different parts of the world.

A **factor** is something which makes a thing happen or be as it is. We are going to examine the factors which decide the kind of climate a place has. These factors include:
- Latitude - how far north or south a place is from the Equator.
- Altitude - how high a place is above sea-level.
- The surface at a place - whether land or sea.
- Distance from the sea
- Prevailing winds
- Ocean currents

All these factors have to do with the sun's energy directly or indirectly.

LATITUDE

Fig 6.2

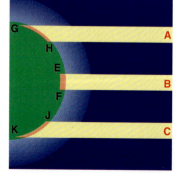

Places at latitudes near the Equator are hot. Places in high latitudes have lower temperatures. The reason for this difference is the curved surface of the Earth. Figure 6.2 shows why. In this example the Earth receives three rays of sunlight, each with the same energy: A, B, and C. Ray B reaches the Earth near the Equator. It falls at an angle of 90° to the surface, so the sun is overhead

VARIATIONS IN TEMPERATURE

here. Notice that Ray B heats area EF. Rays A and C reach the Earth at high latitudes. They fall obliquely on the surface. These rays heat areas GH and JK. Compare the size of the areas heated by the different rays. Rays A and C heat areas larger than that heated by B, therefore areas GH and JK are not as hot as area EF.

There is a second reason why areas GH and JK are not as hot. In the diagram the rays are shown passing through the Earth's atmosphere. Rays A and C pass through a greater depth of atmosphere than ray B. This means that more of their energy is reflected back into space by clouds, so less energy gets through to the ground. This means temperatures are lower at GH and JK.

ALTITUDE

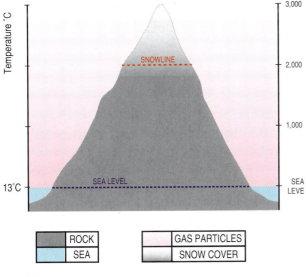

Fig 6.3

The higher a place is above sea level, the lower its temperature. Figure 6.3 shows why. See how there are more gas particles in the atmosphere close to the Earth's surface than there are higher up. It is these gas particles which absorb longwave rays, so more radiation is absorbed at lower levels of the atmosphere. Therefore it is hotter here and colder higher up. The temperature of the atmosphere drops by **6.5°C** for every 1000m increase in altitude.

ACTIVITY 2

1. Which of the following statements are true?
   (a) Temperatures are usually lower in the low latitudes than in the high latitudes. ☐
   (b) The temperature is usually higher at 20° S than it is at 65° N. ☐
   (c) The sun's rays are sometimes overhead at the Equator. ☐
   (d) The temperature rises by 6.5° C for every 500m increase in altitude. ☐
2. Using a diagram explain why the temperature is higher at the Equator than it is at latitude 60° N and 60° S.

THE GEOGRAPHER'S WAY 2

3   If the temperature at sea level is 24°C, work out what the temperature is at 1,000m, 2,000m and 2,500m above sea level.
4   At what height in the diagram in figure 6.3 is the temperature of the air 0°C.
5   Examine figure 6.3 and explain why the upper slopes are covered with snow.

DIFFERENCES IN THE SURFACE

At the seaside on a calm sunny day the beach becomes hot but the water remains cool. The reason for the difference is that land heats and cools down more quickly than water. Figure 6.4 shows why. The sun's rays fall on a coastline. Notice how rays A and B penetrate the sea and heat the water quite a long way down. Rays C and D fall on land but cannot penetrate it so their heat is concentrated at the surface. Therefore in summer land heats quickly and becomes hotter than the sea. But in winter the land loses its heat quickly because it is all at the surface. In contrast the sea heats slowly but retains its warmth for much longer. This is because the sea has to lose heat from a great depth. To sum up:

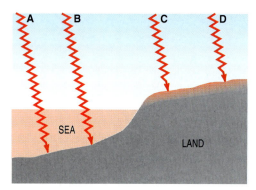

Fig 6.4

(a)   Landmasses heat quickly but lose their heat quickly.
(b)   In summer landmasses are hotter than nearby seas and oceans.
(c)   Seas and oceans heat slowly but keep their heat for far longer.
(d)   In winter seas and oceans are warmer than nearby landmasses.

DISTANCE FROM THE SEA

The sea never gets as warm as nearby land in summer nor as cold in winter. Therefore there is a smaller annual range of temperature at the coast than inland. This can have an important influence on climate. The climate of Western Europe shows this clearly. This is how it happens. The sea warms or chills winds blowing across it. The prevailing wind in Europe is the South-westerly which has crossed the ocean and carries air from the sea. This air is cooler than the land in summer and warmer than it in winter. The wind's greatest effect is felt close to the coast: its warming or cooling influence grows less as it blows inland. Examine the map of Europe in figure 6.5. Valentia has a mild January 7°C

VARIATIONS IN TEMPERATURE

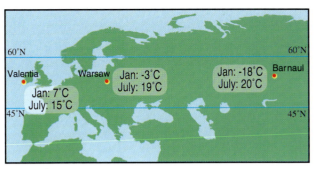

Fig 6.5

and a cool July 15° C. This is due to the ocean's warming effect in winter and its cooling in summer. The annual range of temperature is only 8° C. Moving eastwards across Europe the influence of the sea gets less. There are colder winters, warmer summers and larger annual ranges at Warsaw and Barnaul, which have the same latitude as Valentia. Winters are colder and summers warmer here because they are deeper inland where the influence of the ocean is becoming less and less.

ACTIVITY 3

1   Copy the table in figure 6.6 into your exercise book. Fill in the blank spaces using information from the map in figure 6.5. The values for Valentia are filled in as an example for you.

LOCATION	Valentia	Warsaw	Barnaul
Average January Temperature	7° C		
Average July Temperature	15° C		
Annual range of Temperature	8° C		

Fig 6.6

2   Explain why the annual ranges of temperature at Valentia, Warsaw and Barnaul are different from one another.

WINDS

Winds transfer heat and cold from one area of the Earth to another. The prevailing winds of the North Atlantic are shown on the map in figure 6.7. It shows three prevailing winds: the hot North-east Trade Winds, the warm South-westerly Winds, the cold North-easterly Polar Winds. The South-westerlies and the Polar Winds affect Ireland and most of Europe.

The South-westerly Winds blow between 30°N and 60°N. As they blow from a hotter latitude to a cooler one, they carry heat with them. The warmth they bring greatly affects the climate of Western Europe making it warmer than it otherwise would be.

THE GEOGRAPHER'S WAY 2

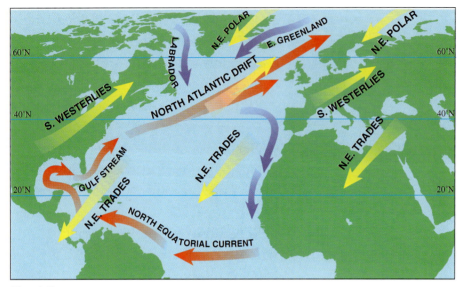

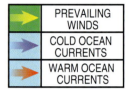

Fig 6.7

The North-east Polar Winds blow out from around the North Pole to about 60°N. These winds make the areas they affect cold. Sometimes they reach as far south as Ireland. When they do they bring very cold weather. In Northern Europe away from the sea their effect is severe.

OCEAN CURRENTS

Winds are an important cause of ocean currents. Prevailing winds blowing across an ocean pull surface water along with them. The winds and the major currents of the North Atlantic show this. Before you read on examine the ocean currents shown in figure 6.7

The north-east Trade Winds blow from the west coast of Africa towards South America. As they do they pull heated equatorial water westwards. This flow of warm water is called the **North Equatorial Current**. When it reaches South America, the flow is deflected north-westwards into the Carribean Sea and the Gulf of Mexico. The warm water builds up here and flows out through the Straits of Florida into the Atlantic as a powerful current called the **Gulf Stream**. About 30°N this comes under the influence of the South-westerly wind which pulls it across the North Atlantic towards Europe. Now it is known as the **North Atlantic Drift** because it flows more slowly. Near Europe, it splits. One branch of this warm current moves in around the coast of Western Europe and on up to the Arctic Ocean. The other moves south past Spain and Africa towards the Equator. This is known as the **Canaries Current.**

VARIATIONS IN TEMPERATURE

The branch of the North Atlantic Drift that flows north has a great effect on West European climates, especially in winter. Because it is warm, it heats the air above it and keeps temperatures higher than they should be. The effect of this warmed air is felt most in coastal regions but it extends deep into the continent. The warm water stops the sea freezing anywhere along the coast of Western Europe.

As the Canaries Current moves south into warmer regions, it seems to become a cold current because the surrounding equatorial water is so much warmer than it. It does not have much influence on climate in Africa because the Trade Winds are offshore here.

The warm currents of the North Atlantic carry water from the Equator to the Arctic. This water must find a way to flow back southwards. It returns in two ways. The first is by surface routes. The Polar Winds pull water from the Arctic Ocean in two cold currents which flow past Greenland. To the west there is the **Labrador Current**, to the east the **East Greenland Current**. The other way is deep down, close to the ocean floor. Here cold currents flow towards the Equator and well up near the coast of Africa.

The Labrador and East Greenland currents affect the climate of Greenland and the North-east of North America. They keep these areas very cold in winter. For example, St. Johns, Newfoundland, latitude $47°$ N, has an average January temperature of $-4.5°$ C. Boston, latitude $42°$ N has an average January temperature of $-3°$ C. These low temperatures cause the sea to freeze as far south as the mouth of the St. Laurence River. This stops shipping for the winter months. Compare this with Europe where the sea is ice-free up to the North Cape, latitude $71°$N.

ACTIVITY 4

1 Match the letters in column X with the number of its pair in column Y.

	X		Y
A	Labrador	1	hot winds
B	Polar winds	2	warm ocean current
C	North Equatorial	3	cold ocean current
D	South Westerlies	4	warm ocean current
E	North East Trades	5	warm winds
F	North Atlantic Drift	6	cold winds

A	
B	
C	
D	
E	
F	

THE GEOGRAPHER'S WAY 2

> 2 (a) Draw a sketch map of the North Atlantic and on it show the main winds and ocean currents.
> (b) Explain how the winds influence the currents.
> 3 Find the following places in your atlas: Newfoundland, St. John's, Boston, Nantes, Rome, St Laurence River, the Great Lakes and the North Cape.
> 4 Winds and ocean currents play an important part in the climate of Europe. Explain what it is.

TEMPERATURE DIFFERENCES THROUGH TIME

Temperatures change through time for many reasons. For instance, clouds and wind can make temperatures warmer or colder. The main causes of temperature change through time are day and night and the seasons of the year. These are predictable because they are caused by the position of the Earth in space, and its regular movement relative to the sun.

DAY AND NIGHT

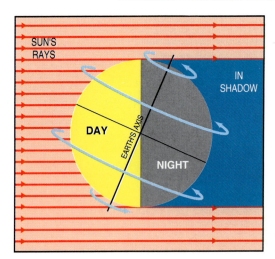

Fig 6.8

Figure 6.8 shows the Earth, its position in relation to the sun, and the rays of the sun falling on the Earth. Imagine a line running through the Earth from the North to the South Pole: call this the **Earth's axis**. This axis is tilted at an angle of $66\frac{1}{2}°$ to the sun's rays. Examine a globe. It usually shows the tilt of the Earth's axis. Use a ruler or metre stick to represent the sun's rays falling on the Earth's surface.

The Earth rotates on its axis once every 24 hours. Try spinning the globe to get an idea of this happening. The rotation causes day and night. Figure 6.9 shows a globe with a light shining on it from the right. This light represents the sun's rays. Notice that only half the globe is lit: the half facing away from the sun is dark. The light and dark represent day and night on Earth. The length of day and night changes during the year at all places on the Earth except the Equator. In Ireland winter days are short and nights are long. The opposite is true in summer; days are long and nights are short.

VARIATIONS IN TEMPERATURE

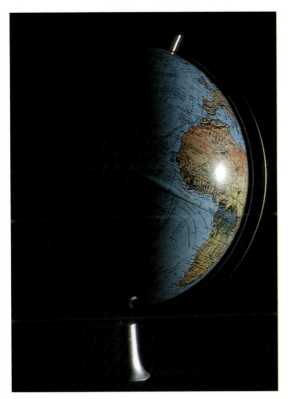

The length of day and night help to decide how much heat a place receives. During daytime the Earth is lighted and warmed by the sun so temperatures rise. During nighttime the Earth receives no sunlight, so temperatures drop as heat radiates out from the Earth into space. This means that in winter when nights are longer than days, there is more cooling than warming taking place so temperatures drop. The opposite is true in summer. Then days are long and nights are short, so there is more warming than cooling and temperatures rise. In this way the temperature seasons are largely due to the length of day and night.

Fig 6.9

HOW THE EARTH ORBITS THE SUN

The length of day and night vary because the Earth makes two different movements in space. The first is its **rotation** on its axis. The second movement is its **orbit** around the sun which takes 365 $\frac{1}{4}$ days, that is one year. Study this diagram carefully. Then do Activity 5 before reading on.

ACTIVITY 5

Examine figure 6.10. Then decide whether each of the following statements is true or false. Answer by ticking a box.

                 T   F

1. The sun orbits the Earth. ☐ ☐
2. The North Pole is tilted towards the sun and the South Pole tilted away on 22nd June. ☐ ☐
3. The South Pole is tilted towards the sun and the North Pole tilted away on 22nd December. ☐ ☐
4. On 21st March and 21st September neither the North nor the South Pole are tilted towards the sun. ☐ ☐
5. On 21nd September the North Pole and the South Pole are not tilted either towards or away from the sun. ☐ ☐

THE GEOGRAPHER'S WAY 2

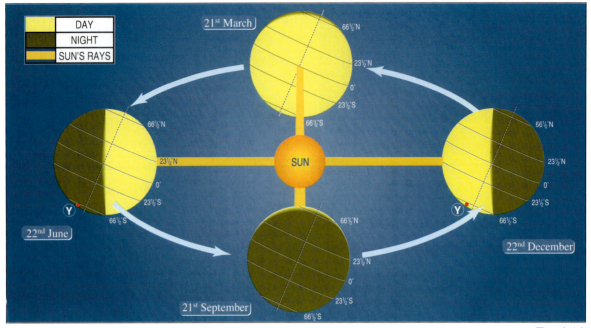

Fig 6.10

THE SEASONS

Figure 6.10 shows the position of the Earth relative to the sun on four important dates. These dates mark approximately the middle of each season of the year. We are going to trace the movement of the Earth as it orbits the sun following the arrows in the diagram. Notice how it takes a year to complete its journey. We will stop to examine its situation each quarter. We begin with December 22nd.

22nd December - Midwinter N. Hemisphere - Winter Solstice

The northern hemisphere is tilted away from the sun. The southern hemisphere is tilted towards it.

The sun is overhead at the Tropic of Capricorn - latitude $23\frac{1}{2}°$S. The heating power of the sun is greatest here.

Between the Arctic Circle $66\frac{1}{2}°$N and the North Pole, there is continuous night. Point W never rotates into sunlight as the Earth spins on its axis. South of the Arctic Circle, the length of day increases reaching 12 hours at the Equator, where day and night are always equal. South of the Equator the length of day continues to increase, reaching 24 hours at latitude $66\frac{1}{2}°$S, the Antarctic Circle. South of this line, there is no night. Point Y never rotates into night.

The northern hemisphere has short days and long nights: Dublin has 7 hours day and 17 hours night.

VARIATIONS IN TEMPERATURE

It is the cold season in the northern hemisphere and the warm one in the southern because heat is gained during day and lost at night.

21st March - Spring Equinox in Northern Hemisphere

The tilt of the Earth remains unchanged. Now it is neither towards nor away from the sun.

The length of day is 12 hours from the North Pole right down to the South Pole, so day and night are of equal length everywhere. This is why it is called **equinox** i.e. equal night.

This is an in-between season because the heat gained in daytime is balanced by the heat lost at night.

22nd June - Midsummer N. Hemisphere - Summer Solstice

The Earth's tilt remains unchanged. The northern hemisphere is tilted towards the sun. The southern hemisphere is tilted away from it.

The sun is overhead at the Tropic of Cancer, latitude $23\frac{1}{2}°N$. The heating power of the sun is greatest in this part of the world.

Between 66°N and the North Pole there is continuous day. Point W never rotates into the dark as the Earth spins. South of the Arctic Circle the length of day decreases reaching 12 hours at the Equator where day and night are always equal. South of the Equator the length of day continues to decrease till the Antarctic Circle $66\frac{1}{2}°S$ is reached. South of this latitude there is no day. Point Y never rotates into the lighted half of the Earth as it spins.

The northern hemisphere has long days and short nights. Dublin has 17 hours day and 7 hours night.

It is the warm season in the northern hemisphere and the cold one in the southern hemisphere.

21st September - Autumn Equinox in the Northern Hemisphere

The situation of the Earth is exactly the same as on 21st March except that the Earth is now on its way back to the December starting point. In the northern hemisphere days will continue to get shorter till they reach their minimum length in midwinter. In the southern hemisphere spring will be followed by summer with maximum daylight.

THE GEOGRAPHER'S WAY 2

ACTIVITY 6

1. Match the letters in column X with the number of its pair in column Y.

X	Y
A spring equinox	1 21st September
B winter solstice	2 21st March
C summer solstice	3 22nd June
D autumn equinox	4 22nd December

A	
B	
C	
D	

2. Examine figure 6.11 which shows the position of the earth relative to the sun on a particular date. Decide whether each of the following statements is true or false.

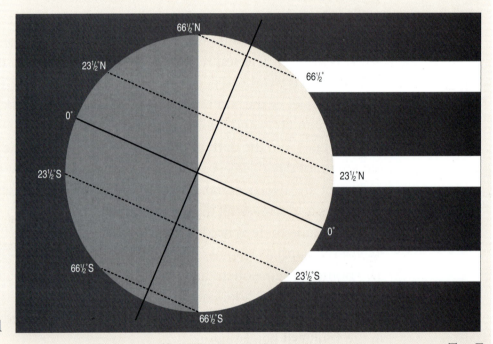

Fig 6.11

(a) The sun's rays are making an angle of 90° with the Equator.
(b) The amount of daylight decreases as you move southwards.
(c) The south Pole has continuous daylight.
(d) This diagram shows the position of the earth at the summer solstice.
(e) The Equator has twelve hours of daylight and twelve hours of darkness.

3. Describe the two main movements of the Earth.
4. Using diagrams explain why the seasons happen.

VARIATIONS IN TEMPERATURE

REVISION

Rewrite the following text in your copy using words from the box to fill in the blank spaces.

> Gulf Stream   Spring Equinox   North Atlantic Drift   longwave
> orbit   6.5°C   Earth's axis   Labrador Current   24 hours
> rotation   Summer Solstice   365 1/4   East Greenland Current
> shortwave   star   Winter Solstice   North Equatorial Current
> factor   Canaries Current   Autumn Equinox

The sun is a _____. The sun's rays are _____ ones. The heated ground gives out _____ radiation. Temperature drops by _____ for every 1000 metres increase in altitude. Something which makes a thing happen or be as it is, is called a _____. The _____ _____ _____ flows just north of 0° latitude. The _____ _____ flows from the Gulf of Mexico out through the Straits of Florida into the Atlantic Ocean. The _____ _____ _____ flows between 30°N and the west coast of Europe. The cold water returning to the Equator along the coast of Northwest Africa is the _____ _____. The cold water flowing down the west of Greenland is the _____ _____ and cold water flowing down the east side is the _____ _____ _____.

The _____ _____ is the imaginary line running from the North Pole to the South Pole. The two movements of the Earth are its _____ on its axis and its _____ around the sun. The rotation takes _____ _____ and the movement round the sun takes _____ days. The important dates in the Earth's movement around the sun are:

   22nd December known as _____
   21st March known as _____
   22nd June known as _____
   21st September known as _____

7 Pressure and Wind

IN THIS CHAPTER YOU WILL LEARN

- The variations in air pressure.
- The relationship between air pressure and wind.
- The locations of the major pressure cells and planetary winds.
- Humidity and relative humidity.
- Air-masses and fronts, both warm and cold.
- How to read isobar maps.

The air has temperature, pressure and humidity. This means it has heat, weight and it holds water vapour gas. These properties are factors in the making of weather. You have studied temperature, and how and why it changes. We now examine pressure and humidity.

AIR PRESSURE

Air pressure is the weight of atmosphere pressing on the surface of the Earth. Air pressure varies everywhere all the time. Listen to weather forecasts and you will hear of changes from low to high pressure and from high pressure to low. These variations are mainly caused by changes in temperature. Knowing the air pressure is important when forecasting weather. Meteorologists measure it constantly, using a **barometer**. The units of measurement are **hectopascals** or **millibars**. Air pressure in Ireland usually has a value between a 'low' of 950 Hp and a 'high' of 1050 Hp.

LOW PRESSURE AND HIGH PRESSURE

Heating of the air is the usual cause of low pressure. Heated air expands and gets lighter. Light air tends to rise. When air rises its weight pressing on the surface becomes less so pressure decreases. See figure 7.1. Where air is rising, there is a **low pressure centre** or '**low**'.

PRESSURE AND WIND

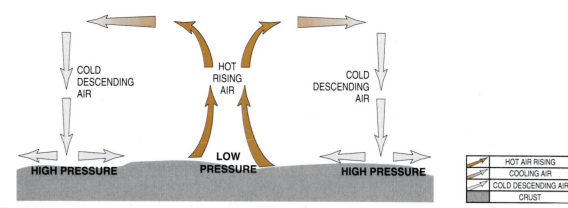

Fig 7.1

Because rising air cools, it makes clouds form. 'Lows' tend to be cloudy and rainy. Another name for a 'low' is a **depression**.

Cooling of the air is the usual cause of high pressure. When air cools it contracts and becomes heavier. Cold air tends to sink and presses more heavily on the surface. This causes higher pressure. Where air is sinking, there is a **high pressure centre** or '**high**.' Cold air is usually drier than warm air, so 'highs' tend to have clear, sunny weather. Another name for a 'high' is an **anticyclone**.

Heavy air spreads out close to the surface. It blows from 'highs' to 'lows'. This movement of air is **wind**. If there is a small difference in pressure between the 'high' and the 'low', the wind will be gentle. If the difference is great, there will be a gale or storm. The difference in pressure between two 'centres' is called the **pressure gradient**. Forecasters can work out facts about winds without being on the spot if they know the location of 'highs' and 'lows' and what the pressures are at each point. From the pressure gradient they tell whether the wind is strong or weak. They can tell the wind direction because winds always blow out from 'highs' and in towards 'lows'.

Because air pressure depends so much on temperature, we can draw two useful conclusions. Regions near the Equator have constant low pressure because it is always hot there. At the Poles there is a constant high pressure cell because it is always very cold there. The word **cell** is used for a large area of pressure. The important pressure cells are shown in figure 7.2. Do Activity 1 based on this.

THE GEOGRAPHER'S WAY 2

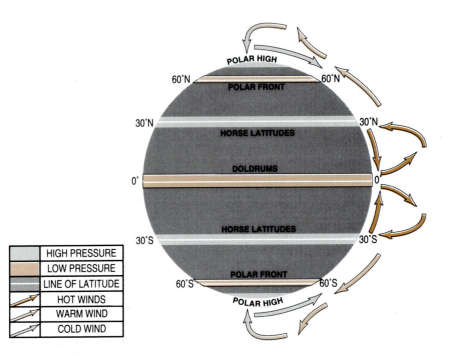

Fig 7.2

ACTIVITY 1

Examine figure 7.2, then do the following:

1. Match the letters in column X with the numbers of their pairs in column Y.

X	Y
A Doldrums	1 Polar Highs
B Horse Latitudes	2 Equatorial Area
C Polar Fronts	3 Around 30° N and 30° S
D North and South Poles	4 Around 60° N and 60° S

A	
B	
C	
D	

2. Write out these sentences omitting the incorrect word.
   (a) There are four/three major low pressure cells on the Earth.
   (b) Ireland with latitude from about 51°N to 55°N is more likely to have high/low pressure often.
   (c) The Horse Latitudes are found 30° on either side of the North Pole/Equator.

3. Describe what happens to the air
   (a) in Equatorial regions   (b) in Polar regions.

PRESSURE AND WIND

THE MAJOR PRESSURE CELLS

Figure 7.2 shows there are four major high pressure cells and three major low pressure cells around the Earth. These are :

HIGHS	LOWS
North Polar High 90°N	Doldrum Low 5°N to 5°S
South Polar High 90°S	North Polar Front 60°N
North 'Horse Latitude' High 30°N	South Polar Front 60°S
South 'Horse Latitude' High 30°S	

Doldrums and the Horse Latitudes   Figure 7.2 shows hot air rising at the Equator causing a low pressure cell at the **Doldrums**. This air cools and spreads out high in the atmosphere. Having cooled, it sinks to the surface around latitudes 30°N and 30°S, called the **Horse Latitudes**   Because the air is sinking, these are areas of high pressure. From the Horse Latitudes air blows out in two directions. Some blows towards the Equator as the Trade Winds; some blows towards the low pressure cell at the Polar fronts as the South-westerly and North-westerly Winds.

Polar Highs and Polar Fronts   The Poles have constant high pressure. From them air spreads out as the Polar Winds. At the Polar Fronts warm air from the Horse Latitudes meets this colder air. When warm air meets colder air, the boundary between them is called a **front**. Because warm air is lighter, it rises over the cold air when they meet. This causes low pressure in the atmosphere. This explains why there is a low pressure cell at the Polar Fronts in the region of latitudes 60°N and 60°S. Note that the air which rises at the Polar Fronts sinks back to Earth at the Poles contributing to the high pressure cell there.

THE PLANETARY WINDS

The **planetary winds** are winds which blow between the major cells of high and low pressure. They are called planetary because they blow on a scale which affects the whole planet Earth. You already know their names because these were the winds which 'prevailed' in Europe and helped to create the currents of the North Atlantic and Arctic Oceans. They were also mentioned when the major pressure centres

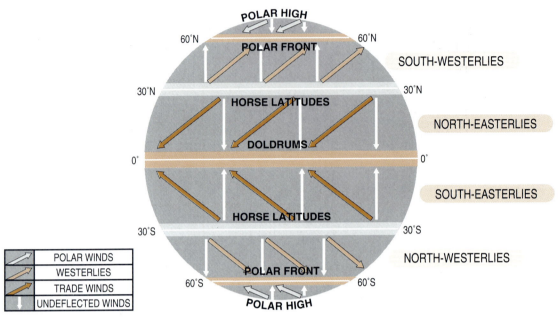

Fig 7.3

were examined. These winds are very important in determining the climate of different parts of the world. The planetary winds:

Planetary Winds/N. Hemisphere	Planetary Winds/S. Hemisphere
The North-east Trade Winds The South-westerly Winds The North-east Polar Winds	The South-east Trade Winds The North-westerly Winds The South-east Polar Winds

When these winds blow from the major 'highs' to the nearby 'lows', they do not blow straight from one to the other. They are deflected to the right in the northern hemisphere and to the left in the southern hemisphere because the Earth is rotating. The white vertical lines in figure 7.3 show how the winds would blow if the Earth did not rotate. The arrows indicate the directions the winds actually take. Notice that in each hemisphere the Polar Winds and the Trade Winds blow in the same direction. Study the wind systems well, because if you understand them you will find it easier to learn the different climates.

PRESSURE AND WIND

ACTIVITY 2

Study figure 7.3 then do the following:
Tick a box to show whether each of these statements is true or not.

		T	F
1	The Trade Winds blow towards the Horse Latitudes.	☐	☐
2	Wind is a movement of air from a high to a low pressure centre.	☐	☐
3	The Westerlies blow towards the Horse Latitudes.	☐	☐
4	The Westerly Winds are the North-westerlies and the South-westerlies.	☐	☐
5	In each hemisphere the Polar and Trade Winds have the same direction.	☐	☐

REVISION 1

Rewrite the following text into your copy using words from the box.

> planetary winds   depression   'high'   hectopascals
> Doldrums   pressure gradient   low pressure centre   cell
> anticyclone   air pressure   front   wind   Horse Latitudes
> millibars   barometer   'low'   high pressure centre

The weight of the air is _____ _____ and the instrument used to measure it is a _____. The units of measurement used to measure the weight of the air are _____ or _____. When air is rising there is a _____ _____ _____ or _____ which is also known as a _____. Where air is sinking there is a _____ _____ _____ or _____ which is also known as an _____. The movement of air from high to low pressure is _____. The difference in pressure between two pressure centres is the _____ _____. A large area of pressure is called a _____. At the Equator there is a low pressure cell called the _____. At 30°N and 30°S there are high pressure cells called the _____ _____. When warm air meets cold air the boundary between them is a _____. The _____ _____ blow between the major cells of high and low pressure.

HUMIDITY

Humidity is the amount of water vapour gas in the air. The water vapour in air is mainly the result of **evaporation** which changes liquid water into a gas. **Condensation** is the opposite of evaporation. It changes water vapour gas into liquid water. There is a limit to the amount of water vapour air can hold. When air reaches the point when it can hold no more water vapour, it is said to be **saturated**. The

relative humidity (**RH** for short) tells how wet the air is. It is measured with an instrument called a **hygrometer**. The wetness is stated as a percentage of the amount required to make the air saturated. If the relative humidity is 90%, then the air is $^9/_{10}$ saturated. It would take another 10% water vapour to saturate the air. If the R.H. is 100% the air is completely saturated, and there is no 'drying' at all. An R.H. of 0% means the air is completely dry. Evaporation is then intense. In practice, the atmosphere is never as dry as this; there is always some water vapour in it.

Humidity is important in the formation of cloud and rain. Examine figure 7.4 carefully. In the diagram the air at ground level has a R.H. of 80% i.e., it is holding 4/5 of the water vapour it could hold. The air is made to rise. As it rises it gets colder. The result is that the R.H. percentage increases because cold air can hold less water vapour than warm air. It is now nearer to saturation point. If the air goes on rising, it continues to chill. If it goes high enough, saturation point is passed and condensation begins. Tiny droplets become visible and cloud begins to form. Notice that the R.H. at the bottom of the cloud is 100%. Inside the cloud millions of cloud droplets join up to form rain droplets. These fall when they become too heavy to stay up in the air.

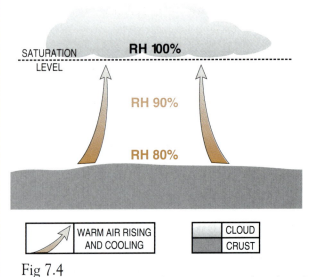

Fig 7.4

ACTIVITY 3

Match the letters in column X with the numbers of their pairs in column Y.

X		Y	
A	Saturated Air	1	0% relative humidity
B	Wet air	2	100% relative humidity
C	Completely dry air	3	21% relative humidity
D	Dry air	4	86% relative humidity
E	Very poor clothes drying	5	94% relative humidity

A	
B	
C	
D	
E	

AIR MASSES AND FRONTS

The atmosphere near the surface is made up of many separate bodies of air. These are called air-masses. An **air-mass** is a large body of air, perhaps hundreds of kilometres wide, which has the same heat, pressure and humidity. An air-mass may be hot or cold and either wet or dry. Warm air-masses come from the tropics and are called **tropical**. Cold air-masses come from near the Poles and are called **polar**. Dry air-masses form over land and are **continental**. Wet air-masses form over seas and oceans and are **maritime**. The table in figure 7.5 shows the air-masses which affect our Irish weather.

AIR-MASS NAME	ABBREVIATION	TYPE	SOURCE
Tropical Maritime	TM air	Warm Wet	Atlantic Ocean
Tropical Continental	TC air	Hot Dry	North Africa
Polar Maritime	PM air	Cold Wet	North Atlantic
Polar Continental	PC air	Cold Dry	North Asia

Fig 7.5

The prevailing winds in Ireland are the South-westerlies, so Ireland is often affected by Tropical Maritime (TM) air-masses from the Atlantic. We also get many Polar Maritime (PM) air-masses. Both of these are wet, so our weather is usually humid. Sometimes continental air-masses spread to Ireland from Europe, Asia and Africa. In winter if there are North-easterly winds, Polar Continental (PC) air brings very cold weather. In summer an occasional Tropical Continental (TC) air-mass may reach us from North Africa bringing hot dry weather.

Ireland's weather is very changeable because the country is close to the Polar Front. Here warm air-masses from the Horse Latitudes meet cold ones coming from the polar region. The Polar Front is not a straight line separating cold and warm air. It forms a wavey line which bulges north or south according as warm air pushes back cold air, or cold air is strong enough to push back warm air. At the same time the air-masses at the Polar Front are usually travelling from west to east. Think of them as a series of warm or cold air-masses snaking around the Earth north and south of latitudes 60°N and S as shown in figure 7.6. This wavey movement makes many different air-masses cross Ireland, each bringing its own weather. In one year as many as ninety air-masses may reach us, so it's little wonder we have changeable weather.

THE GEOGRAPHER'S WAY 2

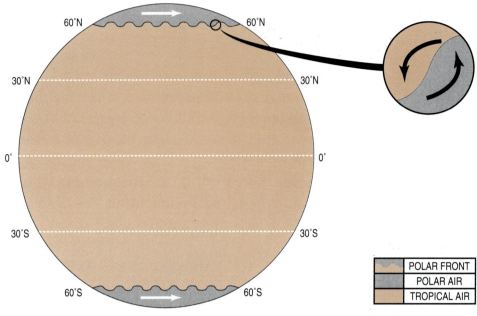

Fig 7.6

WARM AND COLD FRONTS

The air-masses near the Polar Front don't all travel at the same speed as they move eastward. Some are slow-moving and allow the air-mass ahead to remain in an area for a while. More often, the one behind is travelling faster so it catches up with the one ahead. When this happens, a boundary or front forms at the point where the two air-masses meet. No two air-masses are the same, so the one behind is either warmer or colder than that ahead. If the air moving in is colder, there is a **cold front**. If it is warmer, then it is a **warm front**. Each type of front behaves in its own way as it overtakes the air-mass ahead. A definite pattern of weather change is associated with the passing of each type of front, involving temperature change, cloud and often rain. We will examine these patterns now. They will be studied in more detail when we study frontal depressions in Chapter 8.

Warm Front Pattern   At a warm front warmer air is replacing cold air. When they meet the warm air is forced to rise. As it rises it cools and condensation occurs producing clouds and often rain later on. Figure 7.7 shows the weather pattern associated with warm fronts. At A ahead of the warm front: temperatures are cold, the sky is beginning to cloud over with high cirrus cloud, pressure begins to fall. At B the cloud has become lower and is usually stratus type. Perhaps it is just beginning to

PRESSURE AND WIND

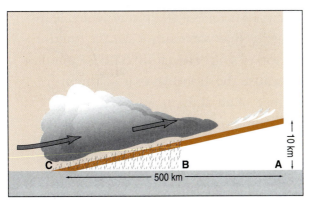

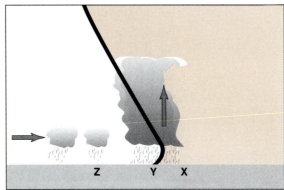

Fig 7.7   Fig 7.8

rain. The word '**nimbo**' or '**nimbus**' is used to indicate that rain is actually falling from a cloud. In this case it is **nimbo-stratus**. Pressure continues to fall. At C which is at the front, the temperature rises, the cloud is low and there is often drizzly rain which continues for a while. Pressure is low but it probably stops falling.

Notice that the slope of the front above the ground is a long gentle one. This means that you can see the cirrus cloud of a warm front long before the front reaches you. High wispy cirrus is one of the most reliable signs that a weather change for the worse is on its way. The symbol on weather maps for warm fronts is shown below the diagram.

Cold Front Pattern At a cold front colder air is replacing warm air. When they meet the cold air wedges under the warm air because it is heavier than it. The warm air is forced to rise quickly, cooling occurs, clouds build up rapidly and rain soon follows. Figure 7.8 shows the weather pattern associated with cold fronts. At X temperatures are not cold and the sky may be cloudy with mainly stratus or cumulo-stratus cloud. Pressure is rather low. At Y which is at the front, there is a sudden drop in temperature. Deep cloud masses move across the sky, heavy rain begins and there may be a strong gusty wind. Because the rain is falling from cumulus cloud, the cloud type is **cumulo-nimbus**. There is a sharp drop in pressure. At Z, behind the cold front, it is cool or cold and pressure is rising. The sky begins to clear except for large cumulus clouds which may give heavy showers of rain or hail. It is a **sunshine and showers** kind of weather.

THE GEOGRAPHER'S WAY 2

Notice that the slope of the cold front is a steep one which leans back from ground level. This means that you cannot see the build-up of cloud till the front is almost on top of you. The cloud type is cumulus and the clouds appear black because the cloud layer is so thick. Sometimes the sudden disturbance of air at the front causes a thunderstorm. There is usually cumulo-nimbus cloud when a thunderstorm happens. The symbol on weather maps for cold fronts is shown below the diagram.

ACTIVITY 4

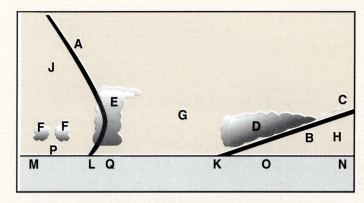

Fig 7.9

1 Examine figure 7.9 then do the following:
   (a) Name the fronts at A and B.
   (b) Name the cloud types at C, D, E and F.
   (c) Is the air warm or cold at each of the points G, H and J?
   (d) Is temperature rising or falling at K and L?
   (e) Is pressure rising or falling between N and K, and L and M?
   (f) What is the weather like at O, P and Q?

Fig 7.10A

Fig 7.10B

110

2. (a) Identify cirrus and cumulo-nimbus cloud which appear in the photographs in figure 7.10.
   (b) Decide which of the photographs indicates the following: an approaching warm front; a cold front has passed.
3. Describe the weather you are likely to get in summer if a tropical continental air mass is over Ireland.
4. Compare and contrast tropical maritime and polar maritime air masses under these headings:
   temperature, pressure, humidity, likely weather in winter.
5. Draw annotated diagrams of a warm front and a cold front.

PLOTTING PRESSURE ON MAPS

The patterns of weather change associated with each type of front are reliable. Therefore forecasters can use them as a basis to make predictions. To do this they have to know where the air-masses are, their type, where the fronts are between them, the direction and speed of the air-masses. This means plotting information on weather maps. In Book One you learned to use isolines to plot temperature and other information. Now we use this method to give the 'pressure picture' of the atmosphere to show where 'highs' and 'lows' are and the wind blowing between them.

The pressure in an area is shown on a map by isobars. An **isobar** is a line on a map joining places with the same pressure. 'Iso' means equal and 'bar' means weight. Isobars operate in the same way as the other isolines, such as isotherms, isohels and contours. The units of measurement on isobars are hectopascals or millibars. When plotting isobars only the isoline for every fourth hectopascal is shown to avoid cluttering up the map. The counting runs up from 1000 Hp and down. Pressure is considered low when less than 1000 Hp and high when above it. High and low pressure centres show up on weather maps as closed figures containing the highest or lowest Hp values for the area. The letters H or L are sometimes used to indicate them. The other isobars are plotted around the centres. If the isobars are plotted close together, pressure is changing quickly and there is a steep pressure gradient. If they are far apart, there is a gentle pressure gradient. From the isobar lines and the pressure gradient they show, you can tell if winds are strong or weak at a particular location.

THE GEOGRAPHER'S WAY 2

Wind blows in towards a 'low' or depression because air is rising here. To take its place, air is being sucked in from areas of higher pressure. The inward-moving air is deflected to the right, so wind spirals in towards the low pressure centre in an anticlockwise spiral. The direction of the wind more or less follows the isobars around the 'low' so wind direction can be estimated.

Wind blows out from a 'high' or anticyclone because the air is descending here. The outward-moving air is deflected to the right so wind spirals out from the centre of a 'high' in a clockwise direction. The direction of the wind more or less follows the isobars around the 'high' so wind direction can be estimated.

ACTIVITY 5

Examine the weather map in figure 7.11, then do the following:

1 Tick a box to show whether each of these statements is true or not.   T   F
    (a) The pressure at P is 1012 Hp. ☐ ☐
    (b) The pressure at Y is 1004 Hp. ☐ ☐
    (c) The pressure at T is 984 Hp. ☐ ☐

PRESSURE AND WIND

                                                                                                  T F

    (d) The pressure at Z is 1000 Hp. ☐ ☐
    (e) The pressure at L is 1004 Hp. ☐ ☐
    (f) The pressure at M is 994 Hp. ☐ ☐
    (g) The pressure at B is less than 984 Hp. ☐ ☐
    (h) The pressure at A is lower than the pressure at C. ☐ ☐
    (i) The pressure at B is lower than the pressure at D. ☐ ☐
(j) Wind is moving anti-clockwise around A. ☐ ☐
(k) Wind is moving clockwise around B. ☐ ☐
(l) Wind is moving anti-clockwise around C. ☐ ☐
(m) The pressure at A is higher than the pressures at B, C and D. ☐ ☐
(n) There are two depressions and two anti-cyclones on the map. ☐ ☐
(o) The strongest winds are blowing around B. ☐ ☐
(p) The lightest winds are blowing around C. ☐ ☐

2 Identify the type of pressure cell at A and B. Give two reasons in each case.
3 As one moves from A to B wind speed increases. What is the evidence for this on the map?
4 Estimate the wind direction at the following locations: Y, P, Z, T, M, L.

REVISION 2

Rewrite the following text into your copy using words from the box to fill in the blank spaces.

> tropical continental   isobar   cold front   saturated   polar
> relative humidity   condensation   sunshine and showers   nimbus
> warm front   hygrometer   air-mass   continental   cumulo-nimbus
> tropical maritime   evaporation   maritime   polar maritime
> polar continental   nimbo   tropical   nimbo-stratus

_____ is the changing of liquid water into gas. The opposite of this is _____. When the air can hold no more water vapour it is _____. The wetness of the air is measured with a _____. The _____ _____ tells us how wet the air is. The words _____ or _____ are used for clouds from which rain is falling. The stratus cloud which brings rain at a warm front is called _____. When a thunderstorm happens there is usually a _____ cloud. A large body of air with similar characteristics is an _____. Hot air-masses are called _____. Cold ones are called _____. _____ air-masses are ones which come from land areas. _____ air-masses come from over the sea. Warm wet air-masses are called _____ _____. Warm dry air-masses are called _____ _____. Cold wet air-masses are called _____ _____. Cold dry air-masses are called _____ _____. Where warm air meets cold air there is a _____ _____. Where cold air meets warm air there is a _____ _____. The changeable weather which arrives after a cold front is called _____ and _____ weather. A line on a map joining places with the same pressure is an _____.

8 Climate

IN THIS CHAPTER YOU WILL LEARN

- The use of composite graphs.
- The workings of the Equatorial Climate.
- Descriptions of Hot Desert and Savannah Climate.
- The workings of the Cool Temperate Oceanic climate including frontal depressions.
- Descriptions of the Warm Temperate Oceanic and Tundra climates.
- The workings of the Boreal climate.

Climate is the weather you expect to get at a place. In Chapters 6 and 7 you learned the importance of temperature, humidity and air pressure in the making of weather and climate. You also studied the factors which influence climate: latitude, altitude, prevailing winds, distance from the sea, ocean currents, cloud. Now we examine some of the main climates of the world, using these ideas.

In Book One you learned there are three climatic zones. These are:

    a Tropical Zone located between 30°N and 30°S,

    a Temperate Zone located between 30°and 60°N and S

    a Polar Zone located between 60°and 90°N and S.

Within the climatic zones there are different climate types. For example, in the Tropical Zone, there is an Equatorial Climate, a Savannah Climate and a Hot Desert Climate. We begin our study by taking a close look at the Equatorial Climate.

ACTIVITY 1

SINGAPORE LATITUDE 1° 20' N												
Month	J	F	M	A	M	J	J	A	S	O	N	D
Temperature (°C)	26	26	27	27	28	27	27	27	27	27	26	26
Rainfall (mm)	170	190	185	175	170	170	190	180	200	250	250	255

Fig 8.1

Examine the climate statistics for Singapore in the table in figure 8.1, then do the following exercises.

1 For which elements of climate are statistics given in the table?

2 Find the maximum and the minimum average monthly temperatures.

3   Work out the annual range of temperature.
4   Calculate the total annual rainfall in millimetres.
5   Is there a dry season or does rain fall all year round?

COMPOSITE GRAPHS

Because temperature and rainfall are the principal elements of climate, it is useful to plot them together on the same graph. This graph is called a **composite graph** because it is composed of two different graphs, in this case, a temperature trend graph and a rainfall bar graph. Having a composite graph allows you to study together the trends in temperature and rainfall during the year and see relationships between them.

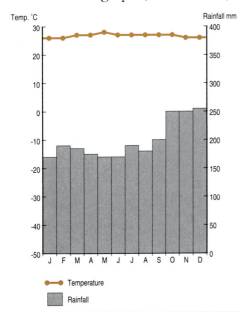

The statistics for Singapore are plotted on a composite trend and bar graph in figure 8.2. Read it in the same way as you read trend graphs and bar graphs. Be careful, though, because the temper-ature scale is shown on one of the vertical axes and the rainfall scale is shown on the other. Also, make sure you know where 'zero' is on both scales.

Fig 8.2

ACTIVITY 2

Examine the composite graph in figure 8.2, then do the following exercise.

1   On the temperature axis give: (a) the highest temperature (b) the lowest temperature.
2   Does rainfall or temperature use the 'horizontal' axis as zero? If either does, state which one.
3   Would you describe the temperature trend as:
    - rising rapidly, then falling
    - falling slowly, then rising
    - remaining fairly constant with little change?

State the trend in a sentence using the phrase you think is correct.

EQUATORIAL CLIMATE

Singapore has an Equatorial Climate. Like all places at or near sea-level close to the Equator it is hot. Temperatures are in the mid or upper twenties all year. They vary little, so the annual temperature range is very small, usually not more than a few degrees. Rain falls throughout the year and the total annual rainfall is high, usually over 2000mm. Because it is always hot and rainy, the Equatorial climate is a 'one season' climate.

Fig 8.3

→	HOT AIR
→	WARM AIR
→	COOL AIR
→	COLD AIR

☁	CLOUD
╱╱	RAIN
▓	CRUST

The word to describe the Equatorial Climate is **monotonous**. The reason is that most days usually have the same pattern of weather. The day begins bright and sunny. Soon it is hot with intense evaporation. The moist air rises with the heat causing **convection currents** which carry it high into the atmosphere. Here it spreads out, cools and condenses to form vast cumulus clouds which build to a height of 8 to 10 kilometres during the morning. These clouds become heavy with rain. See figure 8.3 which illustrates this. By midday the sky is overcast and very heavy rainfall follows. There is often thunder and lightning due to the build-up of electricity in the clouds. The rain eases off towards evening, leaving the countryside saturated. At dawn the pattern begins again. The hot sunshine sets evaporation going and convection starts again. This is the weather people expect all year in lowland equatorial areas.

CONVECTION RAINFALL

Rainfall like this which is caused by strong heating of the air is known as **convection rainfall**. When the rising air cools to saturation point (100% R.h.), rapid condensation occurs. Clouds form, followed by rain which is often a downpour. Convection is the main cause of rainfall in warm and tropical countries. In temperate lands convection rain happens mainly in summertime when temperatures are high. Convection is associated with cumulo-nimbus clouds and thunderstorms.

THE GEOGRAPHER'S WAY 2

LOCATION

Equatorial Climates are found between 10°N and 10°S of the Equator. Important locations which have an Equatorial Climate are: the Amazon Basin, the Zaire Basin, Malaysia and Indonesia. These areas are shown

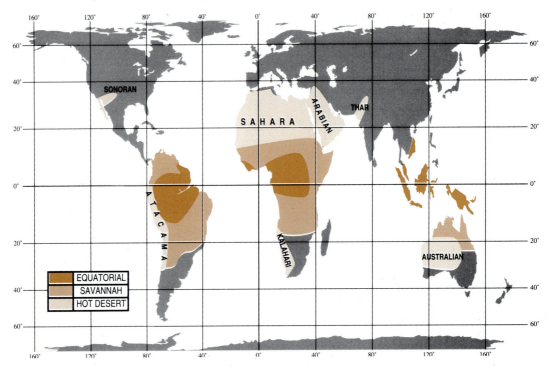

Fig 8.4

on the map in figure 8.4. The true Equatorial Climate is only found at places which are at or close to sea-level. Altitude reduces temperature by about 6.5°C for every 1,000 metre increase in height. This factor moderates the heat at places which are high above sea-level, even if they are situated right on the Equator.

The planetary winds at the Equator also contribute to the hot wet Equatorial Climate. The strong heating of the air near the Equator creates the Doldrums low pressure cell. The North-east and South-east Trade winds meet at the Doldrums causing a front where air is forced to rise into the atmosphere. This air is moist. As it rises the air cools, leading to condensation, thick cloud and heavy rain. The development of convection currents in the atmosphere at the Doldrums also produces severe thunderstorms.

Temperature, humidity and pressure remain more or less the same throughout the year in equatorial regions. This causes the 'sameness' or monotony so typical of the Equatorial Climate

CLIMATE

OTHER TROPICAL CLIMATES

The **Equatorial Climate** is a hot, wet tropical one. There is also a hot dry tropical climate. This is usually called the **Hot Desert Climate**. The Sahara, Kalahari, Sonoran, Australian, Atacama, Arabian and Thar deserts are all hot deserts which have this climate. Find these on the map in figure 8.4. Notice that all of them are situated towards the western side of continents.

These deserts are caused by dry, cool air descending from the upper atmosphere at the high pressure cell of the Horse Latitudes. Because of its dryness this air gives cloudless skies. This allows the sun to shine strongly throughout the year giving very high daytime temperatures. This climate is found on the western side of continents because here the Trade Winds are always offshore. This prevents the sea influencing the climate. The Hot Desert Climate is a 'one season' climate because it is always hot and dry, but in the summer temperatures are hotter because then the sun is higher in the sky.

Between the hot wet Equatorial Climate and the hot dry Hot Desert Climate there is a hot climate which has a wet and a dry season called the **Savannah Climate**. This climate is caused by the movement northwards of all the pressure and wind belts around June and their southward movement around December. Because of this movement the Savannah areas are affected by the wet Equatorial Climate for part of the year and by the dry Hot Desert Climate for the rest of the year. This gives the Savannah Climate a wet and a dry season. The Savannah areas are shown on the map in figure 8.4.

ACTIVITY 3

Climate	Location	Temperature		Annual Range	Rainfall		Pressure	Pressure cells	Planetary winds
		Jan	July		Amount	Type			

Fig 8.5

1. Copy the table in figure 8.5 into your exercise book. Make the columns long enough to take information about three climates. Then using information from pages 115 to 119 fill in facts about Equatorial Climate in each of the columns. Keep the table so that you can fill in information about other climates on it later.
2. Using a diagram explain how convection rainfall happens.
3. Explain how latitude, pressure and the planetary winds influence Equatorial Climate.

THE GEOGRAPHER'S WAY 2

TEMPERATE CLIMATES

The Temperate Zone has a number of climate types. We examine first the Cool Temperate Oceanic Climate. Statistics for this climate are given in the table in figure 8.6.

ACTIVITY 4

BELMULLET LATITUDE 54° 14'												
Month	J	F	M	A	M	J	J	A	S	O	N	D
Temperature (°C)	5	6	7	9	11	13	14	14	13	11	8	6
Rainfall (mm)	108	64	82	70	75	80	76	95	108	116	127	131

Fig 8.6

Using the information in figure 8.6 do the following exercise.
1. Find the maximum and minimum average monthly temperatures.
2. Compare the yearly range of temperature at Belmullet and Singapore.
3. Calculate the total annual rainfall at Belmullet.

Fig 8.7

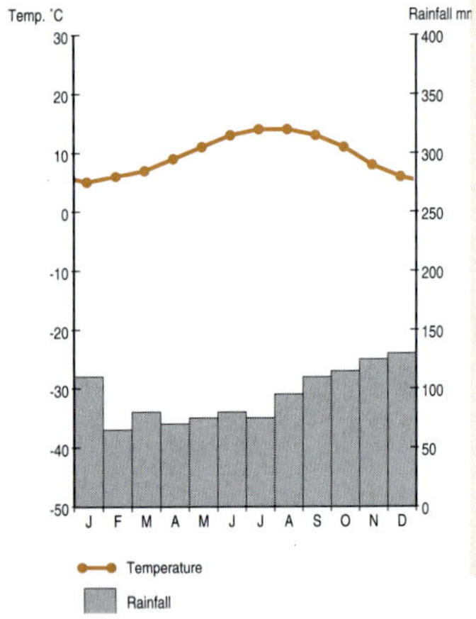

4. Examine the composite graph in figure 8.7, then answer these questions:
   (a) Which of the following statements best describes the trend of average monthly temperature?
   (i) Temperature falls and then rises. ☐
   (ii) There is little change in temperature during the year. ☐
   (iii) Temperatures rise from January till July/August, then they decrease. ☐
   (b) Describe how the rainfall is spread throughout the year.

COOL TEMPERATE OCEANIC CLIMATE

This temperate climate has no extremes of temperature. It is rarely hot or cold. At Belmullet the coldest month has an average monthly temperature of 5°C. The warmest months July and August have an average monthly temperature of 14°C. This gives a small annual range of 9°C, but this is enough to give distinct warm and cool seasons called summer and winter. Rainfall is moderate. At Belmullet the annual total is 1132mm but mountains nearby may get over 2000mm. There is no dry season as rain falls throughout the year.

This climate is very **variable**. A change of weather occurs on average once every four days throughout the year. Sometimes several changes

CLIMATE

happen in a single day as warm and cold fronts cross from west to east. At other times an anticyclone or 'high' settles over an area giving several days or even a couple of weeks of unchanging weather. This happens more often in summer.

LOCATION

The **Cool Temperate Oceanic Climate** is found on the western sides of continents between 40° and 55°N and S of the Equator. Western Europe, Western North America, Southern Chile and New Zealand all have this type of climate. Find these locations on the map figure 8.8. Notice how close the northern and southern edges of this Climatic Zone are to the Polar Fronts at 60°N and S

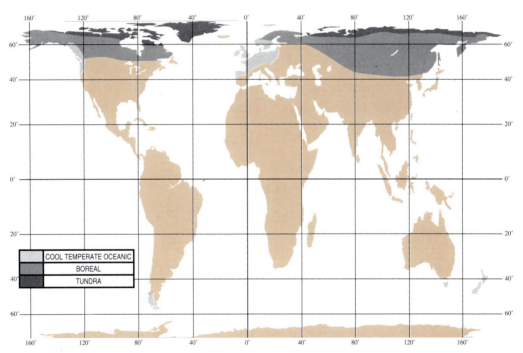

Fig 8.8

EXPLANATION

There are two important influences on this climate. The first is the ocean. This is why the word 'oceanic' is used. The prevailing South-westerly winds blow onshore influencing both temperature and precipitation. For the reasons you have already learned, the ocean is warmer than the land in winter. This warms the air above it which the westerly winds carry inland. This keeps temperatures much higher than they should be. Without this warm oceanic air West European countries would have severe winters with temperatures perhaps 10°C colder than they are. In summer the sea is cooler than the land. This keeps summer temperatures down.

The ocean affects this climate in another way. Oceanic air is usually humid because it picks up water vapour by evaporation on its journey across water. When this air is forced to rise over hills and mountains in its path, it cools causing cloud and relief rainfall. Rainfall amounts due to relief vary with height. Highland areas are wettest with total annual precipitation of 2000mm or more in mountainous parts of Ireland, Scotland, Wales and Northern England. Lowlands and areas in the rain shadow of highlands are much drier with total annual precipitation as low as 500mm.

The second important influence on this climate is the Polar Front. This low pressure cell lies to the north at about 60°N. The Polar Front creates many disturbances in the atmosphere. These cause frequent, often rapid, changes in pressure, wind speed, wind direction, temperature, cloud amount and precipitation. The frontal rainfall they bring causes most of the rainfall in this climate type.

ACTIVITY 5

1. Using data from pages 120 – 122 fill in information about Cool Temperate Oceanic Climate on the table you copied into your exercise book.
2. Explain two ways the ocean influences the Cool Temperate Oceanic Climate.
3. Revise pages 107-110 in Chapter 7 about the Polar Front and warm and cold fronts. Explain how the Polar Front influences the Irish climate.

FRONTAL DEPRESSIONS

Because frontal depressions have such an effect on climate, we will examine them in detail. The frontal depression is the commonest pattern of weather we experience in Ireland. Their disturbing effect on weather is also felt deep into Western Europe. A **frontal depression** is a low pressure centre with two associated fronts: a warm one ahead and a cold one following behind. The depression or 'low' forms along the boundary of the Polar Front as warm and cold air-masses mix. Its development then follows a course which results in a typical frontal situation. Figure 8.9A shows a frontal depression as it often appears on a weather map. Figure 8.9B shows a cross-section along the line A, B, C, D drawn in on the weather map. Examine both these diagrams carefully.

CLIMATE

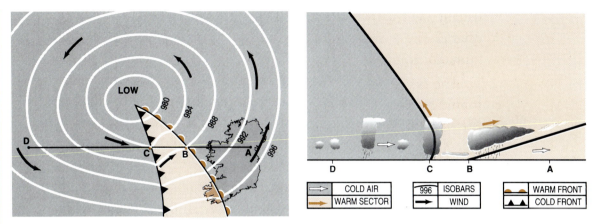

Fig 8.9A

Fig 8.9B

The weather map figure 8.9A shows a depression centred off the west of Ireland. The pressure at the centre is 978 Hp which is quite low. The isobars are tightly packed showing a steep pressure gradient. The anti-clockwise winds are strong because of this. There is a warm front located over the south-west coast of Ireland. There is a cold front located to the west of the warm front. One end of each front lies close to the centre of the 'low '. Between the two fronts there is a wedge of warm air called the **warm sector**. The weather in the warm sector is quite different to the weather ahead of the warm front and behind the cold front.

This pattern of a warm front followed by a warm sector followed by a cold front is typical of a frontal depression. Depressions like these usually travel from west to east across Ireland moving towards North-west Europe. As they do they bring changes of weather as the fronts pass over. We will trace these changes that happen along the line A B C D which appears on both diagrams. If you have learned the patterns of weather at warm and cold fronts, you will find it easy to understand. It is important to follow what is happening on both diagrams.

At A the temperature is low. Pressure is 994 Hp and falling. Wind is south-westerly and fairly strong. Cirrus cloud indicates the approach of a warm front. The weather is dry. The weather begins to disimprove.

Approaching B the cloud becomes lower and thickens. B is at the warm front. Rain is falling from nimbo-stratus cloud. Temperature rises as the front passes. Pressure is 988 Hp and drops sharply at the front. Wind is now from the west. The weather is dull and rainy.

In the warm sector the higher temperature is maintained. The sky is usually overcast with low stratus or nimbo-stratus cloud. There is often drizzle. The weather is 'muggy' with poor drying as the relative humidity is high.

At C there is a cold front. Warm air is pushed up sharply along the front resulting in a band of thick cumulo-nimbus cloud. As the front passes temperature and pressure drop quickly. Pressure is now 984 Hp. Winds have gone round to the north-west. The weather has become cold and blustery with heavy rain.

At D behind the cold front temperature remains low. Large cumulus or cumulo-nimbus clouds grow, giving heavy showers. There may be sunny spells. Pressure is 994 Hp and rising. Winds are becoming northerly. The weather begins to clear giving 'sunshine and showers' but the wind remains chilly.

Weather forecasters can predict the weather in frontal depressions because their pattern is usually fairly constant. Once they know a frontal depression is approaching and its speed, forecasters can tell fairly accurately what the weather will be over the coming hours.

ACTIVITY 6

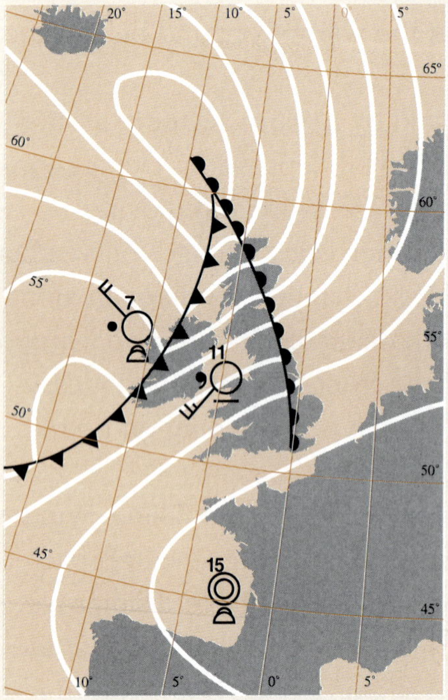

Fig 8.10

1. Examine the weather map in figure 8.10 then decide whether each of the following statements is true or false. Tick the correct box. **T F**
   (a) The centre of a frontal depression is located at 61° 30' N and 10° W. ☐ ☐
   (b) There is a cold front located along the west coast of Ireland. ☐ ☐
   (c) There is a warm front located along the west coast of Britain. ☐ ☐
   (d) The pressure at X is 1004 Hp. ☐ ☐
   (e) The pressure at Y is 1018 Hp. ☐ ☐
   (f) There is a warm sector over France. ☐ ☐
   (g) There are very light winds over France. ☐ ☐
   (h) The steepest pressure gradient is over Britain and Ireland. ☐ ☐
   (i) There is an anticyclone over France. ☐ ☐
   (j) There are South-westerly winds over Ireland. ☐ ☐
   (k) There is a rain belt over Eastern Britain. ☐ ☐

2. Describe the weather at Dublin, Belmullet and Bordeaux.

3. Suggest reasons why the weather varies at Dublin, Belmullet and Paris.

CLIMATE

WARM TEMPERATE OCEANIC CLIMATE

Another climate type in the temperate zone is the **Warm Temperate Oceanic Climate**. This climate is also called **Mediterranean Climate**. It is located on the southern side of the Cool Temperate Oceanic Climate between about 30° and 45°N and S on the western side of continents. The main areas with this climate are: The Mediterranean Basin, Coastal California, Central Chile, the Cape in South Africa and South-west Australia. These areas are shown on the map in figure 8.8. This climate has warm summers with average July temperatures around 20°C. Rainfall is light at about 600mm. Most of the rain falls in winter. Summer is a dry, sunny season. This climate is said to be the most pleasant in the world and it attracts many tourists. The natural vegetation of warm temperate regions is dealt with on pages 138/9.

BOREAL CLIMATE

There are three Polar Climates. Of these the **Boreal Climate** is the most important. It is a cold continental climate. Statistics for this climate are given in figure 8.11. Note that Yakutsk is not very far north but its continental location gives it a climate of great extremes.

ACTIVITY 7

YAKUTSK 62°10'N												
Months	J	F	M	A	M	J	J	A	S	O	N	D
Temperature (°C)	-43	-37	-23	-9	5	15	19	16	6	-9	-29	-41
Precipitation (mm)	23	5	10	15	28	53	43	65	30	35	15	23

Fig 8.11

Examine the climate statistics in figure 8.11, then do these exercises.
1. What are the maximum and minimum average monthly temperatures?
2. Calculate the annual range of temperature. Compare the result with the annual ranges for Singapore and Belmullet.
3. Calculate the total annual precipitation. During which months would snow be the likely precipitation?

THE GEOGRAPHER'S WAY 2

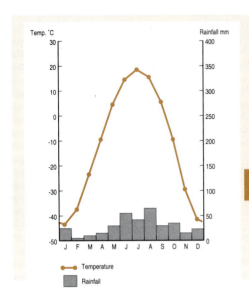

4. When does precipitation reach its maximum? In summer or winter?

5. Examine the composite graph, figure 8.12, then answer the following:

    (a) Describe the temperature trend shown on the graph.

    (b) Is there a relationship between precipitation and the trend of temperature? If there is, explain it.

Fig 8.12

DESCRIPTION

The Boreal Climate has the greatest annual range of temperature in the world. At Yakutsk the average January temperature is an extreme -43°C. The average July temperature is 19°C. This gives an enormous range of 62°C. Most of the precipitation falls in the short summer when maritime air is able to penetrate deep into the continent. Winter is a long dry season.

LOCATION

This climate is found in the North American and Eurasian landmasses between 50°N and 65° N. It stretches as great belts across North America and Alaska to Labrador and across Eurasia from Sweden to Siberia. These areas are shown on the map in figure 8.8.

EXPLANATION

This is the Earth's most extreme climate. The reason for this is that it is the climate of the interior of large continents. The interiors of these landmasses cool down and heat up rapidly with little oceanic influence to moderate heating and cooling. Far from coasts the air is dry so skies are cloudless. Therefore the sun heats strongly in summer. In winter the absence of cloud allows radiation of heat from the surface causing very low temperatures.

CLIMATE

In winter these areas become high pressure centres on account of the intense cold. There is little precipitation because the descending air in the 'highs' is very dry. At Yakutsk only 91mm precipitation falls in six winter months. Most of the rain falls in the short summer when heating of the land surface causes convection. Some convection rain falls but most is frontal. Convection causes maritime air to be sucked into the interior of the continent. This moist air produces frontal situations when it collides with continental air-masses

ACTIVITY 8

1. Using data from pages 125-127 fill in information about Boreal Climate on the table you have already drawn into your exercise book.
2. Explain how a continental location affects Boreal Climate.

TUNDRA CLIMATE

The **Tundra climate** is a polar one. It is found in a narrow strip along the northern edge of the Boreal Climate belts between 70° and 80° N. Because these areas lie inside the Arctic Circle, there is prolonged daylight during the short summer, giving cool temperatures between 6° and 9°C. Winter is long and very severe on account of the long Arctic night. In January temperatures reach below - 30°C except along the coasts where maritime influences have a moderating effect. Some rain falls in summer but precipitation is generally low and falls mainly as snow. In the southern hemisphere only a few isolated places along the edge of the Polar Desert of Antarctica have a Tundra Climate.

ACTIVITY 9

1. Match each letter in column X with the number of its pair in column Y

X		Y	
A	Hot, dry	1	Equatorial Climate
B	Hot, wet and dry	2	Boreal climate
C	Greatest annual range	3	Hot Desert Climate
D	Hot and wet	4	Savannah Climate

A	
B	
C	
D	

2   Study the climate statistics for stations A, B and C in figure 8.13, then do the following exercises:

Location A

Months	J	F	M	A	M	J	J	A	S	O	N	D
Temperature (°C)	4	5	7	9	12	16	18	17	15	11	8	5
Precipitation (mm)	54	40	37	37	46	45	57	59	49	57	64	48

Location B

Months	J	F	M	A	M	J	J	A	S	O	N	D
Temperature (°C)	-49	-44	-30	-13	2	12	15	11	3	-14	-36	-46
Precipitation (mm)	7	5	5	4	5	25	33	30	13	11	10	7

Location C

Months	J	F	M	A	M	J	J	A	S	O	N	D
Temperature (°C)	26	26	27	28	28	27	27	27	27	27	26	26
Precipitation (mm)	101	66	118	230	394	220	140	102	174	348	333	142

Fig 8.13

(a) Calculate the annual range of temperature for each station.
(b) Calculate the total precipitation for each station.

3   Pupils group together in threes. Using the climate statistics for Stations A, B, and C above, each one plots a temperature line graph and rainfall bar graph for a station. Check each other's work for accuracy. Discuss your graphs comparing and contrasting the climate picture they give.

4   Identify the climate found at each of the locations A, B, C. Give reasons.

5   Describe two of the following: Equatorial Climate, Cool Temperate Oceanic Climate, Boreal Climate.
Use the following headings in your description: Temperature, Temperature Range, Rainfall, Types of Rainfall, Sunshine, Cloud, Seasons.

CLIMATE

REVISION

Rewrite the following text into your copy using words from the box to fill in the blank spaces.

> Boreal Climate   variable   Equatorial Climate   Tundra Climate
> Cool Temperate Oceanic Climate   convection rainfall   climate
> Savannah Climate   frontal depressions   monotonous
> composite graph   Warm Temperate Oceanic Climate
> convection current   Hot Desert Climate   Mediterranean Climate

The weather you expect to get in an area is its _____. When two graphs are put together the result is a _____ _____. The climate in the lowlands between 10° N and 10° S is _____ _____. One word to describe this climate is _____. When hot air rises, spreads out and cools a _____ _____ is formed. Rain caused by such a current is called _____ _____. The dry tropical climate is called _____ _____. The tropical wet and dry climate is called _____ _____. The climate we have in Ireland is the _____ _____ _____. One word to describe this climate is _____. This climate is affected by low pressure cells called _____ _____. On the southern side of the Cool Temperate Oceanic Climate there is the _____ _____ _____ _____ which is also known as the _____ _____. The climate with the highest annual range of temperature is the _____ _____. On the northern edge of the Boreal Climate region there lies the _____ _____.

9 Vegetation

IN THIS CHAPTER YOU WILL LEARN

- The differences between natural and cultivated vegetation.
- The natural vegetation and soil of the Rainforest.
- The natural vegetation and soil of the Temperate Deciduous Forest.
- Description of Warm Temperate Oceanic vegetation.
- The natural vegetation of the Mediterranean lands.
- The natural vegetation and soil of the Boreal lands.
- The relationship between climate, soil and vegetation.

The word **vegetation** means the living cover of plants on the land. Vegetation is an important part of the environment. It may be natural or cultivated. **Natural vegetation** is what grows without human interference. **Cultivated vegetation** is planted and grown by people. In this chapter we will study natural vegetation.

To understand vegetation and how it relates to climate, it helps to know how plants grow. Figure 9.1 illustrates a growing plant. It shows rain seeping into the soil. In the soil the water dissolves nutrients. Water carrying the nutrients moves through the plant to the leaves which absorb carbon dioxide from the air. Using energy from sunlight the leaves change the nutrients and carbon dioxide into sugars which the plant uses as food. It is clear from this account that sunshine and rainfall play an important part in plant growth.

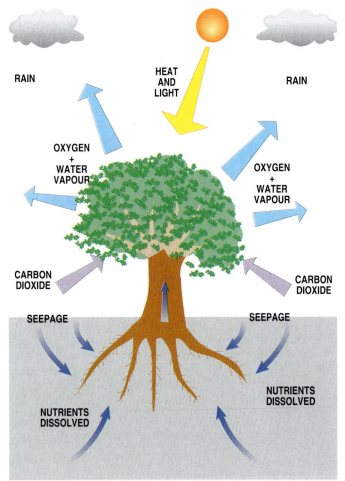

Fig 9.1

VEGETATION

Climate determines the amount of sunlight, heat and water available to plants. Soil determines the nutrients they get. As climates vary round the world, so does vegetation. Likewise, as soils vary from place to place, so does the plant life which lives on them. We will study the soils and vegetation of four climatic regions of the world.

ACTIVITY 1

1. Examine figure 9.2. Do you think the photograph shows natural or cultivated vegetation? Locate evidence to support your conclusion.
2. (a) What are essential for plant growth?
   (b) Using a diagram, explain how a plant grows.
3. Name the five essential ingredients of soil. Refer to Chapter 16 in Book One, if you cannot remember.
4. Explain the difference between natural and cultivated vegetation.

Fig 9.2

EQUATORIAL RAINFOREST

The **rainforest** is the natural vegetation of places with an Equatorial Climate. This climate is ideal for the growth of plants because it is hot and wet, and the growing season lasts all year. There is no dead season because there is always heat and rainfall for growth. These regions have the greatest variety of plants in the world; about one-third of all plant species are found in the rainforests. The high temperatures and heavy rainfall are ideal for large plants such as trees. Typical rainforest trees are tall, broad-leaved evergreens. They are often over 45 metres in height. Their leaves are large and flat, allowing quick conversion of nutrients to food, so growth is rapid. They are evergreen because there is no time when the trees are bare; the leaves die and are replaced all through the year. The rainforest is the source of valuable hardwood species including mahogany, rosewood and ebony. These woods are used in the manufacture of expensive furniture.

In the rainforest there are three vegetation layers. These are shown in figure 9.3. The top or **canopy** layer is made by the crowns of the tallest trees such as the mahoganies and rosewoods. The canopy gets the greatest amount of sunlight and shades the other layers which do not grow so tall. Below the canopy there is an in-between layer of smaller trees and the creepers called **lianas**. The third layer is the **undergrowth** which consists of ferns and fleshy grasses. If the canopy is very dense, little light gets through to the forest floor and vegetation may be absent. The forest floor is often covered with a thick tangle of decaying plant material.

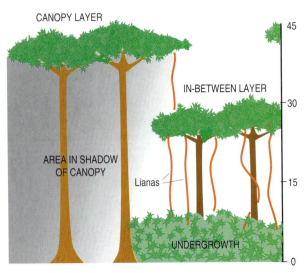

Fig 9.3

ACTIVITY 2

Examine figure 9.4, then do the following.
1. Estimate the height of the canopy and the in-between layer. Use what is in the photograph to help you estimate.
2. Sketch the photograph and indicate two layers of vegetation.
3. Give three pieces of evidence that this is a photograph of an equatorial rainforest.

Fig 9.4

ZONAL SOILS

There are three main climatic zones; tropical, temperate and polar. Each climatic zone has a vegetation and soil type associated with it. Soils associated with climate zones are called **zonal** soils.

Equatorial Zonal Soils   The zonal soils of the Equatorial climate are the **Laterites**. They are the typical **red earths** of the Tropics. The heat and heavy rainfall cause intense chemical weathering which penetrates deep down, so these soils are not shallow. They are very leached because many of their minerals are dissolved and washed out by the frequent downpours. Iron oxides formed by weathering give the soil its red colour. Heat and humidity cause rapid decay of dead plant material but the nutrients are often washed away before they can seep back into the soil.

The equatorial regions appear to be very fertile with lush vegetation. This lushness is deceptive. The fertility depends on the forest's own waste and not on the soil. As leaves fall from the trees and trees die, the plant material is broken down into humus. This humus provides the nutrients on which the trees depend for growth. Many people have been fooled by the richness of the vegetation into believing that laterite soils are very fertile. When they are ploughed and farmed they quickly become useless for agriculture because most of their minerals have been leached away.

Human Response
Hunters and Gatherers   The people who lived in the rainforest were 'hunters and gatherers' or 'shifting cultivators'. The hunters and gatherers lived by hunting animals, fish, birds and insects or by gathering wild plants, roots and fruit. They stayed in one part of the forest till their prey and food supply were exhausted, then they moved on to a new area. These people were completely dependent on their environment.

Shifting Cultivators   These inhabitants of the rainforest cleared a patch of the forest and farmed it for a few years. They usually cleared the forest by burning. This gave the soil a temporary fertility because wood-ash provides **potash**, an important plant nutrient. But its good effect only lasted for a few harvests, then the nutrients were used up or

THE GEOGRAPHER'S WAY 2

washed away. When the soil was exhausted the people moved to a new patch which they cleared for cultivation and started all over again. Eventually they returned to the patch they had started from. In this way they retraced their steps, using and re-using the land over a long period of time. This type of shifting cultivation gave the soil time to become fertile again in a natural way. Shifting cultivators, through knowledge and farming skills, had some control over their environment.

Cash Crop farmers   Colonists from other countries often settled in rainforest areas. They hoped to make their fortune by clearing the land and farming it. They soon found it was difficult to make a success of farming because after a few years the soil became infertile. Then yields could only be kept up if large amounts of fertiliser were put on the land. This used up any profits they made.

ACTIVITY 3

Fig 9.5

1. Describe how shifting cultivators used the rainforest to maintain theirway way of life.
2. Explain why the peoples of the rainforest had to remain 'on the move' rather than settle down in one place.
3. What happened when Europeans tried to colonise the Rainforest?
4. Using figure 9.5 and what you have learned about tropical soils, write a description of a typical laterite soil.
5. Explain how climate plays an important part in the formation of a laterite soil.

VEGETATION

TEMPERATE DECIDUOUS FOREST

Temperate deciduous forest is the natural vegetation of regions with a Cool Temperate Oceanic Climate. Rainfall in all seasons provides plenty of water, and for most of the year there is sufficient heat for trees to grow well. In winter temperatures are too low for growth, so trees develop a deciduous habit. **Deciduous** means having a growing season and a dead season. The trees produce foliage and grow in spring and summer. In autumn growth slows and the trees shed their leaves. In winter growth stops completely.

Most trees in temperate deciduous forests are broadleaved. A few varieties of deciduous conifers are found too, such as the larch. Oaks are the typical species of temperate deciduous forest. Beech, ash and elm are other important species. These do not grow as tall as rainforest trees because there is less heat and moisture.

Their crowns form a canopy but it is lower and much less dense than in the rainforest. Beneath there is a thin undergrowth of smaller trees like hazel and holly. Grass and other plants usually cover the ground. Most of the trees in this forest are hard-woods which mature slowly. Many provide valuable timbers used for furniture-making and construction. Figure 9.6 shows this type of vegetation.

ACTIVITY 4

Fig 9.6

Examine figure 9.6 then do the following exercises.
1. What evidence is there that this is deciduous vegetation?
2. Describe the vegetation in the photograph under these headings: height, shape, leaf-type, colour, species.
3. Find out what oak, elm, ash and beech timber are used for.
4. Suggest reasons why the forest floor in temperate deciduous forest has an undergrowth of smaller trees with a grassy ground cover.

Brown Earth Zonal Soil The zonal soils of temperate deciduous forest are fertile brown earths. The autumn leaf-fall decays into a basic humus, rich in nutrients. This provides good nourishment for vegetation. Soils retain their fertility because the moderate rainfall causes little leaching and the ground water is not very acidic.

Human Response

The mild climate and fertile soils made the temperate deciduous forest regions attractive for human settlement. They have been inhabited for many thousands of years so there has been time for people to interfere with and destroy the natural vegetation. Little of the original woodland of the temperate deciduous forests remains in Europe. In Ireland, the deciduous forests which covered most of the countryside were cut down to make way for farming and to provide fuel and building materials. Possibly the only places where the natural vegetation still exists are tiny isolated islands which people were not interested in farming.

ACTIVITY 5

1. (a) Name the zonal soil of the Cool Temperate Oceanic Climate.
   (b) Revise brown earth soil on page 186 of Book One.
   (c) Are brown earth soils usually found in upland or lowland areas?
2. Explain why the zonal soils of areas with a Cool Temperate Oceanic Climate are fertile.
3. Draw a diagram of a brown earth soil profile. Refer to page 185 in Book One, if you cannot remember how to do this. Is it easy to tell the soil horizons apart in this kind of soil?

BOREAL FOREST

The Boreal Climate has a short summer and a long cold winter. Inside the Arctic Circle there is little sunlight during the winter months. There is not much precipitation. Some rain falls in summer but any winter precipitation falls as snow. These conditions are unfavourable for most plants. Coniferous species which make up most of the boreal forests are adapted to this harsh climate. They have a conical shape which prevents snow building up on the branches and breaking them. This shape also withstands the wind. They are tall and flexible, able to sway in the wind and bend to shed snow. Their leaves are needle-shaped and waxy. This prevents the tree losing water through its foliage. Most

VEGETATION

conifers are **evergreen**. This means they don't have to produce foliage before they begin to grow when the temperature reaches 6°C. As the growing season is short, this helps them survive. Coniferous trees suppress other plants which compete with them for nutrients. They do this by smothering the ground under a thick layer of needles which take years to decay into humus. There is little undergrowth in boreal forest.

Boreal Forests provide enormous quantities of softwood timber. Pine, fir, larch and spruce species produce the red and white **deals** which are used for furniture, household fittings, and construction. Most papers and boards are made with coniferous softwood. The cellulose from these trees is the raw material for products ranging from paints to textiles. Coniferous forests are easy to exploit for two reasons. Firstly, there is little undergrowth. Secondly, the trees grow naturally in **stands** of one particular type of tree. The species are not mixed all through the forest. See page 44 Book One.

ACTIVITY 6

1. Describe a coniferous tree, using the information given above.
2. Explain three ways conifers are adapted to their environment.
3. Name two parts of the world where there are extensive boreal forests. To do this, see boreal climate, Chapter 8.
4. Make a list of the furniture and fittings in your house made from deal timber.
5. Using an encyclopaedia, find out how newsprint is manufactured.

Podzol Soil   Podzols are the zonal soils of the Boreal Forests. Podzol is the Russian word for the colour 'ash-grey'. It was first used to describe the forests of the **taiga**, the huge belt of coniferous forest which stretches across Northern Asia. These soils are so badly leached that they are nearly colourless. Podzols are acid because coniferous trees make soils acidic. As water from rain and snow-melt seeps through the needle-leaves on the forest floor, it becomes strongly acidic. This acid water makes leaching much worse because it removes iron oxide and other chemicals from the soil.

Human Response

The largest wooded areas in the world are found in the Boreal Forests. Much of the forest has survived as natural vegetation. The harsh environment and poor soils have discouraged farming and the permanent settlement which farming brings. The valuable timber resources of the forest are exploited but if cutting is done properly, the forest regenerates naturally. To **regenerate** means to re-create itself. The logging camps of the lumberjacks are temporary settlements because once cutting is finished in an area the teams move off to a new site. Fur trappers live in the Boreal Forests. It is in their interest to preserve the natural environment and its animals because their livelihood depends on it.

ACTIVITY 7

1. Explain why the word "podzol" is a good one to describe the soils which develop beneath the Boreal Forests.
2. Explain why the soils of the Boreal Forest are severly leached.
3. Draw a profile of a podzol. Refer to pages 187/8 in Book One.
4. Investigate the work of a lumberjack in either Canada or Siberia.
5. Find out all you can about the fur trade. Do you think that it is wrong to kill wild animals for their fur? If the animals are bred in captivity, does this change anything?

MEDITERRANEAN VEGETATION

The Warm Temperate Oceanic Climate, or Mediterranean Climate, has dry hot summers and mild moist winters. In summer there are periods of drought, relieved by occasional convection rain which falls during thunderstorms. The vegetation of places with this climate has adapted to survive these unfavourable conditions.

The natural vegetation is broadleaf evergreen trees. The photograph in figure 9.7 shows a fig tree which is typical. Notice that it is not very tall. Its broad leaves have a shiny, waxy surface which prevents too much water being lost due to transpiration. **Transpiration** is the word used to describe how plants and trees breathe out water vapour and oxygen. Trees and plants have adapted by developing long roots. These reach down into the regolith to get at the water stored there during the rainy winter. The vine is an example of a plant of this kind. Some trees have a thick bark which helps conserve the tree's moisture. Cork comes from the bark of such a tree, the **cork oak**. Others, like the olive have tough leathery leaves. Coniferous trees, such as pines, are also common especially in hilly areas. As you know, conifers are well adapted to survive hard conditions, in this case the summer drought. Trees like the lemon and orange are not native to lands with Mediterranean climate but have adapted well to it.

VEGETATION

Fig 9.7

In spite of the difficult climate Mediterranean agriculture produces a number of important products such as cereals, fruits, citrus fruits, wine, and vegetable oils. Some crops, like wheat, olives and vines, suit the climate. Others need irrigation to get them through the summer drought. The river valleys of these regions such as the valleys of the Nile, the Ebro, the Po, the Jordan and the Rhone are very productive. The climate provides plenty of heat and the rivers provide water for irrigation.

Most of the natural forests of regions with a Mediterranean Climate have been cleared. These regions have been settled for many centuries because the climate suits people. The forests were destroyed to make grazing for animals and to provide fuel. Goats and sheep introduced by people did most of the damage. When the forest vegetation was cleared, it was replaced by bushes and shrubs known as **maquis**. This scrubland is useless and almost impossible to reclaim. The destruction of the natural Mediterranean-type forest is an example of how people can damage the environment through ignorance.

ACTIVITY 8

1. Explain how Mediterranean vegetation has adapted to the climate.
2. Explain why the Mediterranean climate suits people but not plants.
3. In your atlas find the five river valleys mentioned in the text. Make a tracing of the Mediterranean basin and the surrounding countries. On it show these rivers and their basins.

THE GEOGRAPHER'S WAY 2

CLIMATE SOIL AND VEGETATION

You now know that there is a relationship between climate, soil and vegetation. Figure 9.1 on page 130 shows this relationship. Revise it carefully and make sure you understand the interactions it shows.

1. Climate provides heat and water.
2. Soil provides the 'home' for vegetation and most of the nutrients it needs.
3. Vegetation takes in carbon dioxide and gives out oxygen.
4. Vegetation returns water vapour to the atmosphere through transpiration.
5. The roots of vegetation protect the soil from erosion.
6. Decayed vegetation renews the nutrients in the soil.

ACTIVITY 9

1. Using information from this chapter and the previous one, fill in the table below in figure 9.8. The map in figure 9.9 shows the locations of A, B, C, D, E, F, G, H.

Location	Climate	Vegetation	Zonal Soil
A			
B			
C			
D			
E			
F			
G			
H			

Fig 9.8

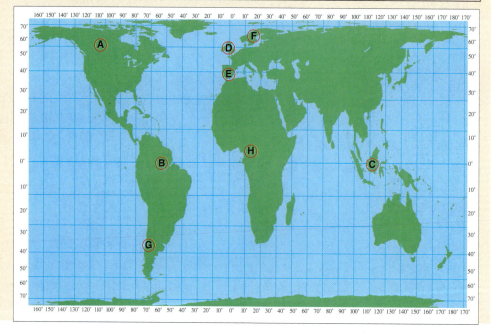

Fig 9.9

2 Using a diagram explain how climate, soil and vegetation interact with one another.

Fig 9.10A

Fig 9.10B

Fig 9.10C

Fig 9.10D

3 Examine the photographs in figure 9.10. Identify the vegetation type or types in each photograph.

THE GEOGRAPHER'S WAY 2

REVISION

Copy the text below into your exercise book using words from the box to fill in the blank spaces.

> maquis   vegetation   transpiration   lianas   evergreen
> rainforest   stands   undergrowth   zonal   natural vegetation
> taiga   deciduous   deals   shifting cultivators   canopy
> red earths   Temperate Deciduous Forest   regenerate
> hunters and gatherers   potash   cultivated vegetation   laterites

The living cover of plants on the land is called _____. The plants which grow without human interference are _____ _____. _____ _____ is planted and grown by people. _____ is the natural vegetation of places with Equatorial Climate. The top or highest layer in this forest is the _____ layer. Below this layer there is the in-between layer which has many creepers called _____. At ground level there is _____. The soils associated with the climate zones are called _____ soils. These include the _____ _____ or _____ of the Equatorial Climate zone. Some people in the rainforest lived as _____ _____ _____ and had no control of their environment. Other inhabitants were _____ _____ who had some control of their environment. They cut down trees to make way for agriculture. They burnt trees which provided the nutrient _____ for the soil. The natural vegetation of the Cool Temperate Oceanic Climate is _____ _____ _____. Having a growing and a dead season is called a _____ habit. Plants which remain green all year round are called _____. The timbers which come from coniferous softwoods are called _____. Large groups of trees of the same species are called _____. The boreal forest of Asia is called the _____. If a forest is properly cut it will _____ itself. The loss of oxygen and water vapour to the atmosphere is called _____. The vegetation which replaced the broadleaf evergreen forests of the Mediterranean when they were cut down is _____.

10 Settlements

IN THIS CHAPTER YOU WILL LEARN

- Development of Irish towns from Norman times to the present.
- Functions of towns.
- Nucleated settlement in the Boyne Valley.
- Nucleated settlement in the Rhine Valley.
- Settlement in the Dutch polders.

A **settlement** is a place where a person or people live. A **nucleated** settlement has houses and buildings together in a cluster round some point or nucleus. Nucleated settlements vary in size from a few farmhouses to villages, towns and cities. Besides a residential function, larger settlements have urban functions like commerce, industry and transport. The map in figure 10.1 shows the distribution of nucleated settlements such as towns and cities in Ireland. The origin of each settlement is indicated by a symbol, so make sure to consult the legend. Larger rivers and land over 100m in height are also shown.

ACTIVITY 1

Using an atlas and figure 10.1 do the following:

1. Find the names and origins of the numbered towns and cities in figure 10.1. Tabulate them in your copy, following this example.

Number	Town	Origin
1	New Ross	Norman

2. Which of the following statements best describes the distribution of Norman towns?
   (a) Norman towns are found only in Ulster and Connacht.
   (b) Most Norman towns are located in Connacht and Munster.
   (c) Most Norman towns are located in Leinster and Munster.
   (d) Few Norman towns are located in Leinster and Ulster.

THE GEOGRAPHER'S WAY 2

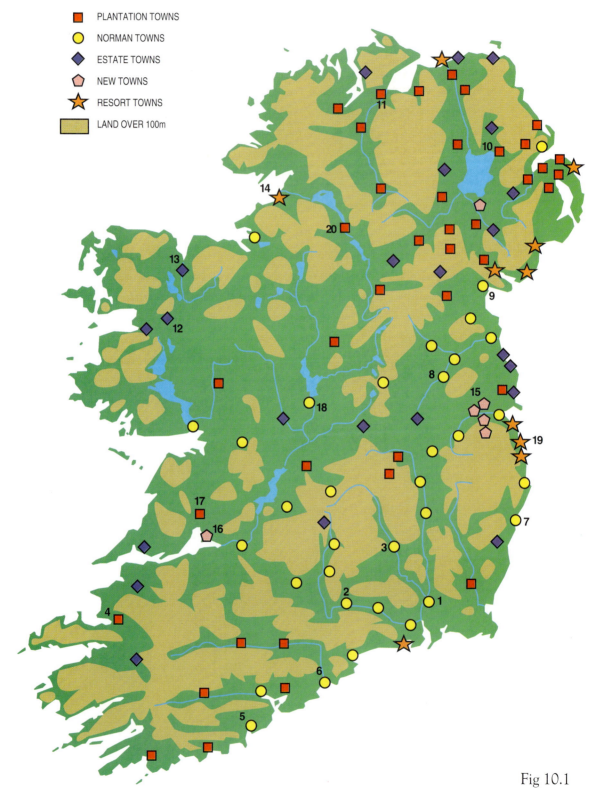

Fig 10.1

3   Which of the following statements best describes the distribution of plantation towns in Ireland?
    (a) Plantation towns are most common in Connacht.
    (b) Most plantation towns are located in Ulster.
    (c) Most plantation towns are found in Connacht and Leinster.
    (d) Plantation towns occur in equal numbers in all four provinces.

DISTRIBUTION OF IMPORTANT IRISH TOWNS

There are few towns on land above 100m so town density above this height is low. There are few towns in West Ulster, Connacht and West Munster. Town density is highest in the eastern half of the country, i.e. East Ulster, Leinster and East Munster. In these areas the density of towns is higher on land under 100m, especially in river valleys and on coastal plains. The way towns are distributed is influenced by a number of factors which include relief, drainage and resources. Historical events also had an important influence on the location of towns.

DISTRIBUTION OF NORMAN TOWNS

In Book One you learned that town settlement was introduced to Ireland by the Vikings. Before that there were no proper towns. The Vikings were pirates and sea traders so most of their settlements became ports located on sheltered estuaries. They didn't build inland towns.

The earliest people to build inland towns were the Normans, who first arrived in Ireland in 1169. For the Normans the main source of wealth was land. They were skilled farmers and on good land they produced a surplus of crops and animals for sale. When they arrived they set about conquering the best land they could find. Fertile brown earths, such as the soils of the river valleys of Leinster and East Munster, were what they were looking for. So it was mainly here the Normans settled. The Normans could do this because they had better weapons and fighting techniques. In particular they used cavalry, whereas the Irish fought on foot.

Having taken an area the Normans built a **motte and bailey**. This was a mound of earth with fences and ditches round it. On top a wooden structure served as a sort of castle. The purpose of the 'motte and bailey' was to defend captured territory. In its shelter a simple settlement formed. Later when the Normans had secured the captured lands they built strong stone castles which often became the nucleus round which towns formed. When they could the Normans took over the coastal port towns founded by the Vikings, providing them with new castles and walls. Some parts of Ireland, especially in the West and Northwest, were never taken by the Normans and life continued there much as it had before the Normans landed.

Norman castles were built at strategic locations. A **strategic location** was a defensive site from which they could control an area. Two common examples of strategic locations are **bridging points** on rivers and **gap sites** in hills or mountains. Kilkenny City is an example of a strategic place and there is a bridging point on the River Nore just below the castle. By their command of bridges the Normans controlled the river routes and roads, and all trade crossing or using the rivers. It also gave them command of the surrounding countryside. Because the Norman towns were defended settlements, they soon became market centres. Traders needed protection and the Norman lords taxed the markets to pay for the protection they provided. The market towns prospered in the shelter of the castles helped by the encouragement of the Norman lords.

The inland towns and the ports were linked by roads so that soldiers and goods could travel easily. Dublin was the chief Norman town and port. It linked Ireland to the Norman territories in Britain and France. The main roads converged on Dublin making it an important nodal point. Dublin became the centre from which Norman Ireland was administered. An **administrative centre** has a 'governing' function. Dublin grew under its new rulers, developing government, church, defence, transport, trade and port functions.

ACTIVITY 2

Using the map, figure 10.1 and your atlas, do the following:
1   Of these river valleys which were important centres of Norman settlement?
        Moy   Foyle   Barrow   Nore   Boyne   Lagan   Suir   Liffey
2   (a)   Suggest reasons why the Normans didn't settle in mountainous areas.
3   (a)   Describe the distribution of Norman settlements in Ireland.
    (b)   Explain their distribution in Ireland.

SETTLEMENTS

By 1500 the large area conquered by the Normans had been reduced to a small territory around Dublin called The Pale and a few towns. The rulers of England at the time, the Tudors, wanted to secure England against their enemies. They feared that Ireland would be used as a base for attacks on them. They decided to conquer Ireland once and for all, and when it was conquered to 'plant' it to make the conquest permanent.

A **plantation** was an organised migration. Land was confiscated from the Irish and given to English adventurers called **undertakers**. The undertakers were granted huge estates of thousands of acres. In return for this land they undertook to bring in English and Scots to settle it. The Irish were driven off to less fertile areas or to the hills.

The first plantation was carried out close to the Pale in Counties Laois and Offaly. Towns such as Philipsburg and Maryborough (now Port Laoise) were established. This plantation was not successful because of poor planning. The next plantation happened in Munster when the lands of the Fitzgerald family were confiscated. This was more successful and resulted in the founding of towns such as Mallow and Clonakilty and the development of others, like Youghal.

The most successful was the Ulster Plantation. The English government had learned from its mistakes. It realised that to be a success a plantation had to be well organised. The settlers had to live in or near defended towns to which they could go for protection when attacked. The towns were also to serve as market, church and administrative centres. The plantation included much of the fertile lowland in Ulster and the plantation towns were spread through the countryside in a dispersed pattern. Plantation towns had a 'grid' pattern with a square or diamond in the centre which served as a market and an assembly point in time of danger. Derry, Draperstown, Moneymore, Enniskillen, Castleblayney, Raphoe and Donegal are a few of the many Ulster towns which trace their origin or development to the plantation.

ACTIVITY 3

Using your atlas and the map in figure 10.1. do the following:
1. Explain how a plantation was organised.
2. Suggest reasons why the density of plantation towns is highest in East Ulster.
3. Find the names of five Ulster plantation towns not mentioned above.

THE GEOGRAPHER'S WAY 2

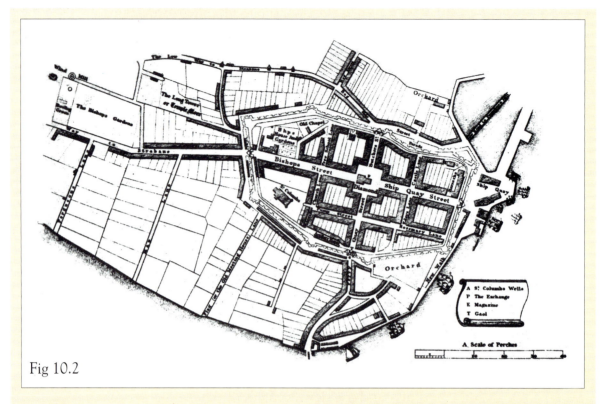

Fig 10.2

4   Study the plan of Derry drawn in 1625, figure 10.2. Pick out three characteristic features of a plantation town and write a sentence or two about each.

ESTATE AND RESORT TOWNS

After the defeat of the rebellion of the 1640's the Cromwellian Government enforced a further confiscation of land known as the Cromwellian Settlement of 1654. This transferred yet more of the ownership of land in Ireland to new foreign settlers. For the Irish it was 'to hell or to Connacht'.

The landlords of the new estates gradually settled in and became rich. They built fine mansions and often created planned villages and towns on their estates. These provided markets and services for the tenants. They were well laid-out. There was usually a market square at the centre, a parish church and perhaps a town hall. Fine views, tree-lined streets and monuments added to the attractiveness of the new settlements. Westport, Edenderry, Blessington and Skerries are a few of the many examples of estate towns.

In the early 19th century the road network was gradually improved. Soon after, railways were introduced revolutionising travel for people and goods. These improved routeways all converged on Dublin increasing its accessibility. **Accessibility** means how easy it is to get to a place. Dublin became the most accessible town in Ireland. This made it easier for the government to rule in a centralised way. It also helped the city develop as the main business centre.

The development of the railway network encouraged the growth of resort towns such as Bray, Tramore and Bundoran. These became holiday centres. Some were at famous beauty spots like Killarney. Most were located where there were good beaches. Promenades and entertainment facilites were built and hotels and guesthouses 'mushroomed' close to the sea front. These resort towns remained very popular until cheap foreign travel and holidays became available in recent years.

TWENTIETH CENTURY TOWNS

As we have seen most Irish towns have a long history. Only a few are twentieth century creations. These are called 'new towns'. A **new town** is a town built in a place where, usually, there was no town before. It is built on a **green field site**. Sometimes the new towns developed where there was a hamlet or village. Shannon New Town in County Clare is an example of a new town built on a green field site. It was created to house and provide services for the employees in Shannon Airport and the Shannon Industrial Estate. Its location was determined by this. Three new towns have been built to the west of Dublin City. These are Tallaght, Lucan/Clondalkin and Blanchardstown. In these cases the new town was built around the nucleus of a small village which already existed. They were built to house some of the growing population of Dublin and provide a better environment for living. They would also help prevent Dublin growing too large.

During the 1960's it was felt that a growth centre was needed to attract new industry and housing developments away from Belfast before it became too congested. A new town called Craigavon was built for this purpose. It was located between Lurgan and Portadown. Craigavon wasn't a great success as it failed to attract much new development.

ACTIVITY 4

1. The photographs in figure 10.3 show three nucleated settlements. One is a resort settlement, one an estate village, and one a new town. Using evidence from the photographs decide which is which.
2. Suggest reasons why the distribution of Irish towns is so dispersed. Refer to historical forces, relief, resources and communications in your answer.

Fig 10.3A

Fig 10.3B

Fig 10.3C

THE FUNCTIONS OF TOWNS

Almost all nucleated settlements have some trade function involving buying and selling. Trade involves transport so they must have some transport function too. People live in the settlement so there is a residential function and perhaps a religious one, if there is a church. But many nucleated settlements are identified by the main function they perform apart from these. For example, we talk about fishing ports and mining towns. Killybegs in Co. Donegal is Ireland's most important fishing port. Its main function is providing services for the fishing industry. Navan is a mining town because Tara Mines is located just outside the town.

We will examine three settlements in the Boyne valley which have different functions. The map in figure 10.4 shows this valley and the three settlements Trim, Navan and Drogheda.

ACTIVITY 5

Examine the map figure 10.4 then do the following:

1. Tick the correct answer. The Boyne river flows from:
   (a) North to South ☐   (c) South-west to North-east ☐   (b) East to West ☐
   (d) South-east to North-west ☐

2. The settlement at the nodal point where the N3 and N51 meet is:
   (a) Drogheda ☐   (b) Trim ☐
   (c) Navan ☐   (d) Slane ☐

Fig 10.4

3. Figure 10.5 is a photograph of Trim, Co.Meath. Examine it, then do the following:
   (a) Name the river.
   (b) Give the location of four different land uses.
   (c) Using evidence from the photograph suggest how the town began.
   (d) Using evidence from the photograph explain how the main function of the settlement appears to have changed over time.

Fig 10.5

Trim This town was founded by the Normans. It was an important defensive settlement guarding a strategic bridging point on the Boyne. Trim Castle is the largest Norman castle in Ireland. It was at the edge of the Pale and so was liable to attack. As time passed the need for defence decreased. Today Trim is a market town for the population of its fertile hinterland. It also has a number of small manufacturing industries. Trim is an example of how a town's main function can change as time passes.

ACTIVITY 6

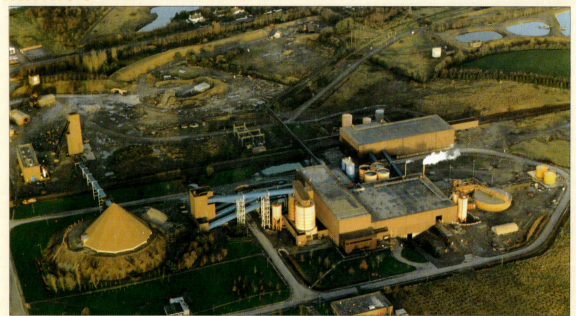

Fig 10.6

Examine the photograph of the Navan mine in figure 10.6. Then do the following:
1   What type of photograph is it?
2   Locate evidence that the mineral is processed at this location.
3   What evidence is there in the photograph to suggest how Navan benefits from this mine?
4   What are the effects of this mine in the local environment?

Navan The photograph shows Tara Mines. Until the discovery of a deposit of lead and zinc ore in the area in the early 1970's, Navan was a market town. It was also a minor manufacturing centre producing carpets and furniture. When the mines opened in 1977 Navan became a mining town. Employment in the town grew as the mine employed many workers. Mining jobs are well paid so the wealth of the town increased. There was more money to spend and businesses prospered. Because the mines contributed so much to the town's prosperity,

Navan became a settlement based on two resources. These were the fertile soils of its hinterland and its ore deposit. This is another example of how a settlement's function can change as time passes. When the lead and zinc resource is exhausted and the mine closes the functions of Navan will change again.

ACTIVITY 7

Fig 10.7

Examine the photograph of Drogheda in figure 10.7. Then do the following:

1. Is the river in the photograph in its upper, middle or lower course? Support your answer with evidence from the photograph.
2. Identify and give the location of three types of transport in the photograph. What conclusion can you draw about Drogheda's functions?
3. Identify and locate five different land uses in the photograph.
4. Give the evidence that Drogheda is a nodal point.
5. From study of the photograph can you tell what products are traded through Drogheda?

Drogheda The town is located at the lowest bridging point on the Boyne. The **lowest bridging point** means the last place where a river is bridged before it enters the sea. Such places are usually important nodal centres as it is the last chance for routeways to converge to cross the river. From the photograph you can see that Drogheda is a nodal point where road, rail and sea routes meet.

The town began as a Viking settlement and continued as a port through Norman times to the present. It is not a big port as it is 5 km from the sea and the river is too shallow for large ships to use. It has lost trade to Dublin which can handle larger ships. The town remains an important market and service centre and it has several manufacturing industries.

THE GEOGRAPHER'S WAY 2

SETTLEMENT IN THE RHINE BASIN

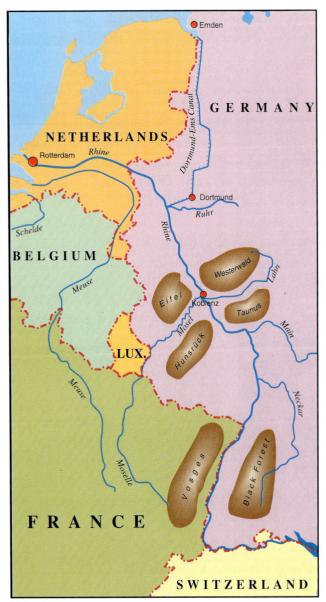

Fig 10.8

The map, figure 10.8. shows the drainage basin of the Rhine. The river rises in the Alps in Switzerland and passes by Germany and France to enter the sea in the Netherlands. These countries are wealthy with prosperous agriculture, mineral resources and many major industries. For centuries the Rhine valley has been the busiest trade route joining northern and southern Europe. Major roads and railways follow the river valley. The river itself is navigable for most of its length. **Navigable** means boats can use it. Huge quantities of raw materials and products are traded along the Rhine making it one of the busiest routeways in the world. We will examine three settlements in the Rhine basin : Koblenz, Dortmund and Rotterdam.

ACTIVITY 8

1. For most of its course the Rhine flows
   (a) South (b) North-east (c) South-west (d) North-west
2. Which of the following rivers is not a tributary of the Rhine?
   (a) Lahn (b) Neckar (c) Scheldt (d) Ruhr (e) Moselle

SETTLEMENTS

Koblenz The name of this town means 'confluence'. It is located in the Rhine Gorge where the Moselle flows into the Rhine. A **gorge** is a steep-sided valley. Koblenz is a nodal point where the Rhine route passing through the gorge meets routes from the Moselle and Lahn valleys. This accessibility has been important in the growth of Koblenz. It is an important market centre for the hinterland on each bank of the river. The surrounding region is very beautiful so the city is well-placed to serve as a tourist centre. The Moselle and Rhine valleys are wine producing areas so Koblenz is an important collecting and distributing centre for the wine industry.

Dortmund This is a resource-based settlement located in the valley of the River Ruhr, a Rhine tributary. Europe's largest coalfield lies beneath the Ruhr valley. This resource of easily-mined coal provided the fuel for the iron and steel industries which grew up around Dortmund. Local iron ore was used at first. Then the iron ore was imported by the Dortmund-Ems Canal which links Dortmund wlth the North Sea. Steel is used in many metal-using industries so these were attracted to the area making 'The Ruhr' one of the great manufacturing regions in Europe. Dortmund grew into an industrial city because of its local coal and the good communications networks which linked it with sources of raw materials and world markets.

ACTIVITY 9

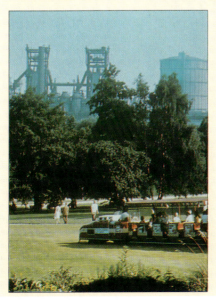

Examine the photograph in figure 10.9, then do the followlng:
1. Describe what you see in the photograph.
2. What is the evidence that the area is polluted. What is the source of this pollution in your opinion?
3. The picture shows steelworks in Dortmond. Are there any similar industries to this in Ireland? Exlain your answer.

Fig 10.9

Rotterdam This is a settlement located at the lowest bridging point on the Rhine. It is the world's largest port. It grew to be so big for these reasons. Firstly, it is situated at the mouth of the Rhine, the world's busiest river routeway. Secondly, its hinterland includes the Netherlands, Belgium, Germany, Luxembourg, France and Switzerland. These are wealthy trading and manufacturing countries. Much of their import and export trade passes through Rotterdam. Thirdly, Rotterdam has excellent communications with its huge hinterland including road, railway, river, canal and air links. Fourthly, the Dutch have linked the port to the North Sea by the 'New Waterway' a large deep canal with no locks. The North Sea is the busiest sea route in the world.

Rotterdam is an entrepôt. An **entrepôt** is a port which serves a number of countries by being a gathering point for exports and a distribution point for imports. For example, Rotterdam is an import entrepôt for oil. Supertankers unload at Rotterdam into storage tanks. Then smaller tankers, barges and pipelines distribute the oil to other countries. Rotterdam serves as an export entrepôt by gathering goods for export from countries in its hinterland. These are then shipped to other parts of the world in large cargo vessels.

ACTIVITY 10 Fig 10.10

SETTLEMENTS

Examine the photograph of Rotterdam, figure 10.10, then do the following:

1. What method of transporting goods are the ships in the foreground using.
2. Contrast the land use in the foreground with the land uses in the background.
3. What facilities are provided for shipping in the area shown?
4. Draw a sketch map of Western Europe. On it show:
   (a) The Rhine and its tributaries.
   (b) Netherlands, Belgium, Luxemburg, Germany, France, Switzerland, Germany and Britain.
   (c) Rotterdam, Dortmund, Koblenz.
   (d) Shade in the hinterland of the Rhine.

THE RHINE DELTA

Much of the Netherlands is a delta formed by the rivers Rhine, Scheldt and Meuse as they entered the North Sea. The delta land is lowlying and flat. Some is below sea level. This makes flooding by the sea and rivers a serious danger. For centuries the Dutch have worked to protect their land from flooding and to add to it by reclaiming new land from the sea. In this century there have been two major reclamation projects. These are the Zuyder Zee project, which we will study, and the Delta Project. The locations of these projects are shown on the map in figure 10.11.

Fig 10.11

THE GEOGRAPHER'S WAY 2

THE ZUYDER ZEE

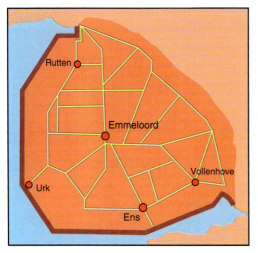

Fig 10.12

The Zuyder Zee was a large shallow sea inlet. The Dutch built a dam across it to cut it off from the open sea. They then reclaimed much of the area inside piece by piece. The reclaimed areas are called **polders**. To reclaim each polder a wide wall or **dyke** was built around it. The dyke was higher than the land it surrounded and it usually had a canal running along the top of it. Water was pumped from the polder into the canal on the dyke. The canal carried the water to the sea. Once the polder had dried, work began to make it suitable for farming. Every aspect of the polder from the size of its population to the number of towns, roads, farms and recreational areas was planned. The planning of settlements is seen on the map of the North-east Polder in figure 10.12.

Fig 10.13

Notice how the largest town Emmeloord is in the centre of the polder so that it is easily accessible from all parts. The smaller towns form a circular pattern around it. This pattern of settlements is designed to provide services as close to people as possible.

The cultural landscape of the Zuider Zee polders is very recent and was planned from start to finish. This is quite the opposite to most cultural landscapes which have developed slowly down through the centuries.

ACTIVITY 11

Examine the photograph of a polder, figure 10.13, then do the following:

1. What type of photograph is it ?
2. Describe the settlement you can see.
3. Describe the land use.
4. Explain how people have helped to shape this landscape.

REVISION

Rewrite the following text into your copy filling in the missing words from the list below.

bridging point	polder	plantation	nucleated
gorge	lowest bridging point	entrepôt	new town
navigable	accessibility	nodal point	gap sites
strategic location	settlement	motte and bailey	dyke
undertakers	green field site	administrative centre	

A place where people live is a_____. When buildings and houses are clustered together there is a_____ settlement. An artificial hill defended by a wooden fence was called a_____ _____ _____. An area which has been drained is called a_____ in the Netherlands. The reclaimed land is surrounded by a wall known as a_____. A port which deals with the trade of other countries is an_____. A_____ is a steep-sided valley. A river is_____ if ships can travel up it. The last point at which a river can be crossed is the_____ _____ _____. A town built where no town existed is called a_____ _____. The site of such a town is called a_____ _____ _____. The ease with which a place can be reached is called its _____. An organised migration which takes land from one group and settles a foreign group on the confiscated land is a _____. The people who undertook to recruit the settlers were called _____. A town or city with governing function is said to be an _____ _____. Towns located at easy crossing points in mountains have _____ _____. A _____ _____ is a point where it is possible to cross a river. Towns located at route centres are called _____ _____. An important defensive location is said to be a _____ _____.

11 The Growth of Towns

IN THIS CHAPTER YOU WILL LEARN

- The morphology of towns.
- The development of Maynooth.
- The development of Dublin.

You have learned how historical events influence the founding and growth of nucleated settlements. Many settlements grow by getting extra functions and a larger population. The extra functions affect the morphology of the settlement. The **morphology** of a settlement is its developing shape. By examining the shape of a town we can learn a lot about it. We will study the town of Maynooth.

The map, figure 11.1, shows the town of Maynooth. This has been taken from a six inch O.S. map. On this kind of map everything is represented by lines and symbols.

Fig 11.1

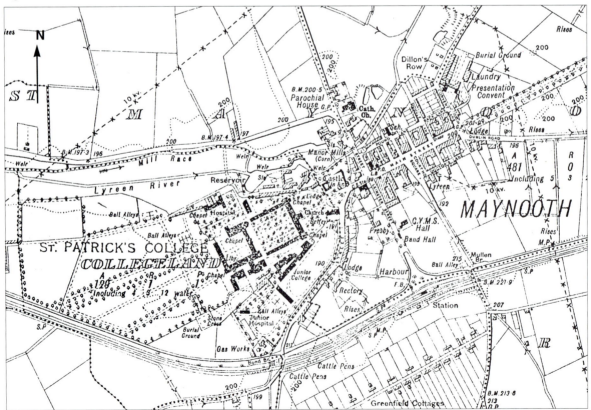

THE GROWTH OF TOWNS

ACTIVITY 1

Examine the map of Maynooth, figure 11.1, then do the following:
1. Identify and give the location of evidence to show that Maynooth was founded by the Normans.
2. Locate evidence to show that Maynooth was an estate village.
3. Locate evidence that Maynooth is a religious and educational centre.

THE DEVELOPMENT OF MAYNOOTH

The town is in a fertile plain about 60m above sea level. A number of streams including the Lyreen meet here. The fertile land attracted the Normans to settle and in 1203 the Fitzgeralds were granted lands by King Henry II. They built a castle, and a small village started to the east of it. Partly because of the troubled history of the Fitzgeralds, this settlement did not grow into a town.

In the 18th century landlords began to develop their estates, building fine houses for themselves and villages for their workers and tenants. The Earl of Kildare, a Fitzgerald, built a mansion called Carton House to the north-east of Maynooth. The Earl thought his unplanned village of Maynooth an eyesore. He decided to redevelop it. To **redevelop** means to pull down what is there and replace it with something new. The Earl rebuilt Maynooth as an estate village. A wide tree-lined main street with a market square was laid out. Roads leading from the main street made a grid pattern with roads parallel to it. This pattern is seen on both sides of Main Street but especially on the northern side. At one end of Main Street a tree-lined avenue led to Carton House.

In 1795 St Patrick's College was opened in Stoyte House at the south-west end of Main Street. This was a training college for Catholic priests. In time it became the biggest seminary in Ireland and was made a university. A 'seminary' is a college for training priests. It is still a seminary but it is also a university for lay people. The founding of the College brought new religious and educational functions. The morphology of the town was affected. Note how the buildings and grounds of St.Patrick's occupy the western end of Maynooth so that further growth in that direction stopped.

The Royal Canal and the railway to Sligo and the West pass to the south of Maynooth. Close to the railway station there are cattle pens and a harbour on the canal. Both show that the town was a market especially for cattle. This function continues as Maynooth has a busy cattle mart. But the canal and railway no longer carry cattle.

To the south of Maynooth there are new housing estates. These are planned settlements. They provide accommodation for people of different kinds. Firstly, there are those who live in Maynooth or have come to settle because of increased local employment. These are residents. Secondly, there is a growing student population. Thirdly, there are commuters. **Commuters** are people who live in one place and travel a distance to another to work. Maynooth is a good location for commuters because it is linked to Dublin by frequent bus and train services. The Maynooth to Dublin road has been improved by building by-passes at Maynooth itself, Leixlip and Lucan. These make commuting by car easier. As commuters settle in Maynooth attracted by its access to Dublin and its pleasant environment, it is getting a new function, that of dormitory town. A **dormitory town** is one where people live and sleep but leave to go to their employment. This function will probably become more important as people move out of Dublin. As a result new housing will be built, further changing the morphology of Maynooth.

ACTIVITY 2

Fig 11.2

THE GROWTH OF TOWNS

Examine the photograph of Maynooth, figure 11.2, then do the following.
1. What type of photograph is it? Using the map, figure 11.1, work out the direction the camera was facing when it was taken.
2. Draw a sketch of the photograph. Divide it into segments as when drawing a sketch map. On your sketch show three different land uses.
3. Draw a sketch map of Maynooth from the map in figure 11.1. On it show: a Norman area, an area of 18th century development, St. Patrick's College, the canal and railway.
4. Using your sketch map as a guide, explain how Maynooth's morphology developed through time.

THE DEVELOPMENT OF DUBLIN

The Viking and Norman Core

Dublin began as a Viking port and stronghold. It continued to have these functions after the Normans captured it in 1170. It soon became the centre of Norman rule in Ireland. Dublin Castle was built in 1204. The old Viking walls were strengthened and extended to defend the new Norman town. The Viking and Norman core of Dublin is shown on the map in figure 11.3. The **core** of a town is the inner or central district which is usually the oldest part. The morphology of the Viking and Norman core is unplanned. The streets are narrow and twisting with no pattern. Find the core on the map and examine it carefully.

Fig 11.3 — VIKING AND NORMAN CORE — GEORGIAN DUBLIN — RIVERS AND CANALS

Fig 11.4

After its early success Norman power in Ireland declined during the 14th and 15th centuries. So did Dublin. The area around the city was no longer safe from the Irish enemy, so the city could not grow beyond its walls. The outbreak of bubonic plague in 1348, the Black Death, greatly reduced the population. It probably killed between a third and a half of the people. By the time Speed's map of Dublin was drawn in 1610, figure 11.4, there had been little growth beyond the walls.

Eighteenth century growth The Tudor conquest and the Plantations ended the decline of Dublin. In the 17th century, there was some improvement in security, and the city began to expand beyond its old Norman walls for the first time.

The continuation of more peaceful conditions prepared the way for the Irish economy to grow in the 18th century. The **economy** means all the activities concerned with the production of goods and wealth. Trade increased, particularly imports and exports. The export of linen and provisions were mainly the cause of the improvement. **Provisions** means foodstuffs, such as salted beef, butter and pork. Dublin port handled much of this overseas trade. New quays were built to handle the growing volume of cargo and shipping. The number of merchants increased. **Merchants** are people who trade in goods usually by importing and exporting them. Coal merchants and wine merchants are examples.

Fig 11.5

The merchants became rich and could afford to buy fine houses in new suburbs to the south-east and north-east of Dublin. These were laid out by 'developers' like Lord Fitzwilliam and Luke Gardiner. Squares and broad streets are a feature of the 18th century suburbs shown on the map in figure 11.3. Look for Fitzwilliam Street, Baggot Street, Leeson Street, Merrion Square, Gardiner Street and Mountjoy Square.

The photograph in figure 11.5 shows an 18th century Dublin street. It is wide and straight. The lines made by the roofs, windows and railings converge at the end leading the eye to a view of a

THE GROWTH OF TOWNS

Fig 11.6

church. The street was planned to give this view. Other streets framed views of the Dublin mountains or other important public buildings. The houses were in terraces. A **terrace** is a group of more than two houses of the same style in a row. Though the houses have the same style they are not identical.

The building style of late 18th century Dublin is called **Georgian** after the three Georges who ruled Britain and Ireland during the 18th century.

As Ireland and Dublin grew prosperous large public buildings such as the House of Parliament (Bank of Ireland today), the Custom House, Trinity College and the Four Courts were built. These were in the classical style which was popular in the Georgian period. This style copied the temples and buildings of ancient Greece and Rome. The photograph of Trinity College in figure 11.6 shows this style clearly. The aristocracy and rich landlords built town houses where they lived during the sessions of the Irish Parliament. For example Leinster House, figure 11.7, which now houses the Dáil (and Seanad) was built by the Earl of Kildare as his town house. By the end of the eighteenth century Dublin was a fine fashionable city, the second largest in the British Empire.

This prosperous phase of Dublin's history came to a sudden end. In 1800 the Irish Parliament voted itself out of existence by the Act of Union. From this date the Irish representatives went to parliament at Westminster. As a result the rich and influential people moved from Dublin to London. By 1820 Dublin had already become less fashionable and prosperous. The impressive development of the suburbs slowed down.

Fig 11.7

THE GEOGRAPHER'S WAY 2

ACTIVITY 3

1. Examine the map in figure 11.3, then do the following:
   (a) Identify and locate three Georgian squares.
   (b) Contrast the street pattern around Merrion Square with the street pattern in the Viking and Norman core.
2. Examine the photographs in figures 11.5, 11.6 and 11.7. Then do the following:
   (a) Sketch a Georgian terraced house paying attention to the front door and the windows.
   (b) Note how the windows vary in size. Suggest a reason why they do.
   (c) Describe the building materials used in Georgian terraces.
   (d) What simllarities are there between Leinster House and the Trinity College?
   (e) Find a picture of an ancient Greek or Roman temple in the library. What features in Dublin's Georgian public buildings were copied from it ?

Nineteenth and twentieth century Dublin During the l9th century Dublin's population increased. There were several reasons for this. Firstly, people lived longer because a supply of clean water became available, proper sewers were built, and disease control improved. Secondly, many people migrated from the country to the city. The poor, and there were many, lived in wretched conditions. They were housed in tenements close to the city centre. **Tenements** were houses built for one family which became home to a number of families. Often they were large Georgian houses which a rich family had left. Living conditions in tenements were dreadful. Families lived in one room and had to share toilet and washing facilities with other families. Areas with such overcrowded housing were known as **slums**. Much of old Georgian Dublin north of the river Liffey and along the quays became slums.

The spread of the suburbs was helped by the building of new transport systems. Railways came first; later there were trams. These allowed the better-off to live in suburbs built round villages like Dún Laoghaire, Howth, Blackrock and Rathgar. From these they commuted to work. Gradually these suburbs became part of the city. Using the map in figure 11.8 count how many suburbs developed around villages on the coast of Dublin Bay.

THE GROWTH OF TOWNS

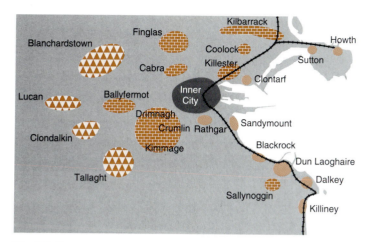

Fig 11.8

The early 20th century brought little improvement. Apart from the spread of the suburbs and growth of a densely populated slum area in central Dublin, the city changed little. It still functioned as a port, and an administrative, commercial and transport centre. There was some manufacturing industry, mainly to supply home needs. Unlike many other large cities Dublin did not become an important industrial city.

Migration from the country continued. Poverty and unemployment remained serious problems. More and better housing was urgently needed. Starting in the 1930's Dublin Corporation began clearing the slums in the city centre. Good housing was built in suburbs like Kimmage and Marino to rehouse tenement dwellers and to provide accommodation for the still-growing population. The map in figure 11.8 shows the names and locations of these new estates.

The population of Dublin grew so rapidly because the city provided a better chance to get a job. The city also attracted people because it was lively, with many cinemas, dancehalls and other social centres. Better education, improved health care and better housing also contributed to the population increase because people were healthier and lived longer. The new estates provided better houses but there was a danger that the city would just sprawl out into the surrounding country. **Urban sprawl** is the uncontrolled spread of a town or city along roads leading to the countryside. To prevent this it was decided to keep the growth of the city to new towns to be built on the western side of Dublin. These new towns included: Tallaght, Lucan/Clondalkin and Blanchardstown .These new towns, already mentioned on page 149, are shown on figure 11.8.

ACTIVITY 4

1. Explain what tenements were.
2. What developments led to the growth of Dublin's suburbs in the 19th century? In what way was the development of some suburbs in the 20th century different?
3. What is urban sprawl?
4. Examine the map in figure 11.8. Identify the new towns around Dublin. Give three reasons why they are located where they are.

REVISION

Rewrite the following text into your copy. Fill in the blank spaces using words from the box below.

redevelop	merchants	core	morphology	provisions
commuters	urban sprawl	dormitory town		
tenement	economy	terrace	Georgian period	

The developing shape of a town is its _____. To _____ is to tear down buildings and replace them with new ones. The original centre of a town is called its _____. People who travel a distance to and from work are _____. A town in which people live but work elsewhere is a _____ _____. Supplies of salted beef, butter and pork were _____. Traders are also called _____. Everything to do with wealth and income is the -_____. The _____ _____ is the period when Britain was ruled by the Georges. A group of more than two houses joined together is a -_____. A house designed for one family but with many families living in it is a _____. When a city or town spreads out into the surrounding countryside in an unplanned way, it is called _____ _____.

12 The Structure of Towns

IN THIS CHAPTER YOU WILL LEARN

- Land uses within the urban area.
- Functional zones within towns and cities.
- Dublin's functional zones.
- Site and location of Paris.
- Functional zones of Paris.

Cities consist of different parts. For example, there are usually a number of land use zones. A **land use zone** is an area with one main type of land use. For instance cities have commercial zones with shops and banks, industrial zones with factories, residential zones with houses and recreational zones with parks and playing fields. In some zones the use of land is densely packed, in others there is more free space. There is also variety in the housing in different parts of the city. There are blocks of flats, detached houses, semi-detached houses, terraces and so on. Some accommodation is modern and of good quality. Other accommodation is old and run-down. Dublin illustrates this variety which is common to most cities. The map, figure 12.1 shows the land use zones in Dublin city. Study it carefully. The way the different parts are arranged is the **structure** of the city. The structure can vary from city to city but usually there is a pattern in the way the parts fit together.

At the centre there is usually a commercial zone with many big stores, banks, company and insurance offices, cinemas and theatres. This commercial zone is called the **central business district** or **CBD** for short. This is the main business area. It is in the most accessible part, close to or at the nodal point for road, rail and bus routes. Shops and offices compete to get space in the CBD. This forces up the price of land so rents are high. Because rents are expensive the maximum use is made of the land and buildings are densely packed. One way to get the most use of land is to have high rise buildings. These are common in the CBD. They allow different land uses on the same piece of land. The photograph in figure 12.2 shows the Irish Life Building in Dublin's CBD. This building has a number of functions. In

THE GEOGRAPHER'S WAY 2

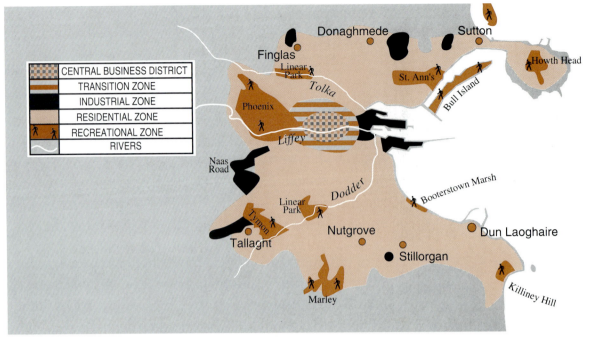

Fig 12.1

the basement there is a car park. On ground level there is a shopping mall. On the higher floors there are various offices. The complex has a residential function because it includes apartments. A swimming pool provides a recreational function.

Dublin's CBD stretches from Grafton Street to O'Connell and Henry Streets, the main shopping areas. Dame Street and College Green is the business area with many banks and insurance companies. The Custom House Docks Scheme is a new financial and shopping centre developed to the east of the CBD and enlarging it.

Moving out from the CBD the land use becomes less intense, and buildings are less densely packed and high. Rents become lower. On the edge of the CBD there is often a mixed zone with industrial and residential functions. Industries are usually small. The housing tends to be old and of poor quality. This mixed zone is called the **transition zone** because it is undergoing change. This is clearly seen in Dublin. On the south side of the city it lies in the area round Aungier Street. On the north side it lies round Ballybough. These were areas where many tenements were located. Most have been cleared. Some tenements were replaced by

Fig 12.2

THE STRUCTURE OF TOWNS

Fig 12.3

blocks of flats like those in figure 12.3. Sometimes offices took the place of tenements. In some places sites have been cleared but remain unbuilt on.

Beyond the transition zone there are residential zones stretching right around the city from Dun Laoghaire to Howth. These zones have housing which varies widely in age, quality and type. The older residential districts are closer to the city centre. The newer estates are on the periphery of the city. The **periphery** means the edge of something. Accommodation in these residential zones ranges from luxurious houses to corporation housing estates.

ACTIVITY 1

1. Examine the photographs in figure 12.4 which show housing in the transition zone. Describe the housing in each photograph under the headings: type, quality and likely age. Look for evidence to help you make a reasoned judgement.

Fig 12.4A

Fig 12.4B

2. The photographs in figure 12.5 are labelled A and B. They show different houses from residential zones. Examine them.
   (a) Which is the older house?
   (b) Using information from the photographs identify and describe the following: the detached house, the terraced houses.

171

Fig 12.5A

Fig 12.5B

Within the residential zones there are suburban shopping centres. Since the 1960's over fifty have been built around Dublin. Shopping centres at Stillorgan, Nutgrove, Tallaght, Finglas and Donaghmede are examples. These were built to provide services for suburban dwellers who did not wish to travel far to do everyday shopping. The shopping centres provide a wide variety of shops and good parking. They were designed to be attractive with restaurants, toilets, pleasant shops and entertainment facilities. Most shopping centres are located at nodal points so access to them is easy.

Recreational zones Recreational areas are scattered through the residential zones. Some of these are parks like Marley Park and St. Anne's Park developed by Dublin County Council. Linear parks have been planned along rivers such as the Dodder and Tolka. The largest recreational zones are Phoenix Park and the Bull Island. Phoenix Park provides for many kinds of recreation with playing fields, open spaces, gardens and a zoo. Bull Island has a beach 5 km long, a bird sanctuary and a golf course. These large recreational zones are in the suburbs where land values are cheaper. Near the city centre parks and recreational areas are small. Find the names of two small parks in the Georgian part of Dublin? (See page 163)

THE STRUCTURE OF TOWNS

Industrial zones These are areas where factories are concentrated. In Dublin the old industrial zone was mainly around the port. Gradually traffic in this area became very congested and modern industries lacked the space they needed for growth. Now modern industrial zones have been created on the periphery of the city on greenfield sites where land is cheap and communications are good. These provide plenty of room for expansion. Modern industrial zones now ring the city, for example at Dun Laoghaire, Sandyford, Walkinstown, Tallaght, Finglas and Santry.

ACTIVITY 2

Fig 12.6A

Fig 12.6B

Fig 12.6C

Fig 12.6D

1. Examine the photographs in figure 12.6. Match the letters on the photographs with the land use zones listed below.

Letter	Land use zone
	Recreational
	Transition
	Industrial
	Central Business District

173

THE GEOGRAPHER'S WAY 2

2 Draw a sketch map of an imaginary city. On it show five different land use zones. Describe each of the zones shown on your map.

3 Draw a sketch map of Dublin and on it show three functional zones. Describe each of the zones.

URBAN TRAFFIC

Large cities like Dublin need efficient transport networks. Most trade depends on transport. The CBD and industrial zones require easy and rapid access. Large numbers of city workers commute from the suburbs or beyond to their workplaces. The flow of traffic is not the same throughout the day. There are 'rush hours' in the morning and evening when people go to and from work. The volume of traffic 'peaks' during rush hours and transport networks must be able to take it. At other times traffic is lighter and transport systems may be under-used.

ACTIVITY 3

Examine the photographs in figure 12.7 which were all taken from the same place but at different times of the day. The camera was pointing towards Dublin. Match the letters on the photographs with the times of day.

Letter	Time of day
	Morning rush hour
	Mid-morning
	Evening rush hour

Fig 12.7A

Fig 12.7C

Fig 12.7B

THE STRUCTURE OF TOWNS

PARIS

Paris is one of the world's most famous cities. It is the capital of France. Paris illustrates very well many of the points made about cities so we will use it to revise the ideas in this and the last chapter.

THE SITE OF PARIS

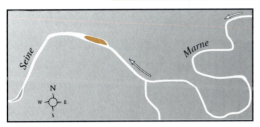

Paris was developed by the Romans. The map in figure 12.8 shows the site of the Roman core of Paris. Examine it carefully.

Fig 12.8

ACTIVITY 4

Use the map in figure 12.8 to complete the text.

| site | defend | cross | confluence | flood plain |

The _____ of a town is the land it is built on. The site of Paris is located close to the _____ of the rivers _____ and _____. Here there were _____ in the river which made it easy to _____ the settlement and to _____ the river. The island is called the _____ _____ _____ _____. The town is built on a _____ _____.

LOCATION OF PARIS

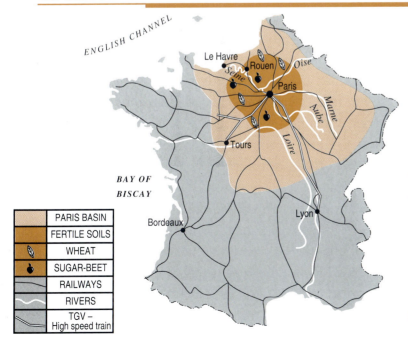

Paris was an excellent site for a Roman town. It was easy to defend as it was on an island. It was also good for trading as it was at a crossing point on the river. The development of Paris into a major city was not due to the advantages of its site but to the advantages of its excellent location. The map in figure 12.9 shows the location of Paris. Examine it carefully.

Fig 12.9

THE GEOGRAPHER'S WAY 2

ACTIVITY 5

Use the map and legend in figure 12.9 and the words to complete the text.

| hinterland | converge | nodal | central | increased | market |
| rail network | temperate | route centre |

Paris is located in the _____ _____. This is a very rich agricultural area with _____ soils. The _____ climate is ideal for growing crops such as _____ and _____. Paris's _____ location made it the most important _____ point and _____ centre in the Paris Basin. Routeways following the valleys of the rivers _____, _____, _____ and _____ converged on Paris linking it to this rich agricultural _____. Later Paris became the central point of the _____ _____. This _____ the size of its hinterland still further. Today all the high speed _____ rail routes and air routes _____ on Paris making it the most important _____ _____ in France.

FUNCTIONAL ZONES

Under the French kings, Paris became by far the biggest city in France and the centre of government. In the 19th century it became an important industrial city as did most large cities at that time. Today, it is the single biggest industrial centre in Europe with a huge population of about ten million people. It is also famous for its many recreational functions, including theatres, cinemas and many artistic activities. Paris like most cities has a number of land use zones. The map in figure 12.10 shows the functional zones in Paris. Examine it carefully.

The CBD is in the centre around the Ile de la Cité on the site of the original Roman town. In modern times this area became so congested that a number of districts with large offices and shops were developed in the suburbs. These were planned to attract growth away from the old central district. These developments are like small CBD's. 'La Défence' is the most famous of these new CBD's. It and other new growth centres are shown on the map in figure 12.10.

There are a number of industrial zones. There is a heavy industry zone in the north-east suburbs with car and train factories. **Heavy industry** makes products which are big and heavy, for example ships, trains, large machines and so on. Close to the Seine there are port industries which process imported raw materials which come up the

THE STRUCTURE OF TOWNS

river by barge from the sea ports of Le Havre and Rouen. These include oil refining. There are also industrial zones on the periphery where many different products are manufactured like electronic goods and foods.

There are many residential zones spread through the city. The population density is very high because most Parisians live in apartment blocks which are usually five or more storeys high. Housing, too, is densely packed because land values and rents are expensive. As

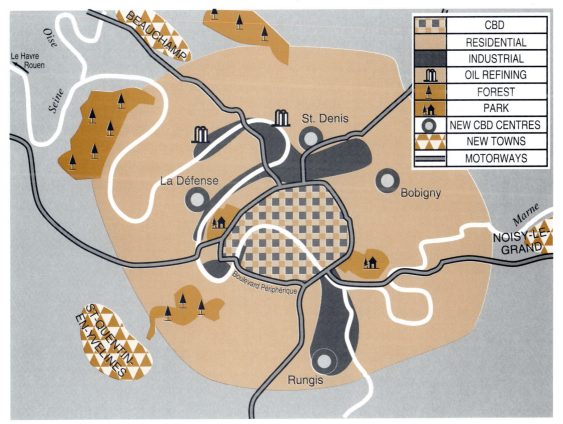

Fig 12.10

in most cities, accommodation varies in quality. There are very fashionable 'quartiers' but also some 'bidonvilles' which means literally 'tin-can towns'. With such a large population, transport, traffic and 'rush hour flows' are a serious problem. A large 'ring road' system called the 'Peripherique' relieves traffic congestion though there are often traffic jams during rush hours.

The recreation zones in and around Paris are usually parks or forests. With such a high density of population the pressure on these zones is very great. For this reason it is planned to keep new building schemes away from the Seine. As in Dublin new towns have been built to draw some of the population away from the city centre. These new towns are shown on the map in figure 12.10.

THE GEOGRAPHER'S WAY 2

ACTIVITY 6

1. Use the map and legend in figure 12.10 and the words to complete the text.

| imported | suburbs | density | Roman core |
| congestion | apartments | centre | |

Paris's CBD or Central Business District is located around the Ile de La Cité which is the old _____ _____. There are also smaller CBD's in the _____ because the main CBD became too congested so in some cases CBD functions were developed in the suburbs. _____ _____ is one of these outer CBD's. There is an _____ zone in the North-east suburbs with car and train factories. Close to the _____ there are port industries which process _____ raw materials which come up the river from the sea-ports of _____ and _____ _____. One of these port industries is _____ _____. Most of the residential zones have a very high _____ of housing due to people living in _____ rather than houses. Due to the large population and its high density there is much traffic _____. The large ring road called the _____ _____ runs around the _____ of Paris relieving traffic congestion. Recreation zones are usually _____ or _____ and are increasingly located along the Seine.

2. Draw a sketch map of France. On it show the following:
   The Atlantic and Channel coastlines
   The Rivers Seine, Marne and Oise
   The cities Paris, Rouen and Le Havre
3. Describe the site of Paris using a sketch map.
4. Draw a sketch map of the Paris region. On it show the following:
   the Rivers Seine and Marne, the CBD, La Défence, two industrial zones, a recreational zone.

REVISION

Rewrite the following text using the words in the box to fill in the gaps.

| heavy industry | structure | transition zone |
| central business district | periphery | land use zone | CBD |

An area with one main type of land use is a _____ _____ _____. The zone of large offices and shops at the centre of most towns is the _____ _____ _____ or _____ for short. The _____ of a town is the way its different parts are arranged. A zone in which land use is changing rapidly is a _____ _____. The edge of an area is called the _____. _____ _____ produces large heavy products such as trains and ships.

13 Population Growth

IN THIS CHAPTER YOU WILL LEARN

- Growth of the World's population.
- Natural changes caused by changes in the birth and death rates.
- Factors influencing birth and death rates.
- Population change in Ireland, Germany and Brazil.
- Future world population and population projections.

The **population** is the people who live in a place. Governments need to know the size of the population in a country because they organise services, like health-care and education. These must match people's needs and be paid for. Governments must know when the population changes and how fast an increase or decrease happens. This information allows plans to be made for the future. To find the size of the population a government carries out a census. A **census** counts people and gathers information about them. Comparison with previous censuses shows what changes there are and how quickly they are happening.

The United Nations (U.N.) recommends countries to take a census every ten years on the first year of the decade, i.e. 1971, 1981, etc. This enables the U.N. to calculate the world population and the rate at which it is changing. Ireland follows the U.N. recommendation, and in addition a partial census is often taken on the sixth year of the decade. The last full census was taken in 1991, with a partial census taken in 1986.

WORLD POPULATION GROWTH

The population of the world is increasing very fast. This change has important consequences for us so it is important for us to know as much about it as possible. We need to know where it is happening and how rapid it is so that we can plan to cope with it. If the population of an area gets too large for the resources available to it, famine and great hardship may occur.

THE GEOGRAPHER'S WAY 2

ACTIVITY 1

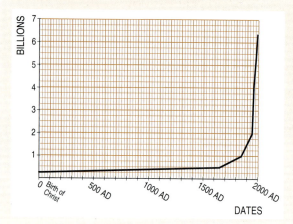

Examine the graph of world population growth in figure 13.1 then answer the following questions. (1 billion is a 1,000 million or 1,000,000,000.)

1. What type of graph is it? Why is this type of graph a good one to show population growth?
2. Estimate the world's population at each of the dates in the following table:

Fig 13.1

DATE	POPULATION	DATE	POPULATION
1 AD (Time of Christ)		1950 AD	
1650 AD		1975 AD	
1850 AD		2000 AD	

3. Between the time of Christ and 1975 the population of the world doubled four times as follows:
   (a) From 250 million to 500 million   (b) From 500 million to 1 billion
   (c) From 1 billion to 2 billion   (d) From 2 billion to 4 billion
   Calculate how long the doubling took in each case.
4. Which of the following statements best describes the growth of world population from the time of Christ to the present?
   (a) The population of the world grew rapidly until 1500 AD and then increased even more rapidly.
   (b) Population grew slowly until 1950 AD and then increased very rapidly.
   (c) Population increased gradually until 1650 AD, then it began to grow more and more rapidly.
   (d) Population rose steadily from 1AD to 1800 AD, then it began to increase rapidly.

The graph shows an estimate of how world population has increased since 1 AD. The graph getting steeper shows that the rate of population growth speeded up as time passed. The steeper the graph the greater the rate of population change. We will analyse this graph.

Between 1 AD and 1650 the graph slopes upward gently, showing that population rose gradually. It took 1650 years to double from 250 million. After 1650 the slope steepens showing faster growth. Population doubled to 1 billion in the 200 years to 1850. After 1850 the growth rate continues to increase so that population doubles to 2 billion by 1950, a period of 100 years. Between 1950 and 1975 the graph is at its steepest. Now world population doubles from 2 to 4 billion in only 25 years. After 1975 the rate of population increase slows slightly. This is shown by the graph becoming a little less steep. We can project the graph into the future to estimate what world population will be. By 2000 AD the graph shows world population may be about 6.3 billion. This very rapid increase in world population is called the **population explosion.**

POPULATION CHANGE

Population changes by increasing or decreasing. Increase or decrease happens for two reasons. Firstly, there may be changes in the numbers of births and deaths. Secondly, people may migrate into or out of an area; this changes the number of the population.

Changes in births and deaths Change due to births and deaths in a population is known as **natural change** because birth and death happen naturally. When studying natural change we use birth rates and death rates. The **birth rate** is the number of births per 1000 of the population. The **death rate** is the number of deaths per 1000 of the population. In 1990 the birth rate for the world was 26 per 1000. This means that 26 children were born for every 1000 people in the world's population. The death rate in that year was 9 per 1000. We use the idea of 'per 1000 people in the population' because we can compare the rates in different places, whether particular areas, countries, or the world.

By subtracting the death rate from the birth rate we can find the rate of natural increase. The **natural increase** is the increase of population caused by there being more births than deaths.

The World's Natural Increase 1990	
Birth rate	26 per 1000
Death rate	9 per 1000
Natural Increase	17 per 1000

THE GEOGRAPHER'S WAY 2

There were 17 more people for every 1000 in the world at the end of 1990 than at the beginning. World population increased naturally by over 100 million in that year.

Usually the population changes by increasing naturally but a natural decrease can occur. A **natural decrease** happens when the death rate is higher than the birth rate. A natural decrease causes a fall in population. If birth and death rates are equal, then the population is said to be **stable**. It does not change by increasing or decreasing.

ACTIVITY 2

Examine these statistics, then do the following:

Country	Birth Rate	Death Rate	Country	Birth Rate	Death Rate
Egypt	31	9	Denmark	11	11
Germany	11	12	Mali	51	19
Brazil	26	7	Bolivia	41	12
Saudi Arabia	42	6	United Kingdom	14	11
India	31	10	China	21	7

(a) Using the statistics calculate which countries have a natural increase, a natural decrease or a stable population.
(b) Rank the countries 1-10 on the basis of their rate of natural change. The country with the highest rate is to be ranked '1'.
(c) Use an atlas to find out in which continent each country is.
(d) Draw two conclusions about natural changes in population from the information in the table.

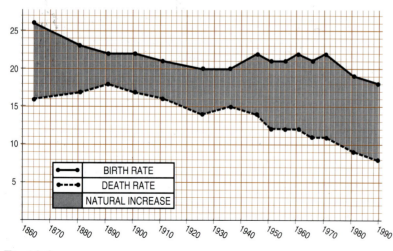

Fig 13.2

The graph in figure 13.2 shows birth and death rates for Ireland since 1864. The solid black line shows the birth rate, the broken line the death rate. The area between shows the natural increase. In 1990 the birth rate was 18 per 1000 and the death rate 8 per 1000, so the natural increase was 10 per 1000.

POPULATION GROWTH

Graphs like this which co-relate two or more different sets of information are useful. Here the birth and death rates are presented together for a period of years. This allows us to relate two things. Firstly, we see how birth and death rates relate to each other. Secondly, we see at a glance the rate of natural increase, a new piece of information, and how it changed over time.

ACTIVITY 3

Examine the graph in figure 13.2 then do the following:
1. (a) What type of graph is it?
   (b) What are the maximum and minimum birth rates shown on the graph? In which years did they occur?
   (c) What are the maximum and minimum death rates shown on the graph? In which years did they occur?
2. Work out the natural increase in each of the following years:
   1864   1891   1951   1971

The graph shows that Ireland had a natural increase in population every year between 1864 and 1990. The size of this increase varied. For example, in 1864 the natural increase was 10 per 1000 but by 1891 it had fallen to 4 per 1000. A change in the rate of natural increase can be caused by a change in birth rate or by a change in death rate. It is important to remember that both can change.

FACTORS FOR NATURAL CHANGE

Natural change in population can be influenced by a number of different factors.

Food Supply We will consider the death rate first. If food is scarce, people are undernourished and unhealthy. Disease increases and the death rate rises. In an acute shortage, called a famine, people die of starvation as they did during the Irish Famine of 1845-47. If the food supply is good, the population is healthy and the death rate is likely to fall. Now, we look at the birth rate. If mothers are underfed and unhealthy, there will be fewer births. When there is enough food, mothers are healthier and there will be more births. So the food supply can affect both birth and death rates.

Fighting and war Death rate rises during wartime because of the killing. War disrupts food supplies so the population becomes underfed and unhealthy. This tends to increase the death rate too. In wartime couples are separated when the men go off to fight. The separation of husbands from wives causes a drop in birth rate. For these reasons countries usually experience a decrease in population in wartime.

Technology   Improvements in technology usually cause population increase. For example, when the Celts developed the iron plough they could till heavier soils than before. The cultivation of more land meant a better food supply, so death rates decreased and birth rates rose. More recently, the improved supply of pure water made possible by 19th century technology reduced death rates in cities, causing a rapid rise in population. Developments in technology during the Industrial Revolution gradually brought improvement in housing and sanitation. These reduced death rates.

Medicine   Progress in medical knowledge and health care cause natural change in population. The discovery of vaccines which protect people against diseases like smallpox, tuberculosis and polio can reduce death rates quickly. The discovery of antibiotics has had a great effect on population by reducing death rates. When a decrease in death rate is caused by medical or scientific progress, the change in natural increase can be quite sudden.

Education   The standard of education affects birth and death rates. The better educated people are, the lower the death rate among them. People know more about disease and hygiene and so can protect themselves. Birth rates also decrease as people become better educated. Parents haven't the same need of a large family to provide workers and people to care for them in old age. Women are in a better position to have a life outside the family and go out to work. Educated people are usually better informed about family planning.

Status of Women   Status means the position someone has in society. The part played by women has an effect on the birth rate. In some societies a woman's role is seen as mother and housewife only. In such societies women may have no choice but to stay within the home, often having large families. In other societies women and men have more equal roles with equal opportunities to work. In such societies many women work outside the home. Women who work away from home have fewer children.

These six factors don't work separately. They usually interact. For example, take a society where there is technological progress. This leads to larger earnings which means better nourishment. As earnings increase people can afford better healthcare and education. This leads to changes in how people think about the status of women. Each of these changes is the result of interaction and has its own effect on the birth rate.

ACTIVITY 4

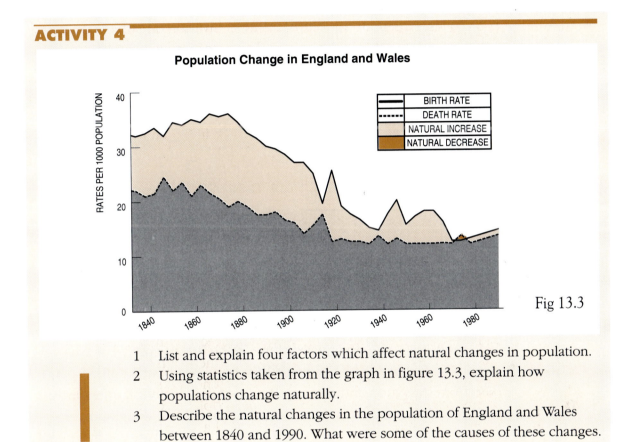

Fig 13.3

1. List and explain four factors which affect natural changes in population.
2. Using statistics taken from the graph in figure 13.3, explain how populations change naturally.
3. Describe the natural changes in the population of England and Wales between 1840 and 1990. What were some of the causes of these changes.

IRELAND'S POPULATION AND EMIGRATION

Between 1864 and 1991 Ireland's population has always had a natural increase. Because of this you would expect the population to have grown. The graph in figure 13.4 shows that this did not happen. In fact, the population fell for most of the period between these years.

THE GEOGRAPHER'S WAY 2

ACTIVITY 5

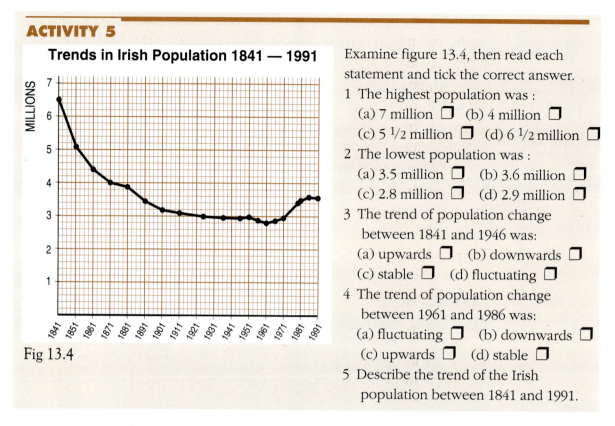

Fig 13.4

Examine figure 13.4, then read each statement and tick the correct answer.
1. The highest population was:
   (a) 7 million ☐ (b) 4 million ☐
   (c) 5 ½ million ☐ (d) 6 ½ million ☐
2. The lowest population was:
   (a) 3.5 million ☐ (b) 3.6 million ☐
   (c) 2.8 million ☐ (d) 2.9 million ☐
3. The trend of population change between 1841 and 1946 was:
   (a) upwards ☐ (b) downwards ☐
   (c) stable ☐ (d) fluctuating ☐
4. The trend of population change between 1961 and 1986 was:
   (a) fluctuating ☐ (b) downwards ☐
   (c) upwards ☐ (d) stable ☐
5. Describe the trend of the Irish population between 1841 and 1991.

The graph shows that the trend in population was downwards from 1841 until 1946. The downward slope in the first twenty years was very steep. The Famine 1845-47 caused this, because about 1 million people died from starvation and disease. But this huge death toll only partly explains the rapid decrease between 1841 and 1861. Emigration also happened on a massive scale. **Emigration** is the outward movement of people from an area or country. During and after the Famine emigration increased greatly as people fled from Ireland. The numbers of people leaving became greater than the natural increase. This caused a decrease in the population.

The high rate of emigration continued for many years and steadily reduced the population. We can see its effect by studying the decade 1891-1901. In this period there were 835,072 births and 639,073 deaths. Subtracting deaths from births, the natural increase was 195,999. This is the number by which the population should have increased. But emigration in the period was 597,325. Because this number was greater than the natural increase by 401,326, we find that the population actually decreased by this number. This pattern of emigration cancelling out the natural increase prevailed for more than a hundred years until about 1960. In the period 1946-51 emigration fell for a short time and a slight rise in population happened. From the graph you can see this increase did not last long.

On the graph the period 1961-1986 shows the first sustained growth in population since the Famine. There are two reasons for the change in trend. Firstly, natural increase continued to be strong with a high birth rate and a low death rate. Secondly, emigration decreased as people began to return to Ireland. This inward migration is called **immigration**. Between 1971 and 1979 the natural increase was 281,035 and immigration added 108,934 people to the population. Taking these figures together the population grew by 389,969 in these years. During the 1980's emigration increased again. The 1991 census shows a return to the pattern of emigration cancelling out any natural increase there was.

ACTIVITY 6

1 Using the information for Ireland in the table, work out the change in population in each of the periods. Note that a **+** sign means immigration and a **-** sign means emigration.

PERIOD	BIRTHS	DEATHS	MIGRATION
1891-1901	737,934	588,391	-396,414
1936-1946	602,095	428,297	-187,111
1971-1981	694,637	333,369	+103,889

2 Explain the changes in the total population which you calculated in Question 1.

THE POPULATION OF GERMANY

After World War 2, Germany was divided into two states called East Germany (German Democratic Republic) and West Germany (Federal German Republic). In 1990 they were united again to form a single Germany. The graph in figure 13.5 shows the populations of East and West Germany from 1950 and the population of Germany reunited since 1990.

ACTIVITY 7

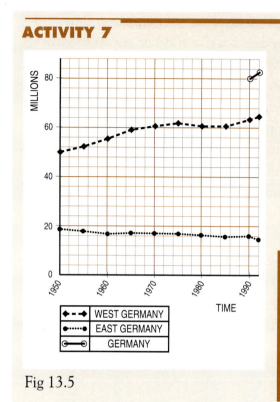

Fig 13.5

Examine the graph in figure 13.5 then do the following.
1. What type of graph is it?
2. Why was this type of graph used? Give two reasons.
3. Describe the trends in population in East and West Germany between 1950 and 1990.
4. By comparing the population graphs of the two countries find three contrasts between them.
5. What was the population of Germany in 1992?
6. After East and West Germany were united there was internal migration within Germany. Using evidence from the graphs decide whether the direction of this movement was mainly from East to West Germany or from West to East Germany. Give two reasons for your decision.

After Germany was divided, East Germany became a communist state. Many did not want to live under this kind of government as they were less free and had a lower living standard. These acted as 'push' factors causing people to migrate from East to West Germany. Other factors 'pulled' them to West Germany: jobs, higher wages, better living standards. Families had been split up when the country was divided. The desire to be re-united pulled many to West Germany which had the larger population. This movement contributed to the growth of population in West Germany and reduced the numbers of East Germans.

The high rate of emigration from East Germany worried the government there. In 1960 it closed the border between the two Germanies preventing further migration. The West German economy was growing rapidly and many jobs had been filled by Germans from the East. With the border closed a shortage of workers developed in West German industry. To meet the demand the West German government encouraged people to migrate from countries like Turkey, Italy, Greece, Poland, and Romania. This immigration caused the population in West Germany to continue to rise during the 1960s despite a sharp decrease in birth rate. The immigration of foreign workers cancelled out the natural decrease which should have happened.

POPULATION GROWTH

After 1970 the population in West Germany stabilised. It then began to decrease slowly as immigration grew less and the birth rate declined to become one of the lowest in the world. Since 1990 the birth rate in West Germany has shown a small increase, causing a growth in the population of Germany as a whole. This trend is shown in the graph. In East Germany the population has continued its slow decrease. The rate of decline sharpened after 1990 as people crossed to the West to get jobs and re-join their families.

The population of Germany is now 80.5 million. This number will probably not increase much. The death rate at 12 per 1000 is higher than the birth rate at 11 per 1000, so there is actually a natural decrease. Many of the 6.5 million foreigners in Germany were brought in as 'guest workers'. These are now being encouraged to return to their homelands. This should cause a decrease in population. If there is a need for workers in the future, it will probably be met by migration from the old East Germany.

ACTIVITY 8

Use the knowledge and skills you have learned studying the populations of Ireland and Germany to find out about the population of Brazil.

POPULATION OF BRAZIL

Year	Population in millions	Birth rate per 1000	Death rate per 1000
1950	53.4	45	15
1970	95.8	36	11
1992	154.1	26	7

Study the table giving population statistics for Brazil, then do the following:
1. What was the change in population between 1950 and 1970 and between 1970 and 1992?
2. What was the natural increase per 1000 in 1950, 1970 and 1992?
3. Describe the trends in the birth rate, death rate and natural increase between 1950 and 1992.
4. Suggest two reasons for the trend you identify in the natural increase.
5. (a) Contrast Brazil's population with the Irish population under the headings: size; birth rate; death rate; natural increase.
   (b) Suggest reasons for the contrasts you identify.

THE GEOGRAPHER'S WAY 2

WORLD POPULATION - THE FUTURE

The growth in world population is very fast. It is not spread evenly. Some areas have low rates of growth; in others population is growing very quickly. The map in figure 13.6 shows the variations in natural increase.

ACTIVITY 9

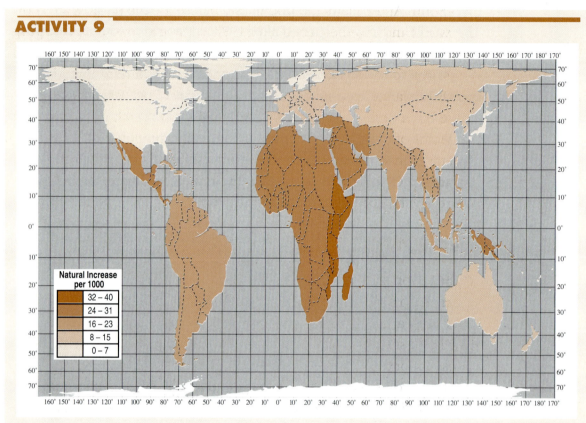

Fig 13.6

Study the map in figure 13.6 then do the following:
1. Decide whether each of the following statements is true or false. Place a tick in the correct box.
                                                                                                                  T F
   (a) The natural increase in South America is between 16 and 23 per 1000.
   (b) The natural increase in most of Africa is between 32 and 40 per 1000.
   (c) Southern Asia has a higher natural increase than Northern Asia.
   (d) Northern Europe has a lower natural increase than Oceania.
   (e) Asia has the largest natural increase.
2. Write a description of how natural increase varies around the world.

POPULATION GROWTH

Natural increase is highest in Africa. Central and South America and Southern Asia also have large natural increases though not as large as Africa's. The lowest natural increases are in Europe, North America and Japan. North and East Asia and Oceania have fairly low natural increases.

Most growth in world population will happen in Africa, Central and South America and Southern Asia. These are the poorest areas of the world and together are called the **Third World**, or the **Developing World**. The cause of the rapid growth in these areas is their high birth rates. The following developing countries have a birth rate of 50 per 1000: Tanzania, Zambia, Rwanda, Côte d'Ivoire and Yemen. Each of these has a death rate of 16 per 1000 or less. The result is large natural increases of over 30 per 1000 per year. Such natural increases are much greater than in the First World countries of North America, Europe, Japan and Oceania. The **First World** or the **Developed World** is the name given to the richer areas of the world.

POPULATION PROJECTIONS

Population projections forecast how population will probably change. To make a projection of world population you need to know how birth and death rates are likely to change. Death rates are fairly low in most countries, whether they are developed or not, so death rates will probably not change much. Therefore death rate change is not likely to be an important factor in deciding future population. In First World countries birth rates are already low, so they won't change much either. On the other hand, birth rates are high in the Third World, so here there is plenty of room for change. For example in Eastern Africa birth rates range between 32 and 40. Future world population depends mainly on how birth rates change in these countries and how quickly. There is no agreement on what these changes are going to be or how quickly they will happen, so there are many different forecasts of the future size of world population.

Fig 13.7

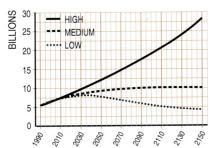

Three different projections are shown on the diagram in figure 13.7. The solid line is a pessimistic projection which forecasts the population to be close to 30 billion people by 2150 AD. Such an enormous population will put great pressure on the Earth's resources and environment to provide basic needs and space for so many. The dashed line shows a medium projection. It forecasts that world population will stabilise at 10 billion by 2150 AD. The Earth could probably support such an increase though there would be more pressure on resources and environment than at present. The dotted line is a very optimistic projection which forecasts that both birth and death rates will fall. It predicts that world population will decrease to 4 billion by 2150 AD. This seems unlikely but it must be remembered that future population depends on human behaviour and this can be very unpredictable.

CARTOONS

A **cartoon** is a drawing which conveys a message. In some cases the message is funny, in others it is serious. Cartoons are effective because they present an image or picture which sticks in our mind. They can sometimes shock us into thinking about something. Cartoonists, the people who draw cartoons, think carefully about how to get their message across before they draw a cartoon. To understand the message of a cartoon it is important to observe and analyse it carefully. The cartoon in figure 13.8 deals with the issue of world population.

ACTIVITY 10

Fig 13.8

POPULATION GROWTH

1. Examine the cartoon in figure 13.8 carefully, then do the following:
   (a) Which hemisphere of the Earth is shown?
   (b) What lies beneath the Earth?
   (c) What, do you think is the message of this cartoon about the Earth's population? Use evidence from the cartoon to support your answer.
   (d) Is the message of the cartoon pessimistic or optimistic? Explain your choice.
2. (a) Describe three different predictions of the world's future population.
   (b) Explain why population predictions can vary so much.

REVISION

Rewrite the following text into your copy using the words in the box to fill in the blank spaces.

population projections	First World	stable	census	emigration
Developed World	birth rate	Developing World		
death rate	natural decrease	immigration		
cartoon	natural increase	Third World		
population	billion	natural change		

The number of people in a country is its _____. A _____ is a counting of the number of people in a country. A thousand million is a _____. The number of births per thousand of the population is the _____ _____. The number of deaths per thousand of the population is the _____ _____. If there is a difference between the number of births and the number of deaths then there is a _____ _____ in the population. If there are more births than deaths, there is a _____ _____ but if there are more deaths than births, there is a _____ _____. If births equal deaths then the population is _____. People migrating out of a country is _____. People migrating into a country is _____. The poorer areas of the world including Africa, Central and South America and Southern Asia are called the _____ _____ or the _____ _____. The richer part of the world including North America, Europe, Oceania and Japan is called the _____ _____ or the _____ _____. Predictions of future population changes are called _____ _____. A _____ is a drawing with a message.

193

14 Population: Density and Distribution

IN THIS CHAPTER YOU WILL LEARN

- How to calculate population density.
- Density and distribution of world population.
- Population distribution in Ireland, Sweden and Brazil.
- Problems of high population densities in Calcutta and Hong Kong.
- Problems of low population density in Mali.

The map in figure 14.1 shows how population is distributed in the world. It gives the population densities for different areas. The **population density** is the number of people in a stated area. In this case it is the number of people per square kilometre. To find the population density divide the population by the area. The population density of Ireland is calculated as follows:

$$\frac{\text{Ireland's population}}{\text{Ireland's area}} = \frac{3,500,000}{70,000 \text{ km}^2} = 50 \text{ people per km}^2$$

This means that if the population is spread evenly throughout Ireland there will be 50 people in each square kilometre.

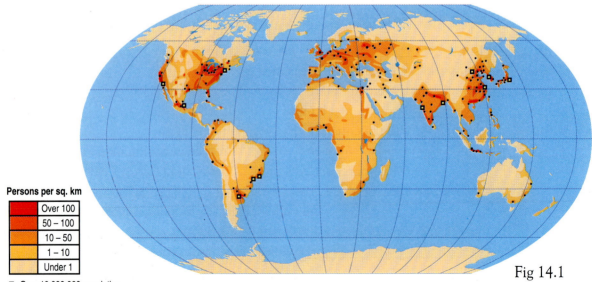

Persons per sq. km
- Over 100
- 50 – 100
- 10 – 50
- 1 – 10
- Under 1

▫ Over 10,000,000 population
• 5,000,000 – 10,000,000 population
· 1,000,000 – 5,000,000 population

Fig 14.1

POPULATION: DENSITY AND DISTRIBUTION

ACTIVITY 1

1. Revise the ideas of density and distribution, Book One, pages 275/277.
2. Using these figures, calculate the population density for each country.

COUNTRY	POPULATION	AREA
Mexico	90,000,000	2,000,000 km^2
Paraguay	4,400,000	400,000 km^2
Mali	9,000,000	1,250,000 km^2
Thailand	55,000,000	500,000 km^2
Netherlands	15,000,000	37,000 km^2

3. Using an atlas, find in which continent each country is located.
4. If the area of a country is 300,000 km^2 and its population density is 18 per km^2, calculate its total population.
5. Examine the map in figure 14.1, then do the exercise by ticking the correct answer. Use this information to decide the correct answer:

    Population density < 50 per km^2 is low.
    Population density 50 – 100 per km^2 is medium.
    Population density > 100 per km^2 is high.

    (a) In Australia population densities are mostly
    (i) low ☐   (ii) very high ☐   (iii) medium ☐   (iv) high ☐

    (b) In Europe the only large areas of low population density are in the
    (i) South ☐   (ii) West ☐   (iii) North ☐   (iv) East ☐

    (c) In most of Africa population densities are:
    (i) above 100 per km^2 ☐   (ii) below 10 per km^2 ☐
    (iii) above 10 per km^2 ☐   (iv) below 1 per km^2 ☐

    (d) The highest population densities in Asia are in the:
    (i) North and East ☐   (ii) North-east and South-west ☐
    (iii) South and East ☐   (iv) North and Centre ☐

6. Write a description of the population distribution in the world. Use the instructions for describing a distribution given in Book One, page 277.

WORLD POPULATION DENSITY AND DISTRIBUTION

There are four large areas of high population density. These are Europe, the North-east of North America, Southern Asia and Eastern Asia. There are several reasons for the high densities in these areas. Some are to do with the availability of resources, others are to do with history.

Europe The temperate climate fertile plains and network of river routeways made Europe an attractive location for people to settle since early times. Slowly the population grew. Improved knowledge and the discovery of local coal and ore provided the resources which made possible the Industrial Revolution. This revolution enabled some European countries to control large parts of the world through their superior knowledge and skills. Great riches flowed to Europe. This new wealth caused the death rate to decrease and population grew rapidly. Europe also attracted many immigrants who came to seek work and prosperity.

North-east of North America The climate soils and landscapes of this region are like those in Europe. For this reason the area around New York was called New England by its first British settlers. The region received many immigrants from Europe during the 19th and early 20th centuries. Some of these migrants brought technology and industrial skills with them as well as their different cultures. Wealth grew rapidly as farming and industry exploited the huge resources of the continent. This drew in more immigrants anxious for a better life. It soon became an area of increasingly dense population.

Eastern and Southern Asia This area consists mainly of two countries, China and India. Between them they have more than half the world's population. The high population densities here are due to similar causes. These were the first areas where farming developed. They have been cultivated for thousands of years, specially their fertile flood plains. Rivers like the Hwang Ho and Yangste Kiang in China and the Ganges and Indus in India flood each year. As with the Nile, the floods deposit **alluvium** which fertilises the soil. This makes the land produce large harvests, especially rice. Because they had a reliable food supply, these areas attracted settlement over many centuries, so population density increased. The fall in death rate due to recent progress in medicine and health care has made population grow more rapidly still.

Agriculture here is mostly subsistence farming which produces just enough food for farmers and their families. They use the land **intensively** which means they try to get as much from it as possible. The farms are small and the level of technology is low; most of the work is done by hand. This intensive farming of rich land can create rural population densities as high as 750 per km^2.

There are very low densities of population in areas unsuitable for settlement. They may be too cold, too mountainous or too dry for people to settle. Antarctica, Siberia, Greenland and Northern Canada

POPULATION: DENSITY AND DISTRIBUTION

are too cold to attract many people. Nomads such as the Inuits in Canada and the Lapps in Norway and Sweden populate these regions but their numbers are small. Population densities are less than 1 per km². High mountain regions like the Himalayas, Rockies and Alps are unsuited to human settlement because they are too cold and exposed.

Some regions have low population densities because they are too dry. These are the deserts. They include the Sahara and Kalahari Deserts in Africa, the Atacama Desert in South America, the Arabian Desert, the Gobi Desert in Asia and the Australian Desert. Nomads inhabit these regions as do oasis-dwellers. An **oasis** is a place in a desert where ground water comes to the surface. Settlements developed at oases because the water was used for farming. Oases also became trading centres because desert travellers converged on them to get water on their journeys. Even though some people inhabit the deserts they are few, so densities are very low at about 1 per km².

ACTIVITY 2

Fig 14.2A

Fig 14.2B

Fig 14.2C

1. Examine the photographs in figure 14.2 then do the following:
   (a) Using evidence from the photograph decide whether the population density is likely to be high or low in each of the areas shown.
   (b) Using evidence from the photograph, suggest in which part of the world each photograph was taken. Explain.
2. Use your atlas to find out where the deserts mentioned in the text are.

THE GEOGRAPHER'S WAY 2

POPULATION DISTRIBUTION IN IRELAND

Just as the population of the Earth is unevenly distributed, so in countries there are areas of high and low population density. Ireland is a small country but there are marked differences in the densities of its population in different parts.

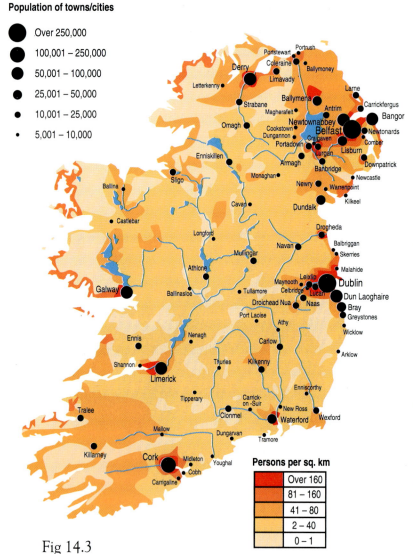

Fig 14.3

Examine the population distribution map in figure 14.3 then do the following:

1. Name five areas with population densities over 160 per km^2.
2. Name five mountain ranges where population density is less than 1 per km^2.
3. Which of the following statements best describes the population distribution?
   (a) The highest densities are in the Central Lowlands and the lowest densities are in coastal areas.
   (b) High densities are only found in coastal locations whereas low densities are found in mountainous and inland areas.
   (c) The lowest densities in Ireland are between 2 and 40 people per km^2 and the highest densities are between 81 and 160.
   (d) Ireland's highest densities are along the south coast: as one moves northwards population densities decrease.

The highest population densities are in and around the main cities and towns: Dublin, Waterford, Cork, Limerick, Galway and Drogheda. The next highest densities are found in a narrow strip along the west coast in Donegal, Sligo, Mayo, Galway, Clare and Kerry. Most inland areas have low densities. The lowest densities are found in the mountains.

The low densities may be for different reasons. In mountains densities are low because there are infertile soils, steep slopes and a

POPULATION: DENSITY AND DISTRIBUTION

climate too cold and wet for human settlement. Population may be low in fertile lowland areas because farms are large and farmhouses are widely scattered giving low densities.

The high densities on the western coastal plain have a number of causes. During plantation times, land was confiscated from the inhabitants who were forced to move west of the Shannon. This caused a rapid increase in the population of Connacht. As Connacht is mountainous, many of the migrants had to settle on the coastal plains where there was the best land they could find. Farms are usually small in the west. A large number of farms in a small area causes a high population density.

Population density may vary within very small areas. Take the area in and around Dublin City. In the CBD densities are low because most buildings are offices, shops and banks. Residential buildings are few. The inner suburbs have high densities because there are many flats there. In the outer suburbs densities are high but decrease as one gets further from the city centre. This is because the houses are larger with larger gardens. Just south of Dublin the densities are very low because of the Dublin/Wicklow Mountains. There are also low densities to the north and north-west because Dublin Airport has blocked the development of suburbs there.

ACTIVITY 3

1. Describe the distribution of population in Ireland.
2. Explain the population distribution of Ireland.
3. Examine the population map of Sweden in figure 14.4A. Using an atlas describe the distribution of population in that country.
4. Using the map in figure 14.4B which shows Swedens resources explain the distribution of population in Sweden.

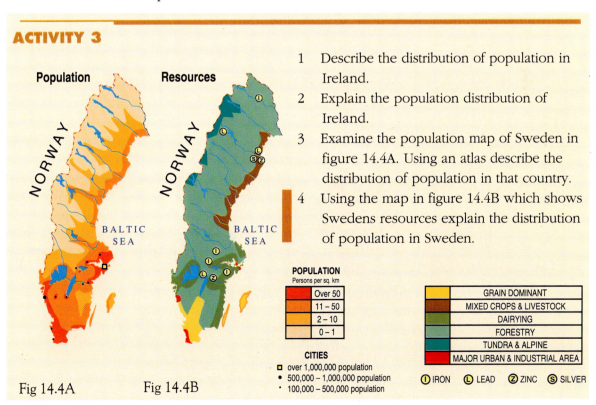

Fig 14.4A   Fig 14.4B

THE GEOGRAPHER'S WAY 2

POPULATION DENSITY - BRAZIL

The Portuguese arrived in North-east Brazil in 1500 looking for land and wealth. They made Brazil a Portuguese colony. A **colony** is a country which is taken over by another and exploited for its benefit. The colonists settled on the north-east coast and then gradually moved southwards. They settled on the coast because they needed ports to ship out the wealth they had taken or produced. Primary products they sent included sugar, rubber, coffee and metals. The largest numbers of Portuguese settled in south-east Brazil because here the climate was similar to the climate in Portugal. Today the largest cities and highest population densities are found here. The colonists gradually moved inland looking for land and minerals but they avoided the Amazon Basin. They found its climate too tiring and unhealthy. Today the population is still expanding inland to the Mato Grosso plateau and into the Amazon Basin. The Trans-Amazonian Highway has given people access to the forest. People are attracted by cheap land and by resources such as minerals and fuels.

The colonisation of Brazil had a drastic effect on the Indians who had lived there for thousands of years before the Portuguese came. It is estimated that there were 5 million Indians in 1500. Now only a quarter of a million remain. The rest were killed or died from diseases brought by the colonists.

ACTIVITY 4

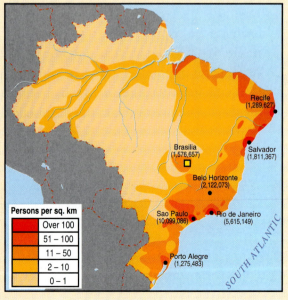

1. Examine the population map of Brazil in figure 14.5 then describe the distribution of population in that country.
2. Explain why the density of population is high in South-east Brazil and low in the Amazon Basin.
3. Explain what a primary product is. Revise pages 35-45 in Book One.
4. Draw a sketch map of Brazil and on it show the distribution of popluation and five cities with populations greater than a million.

Fig 14.5

POPULATION: DENSITY AND DISTRIBUTION

PROBLEMS OF HIGH POPULATION DENSITY

Fig 14.6

Calcutta - overcrowding Calcutta is a city in north-east India with a population of 9.1 million. It is located on the delta of the Ganges River, see figure 14.6. It serves a large hinterland with a population of 150 million. Many poor people migrate to Calcutta looking for work or food. The city hasn't the resources to provide services for them and this creates problems of overcrowding. There is an acute housing shortage and many live on the city pavements. About 3 million live in huts made from mud and timber, called **bustees**. These often collapse when flooded.

Flooding is common because the city is located on a delta and the land is low and flat. Many bustees have no proper water supply or sewerage. This causes dysentery and cholera, deadly diseases which are the result of drinking dirty water. These diseases are common and cause a high death rate.

The government has tried to improve conditions by providing water taps, toilets and street paving in the bustees. Unfortunately what has been done is not enough but there has been progress. The bustee dwellers themselves have helped to improve conditions by working and supporting one another. Local water and sewerage schemes run by community action have achieved a lot to improve living standards.

Fig 14.7 'Calcutta'

Another problem is serious traffic congestion. In most cities about 20% of the land is used for streets. In Calcutta streets use only 6% of the land. This shortage creates huge traffic jams at rush hours. It also makes it even more difficult to provide basic services.

Fig 14.8

Hong Kong – shortage of space The map in figure 14.8 shows Hong Kong, located on the south coast of China. It has a very high population density. Seventy times smaller than Ireland, it has a population of 5.9 million. The average density is 5,200 people per km². Now a British colony, it will be returned to China in 1997.

Hong Kong is an entrepôt for Eastern Asia with important trading and manufacturing functions. It is also a tourist centre. Incomes are higher than in the neighbouring countries of China and Vietnam. This was a pull factor attracting migrants from these countries. Population grew rapidly because of immigration and a high birth rate. The map in figure 14.9 shows that Hong Kong consists of a mountainous peninsula and a number of islands, of which the most important is Hong Kong Island.

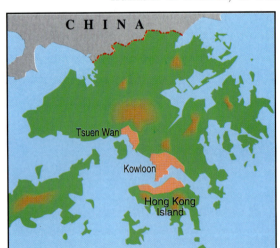

Fig 14.9

There is an acute shortage of open space to use for recreation because there is so much mountain. The rest of the land is covered by settlements or is used intensively for agriculture. The high population density creates a massive pollution problem because so many people produce large amounts of sewage and rubbish. Disposal of waste is very difficult in so small an area. The result is that the sea around Hong Kong Island is severely polluted and a serious health risk.

Although richer than Calcutta, not everybody in Hong Kong shares its wealth. Many immigrants live in shacks clustered on the steep slopes which nobody wants. These settlements are called **shanty towns** and are similar to the bustees of Calcutta. Others live on house boats and are at risk of disease from the polluted water.

POPULATION: DENSITY AND DISTRIBUTION

Fig 14.10

ACTIVITY 5

1. Draw a sketch map of Asia. On it show:
    China, Vietnam, India, the Himalaya Mountains,
    the Ganges River, Calcutta, Hong Kong
2. Examine the photographs of Calcutta and Hong Kong in figures 14.7 and 14.10.
    (a) Write a description of what is seen in each photograph.
    (b) Giving evidence from the photographs, identify and explain two problems in each place caused by high population density.
    (c) Contrast the two areas in the photographs.

PROBLEMS OF LOW POPULATION DENSITY

Low population density creates social and economic problems. These can act as push factors causing people to migrate from an area, so reducing the population density even further. This makes a bad situation worse.

Population densities are generally low in the West of Ireland from Donegal to Kerry, apart from the coastal strip. People's social lives are affected when there are few people living in an area. **Social life** means how people mix with groups within their community. This is important in making them happy and content. Low population density makes it difficult to arrange social activity and there are fewer opportunities for people to meet. This can lead to a low marriage rate and eventually a further decline in population. The maps in figure 14.11 show the distribution of single people between the ages of 25 and 34.

ACTIVITY 6

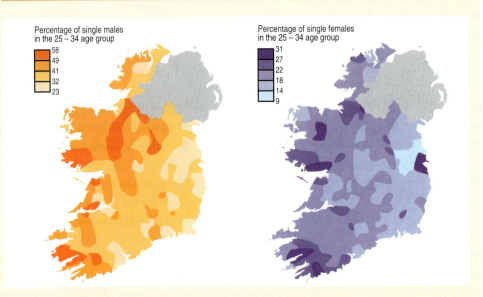

Fig 14.11

Study figure 14.11 then do the following:
1. Which sex has the higher percentage of unmarried adults?
2. Using evidence from the maps decide whether this statement is true, and explain your answer.
   'In the West of Ireland higher percentages of males and females in the 25-34 age group are unmarried than in the East.'

The maps show that in most places there is a higher percentage of unmarried people in the West of Ireland than in the East. This is partly caused by low population density. Few people and low marriage rates make an area less attractive and so act as push factors causing outward migration. As people migrate seeking a better social life, farms are abandoned and the land is left idle. Another problem caused by low population density is the lack of political power which it creates.

Political power is the ability to influence government to get things done or changed. An area of low density has fewer votes and sends fewer representatives to the Dáil. This means that the people of Dublin have more power to get things done, such as building roads, schools, hospitals and so on.

Economic power is the power to buy things. Areas of low density are unlikely to have much economic power. Businesses do not prosper because customers are few and not enough can be sold to make profits. There are fewer services in low density areas: shops, hairdressers, doctors, lawyers, cinemas, dance halls, transport and so on. This also makes the area less attractive and may be a push factor in migration.

POPULATION: DENSITY AND DISTRIBUTION

MALI

Locate Mali in your atlas. Find out the following information about it.
(a) The continent in which it is found.
(b) Identify four of Mali's neighbouring countries.
(c) Name two towns in Mali.
(d) Name a large river which flows through it.

Mali is in Western Africa. It is a large country with a low population density of only 7 per km². The northern part lies in the Sahara Desert, the south is in the Sahel. 'Sahel' is an arabic word meaning fringe. It describes a belt of countries on the southern margin of the Sahara. The Sahel has a savanna climate with a wet and a dry season. The wet seasons are very variable and droughts often happen when the rains fail.

In northern Mali growing crops is impossible due to the desert climate. Animals are reared but they have to stay on the move in search of pasture. This type of farming is called **nomadic pastoralism**. The **Tuareg** people are nomads who live by this type of agriculture. Improvement in health care caused a drop in their death rate, so the numbers of Tuareg increased. The numbers of animals grew as well. This led to overgrazing which destroyed the vegetation in areas near the Sahara. When this happens there is nothing to hold moisture in the soil and it becomes desert. The Sahara Desert is gradually spreading south because of this and a possible drying of the climate. This process is called **desertification**. Because of it, the Tuareg have now been forced to move further south in search of pasture. This brings them into conflict with the settled arable farmers near the Niger River.

Fig 14.12

THE GEOGRAPHER'S WAY 2

The Tuareg have little political power and get little support from the government of Mali because they are few. Most governments don't like nomads anyway because they are difficult to control and tax and the Mali government is no different. It is trying to fix them in permanent settlements. The droughts help the government to do this because the Tuareg animals are killed by drought and this forces the people into the towns in search of food aid. Many never return to their wandering. The Tuareg way of life is unlikely to continue when such a powerless group is faced by a hostile government and a more numerous settled community.

ACTIVITY 6

1. Write a description of Mali under the headings: location, climate, lifestyles, social conflict.
2. What is desertification? Explain two possible causes of it.
3. Explain three reasons why the Tuareg way of life is unlikely to continue much longer in Mali.
4. Find out about the Tuareg people in an encyclopedia. Give an account of their way of life.
5. Examine the photograph of the Sahel in figure 14.12. Identify and explain the processes which are changing this environment.

REVISION

Rewrite the text into your copy using the words in the box.

shanty towns	population density	oasis	desertification
political power	colonists	Tuareg	intensively
economic power	colony	bustees

The number of people per square kilometre is called the _____ _____. When every piece of land is farmed as much as possible it is being farmed _____. An _____ is where water comes to the surface in a desert. A country controlled by another country is a _____. The people who settle in other countries to exploit them are called _____. In Calcutta very low-quality houses are called _____. In other parts of the world large settlements of low-quality housing are known as _____ _____. The power to get into government and get things done is called _____ _____. The power to spend money is called _____ _____. The _____ are nomads in Mali. The gradual spread of the desert is _____.

15 Population Structure

IN THIS CHAPTER YOU WILL LEARN

- Age/sex structure of a population.
- How to study a population pyramid.
- Different pyramid shapes as in the case of Germany and Brazil.
- Migration and its effect on population structure.

Fig 15.1

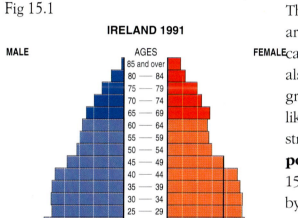

The population of each country has its own arrangement or structure. The population can be divided into males and females. It can also be broken down into different age groups. When a population is broken down like this we see its **age/sex structure**. This structure is best shown on a graph called a **population pyramid** like the one in figure 15.1. Knowing the structure of a population by age and sex helps a government plan for people's needs.

IRELAND'S POPULATION PYRAMID

On the left of the central line the blue bar chart represents males. Each blue bar represents a 5 year age group. The red bar chart on the right represents females. Each red bar represents a 5 year age group.

To find the number of males or females in an age group draw a line from the end of the bar down to the horizontal scale and read off the number. This has been done for the 10 - 14 male age group and the 45 - 49 female age group on the Irish pyramid. From these lines we can tell that there were 180,000 males in the 10 - 14 age group and 90,000 females in the 45 - 49 age group. By examining the Irish pyramid we can tell a lot about the Irish population.

Firstly, the largest age groups are those between 5 - 20. This makes the young population very big.

THE GEOGRAPHER'S WAY 2

Secondly, the 0 - 4 age group is smaller than the 5 - 9 age group, so the number of births must be falling.

Thirdly, there are more females than males in the older age groups from 65 up. Women appear to live longer than men.

Fourthly, taken together young people and the old make up a large part of the Irish population.

USING POPULATION PYRAMIDS

To study a population pyramid do the following:
1. Note its title and date, if it has one.
2. Find out on which side of the central line males and females are shown. Males are usually to the left, females to the right.
3. Note the two horizontal axes ; one to the left of the central line and one to the right of it. Check the units of measurement used on the horizontal axes. Some show actual numbers of people, others show the percentage of the total population in that age group.
4. Find out what age groups are shown on the vertical axis. Usually the population is divided into 5 year age groups: the first age group is 0 - 4 ; the second 5 - 9 ; and so on up.

ACTIVITY 1

Examine Ireland's population pyramid in figure 15.1, following the steps 1 to 4. When you have finished your study you will probably have noticed that the pyramid is really made up of two bar charts on their sides. Do the following:

1. How many males and females are there in the following age groups ?
   0 - 4   10 - 14   35 - 39   65 - 69
2. What is the total population in each of these age groups ?
   5 - 9   25 - 29   75 - 79
3. Given that the population of Ireland was 3.5 million in 1991, work out the percentage of the population which was in the 0 - 14 age group in that year.
4. Using information from Chapter 13, explain why there is a bulge in the pyramid between the ages of 5 and 20.

DEPENDENT POPULATION

A population pyramid shows the dependent population and the economically active population. The **dependent population** is the age groups which depend on others for their survival. There are two sections in the dependent population. These are young people up to the age of 15 years and old people above 65. These are shown by the lightest and darkest shades of blue and red on the pyramid in figure 15.1. The age groups between 15 and 64 are called the **economically active** groups because they contain the 'wealth producers' who support the dependent population.

ACTIVITY 2

Using the pyramid in figure 15.1 do the following:
1 Work out dependent and active numbers. State as actual numbers of people.
2 Compare the number of young dependents with the number of old dependents.
3 List some of the special needs of (a) young dependents (b) old dependents.

DIFFERENT PYRAMID SHAPES

The age/sex structure of the population varies from country to country. Usually there is a great difference in population structure between First World and Third World countries. This difference is seen by comparing the pyramids in figure 15.2.

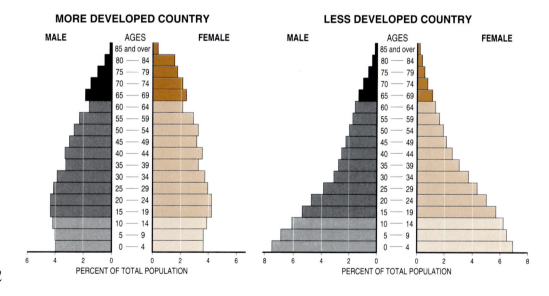

Fig 15.2

The pyramid on the left represents the population structure of developed First World countries. Notice how the pyramid bulges in the economically active age groups. The majority of the population is in the 15 to 65 age groups, the working age groups. The young and old dependent populations are smaller. This means that the wealth-producing population can easily provide for the dependents both young and old.

In the developing country the pyramid has a very wide base. This shows that there is a large percentage of the population in the young dependent age groups. Of the total population 28% is below 10 years of age. There are few people who survive to old age. As age increases a high death rate reduces the population quickly which causes the pyramid to narrow sharply. This shows that there are few people in the economically active age groups. This makes it difficult for the working part of the population to support the large dependent young population and the few remaining old people. This means that many people probably live in poverty.

ACTIVITY 3

Examine the population pyramids of two countries A and B in figure 15.3.

1. Work out the total number of people in the following age groups in each country: 0 - 4   30 - 34   65 - 69

2. Read the statements which follow, then decide which country each applies to. Tick the correct box.

                                                                                             A B

(a) There are 2 million males between 50 and 54 in this population. ☐ ☐
(b) There are 3 million females between 50 and 54 in this population. ☐ ☐
(c) The young dependent population is larger than the old dependent population. ☐ ☐
(d) There is a bulge in the economically active age groups. ☐ ☐
(e) It has the larger of the two populations. ☐ ☐

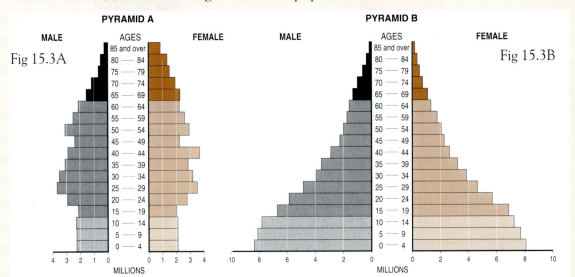

3. Comment on the dependent population in each case.
4. One of the countries is Brazil, the other is Germany. Decide which is which, giving three reasons for your choice in each case.

POPULATION STRUCTURE

Pyramid A represents the German population in 1991. It has a narrow base indicating that the young dependent age groups are small. This is what we would expect in a developed country where the birth rate is very low. The middle of the pyramid has a bulge. This reflects the higher birth rates between 20 and 60 years ago. With the bulge there is a sudden narrowing in the 40 to 50 age groups. This was due to the decrease in the birth rate during the Second World War (1939-1945). There are a large number of people in the older age groups because in a rich country like Germany elderly people are educated, well-fed and get excellent health care. This prolongs life. The narrowing of the pyramid in the 70 - 74 age group is due to the fall in the birth rate during the First World War (1914-1918). The marked difference between the number of males and females over 65 years of age is largely due to males being killed during World War Two.

Pyramid B represents the Brazilian population. The base is very wide indicating a very high birth rate and a large young dependent population. The pyramid narrows quickly because of the high death rates. This leaves a small economically active group to support a large young dependent group and a small number of old people. This results in poverty for many.

SEX BALANCE

Population pyramids also show the balance between the sexes. Usually there are more males in the young age groups and more females in the older ones. This is because death rates are usually higher among males than females. Nature compensates for this with more male births than female. As the death rate is higher among males, by the time old age is reached females are more numerous than males.

ACTIVITY 5

"There is usually an imbalance of males and females in the population in the younger age groups. There are more males than females. But in the older age groups there are usually more females than males."

1. From a study of the population pyramids in this chapter decide whether this statement is true. Give figures to support your answer.
2. Check whether the statement is true in the case of both developed and developing countries. Support your answer with specific figures.

THE GEOGRAPHER'S WAY 2

THE USE OF POPULATION PYRAMIDS

Population pyramids are useful to governments in their planning. The Irish government knows that it must plan for the increase in the number of young adults in the population. This age group needs jobs and third level education so the government must be ready to provide these. As the numbers under ten in the population are falling, there will be less need for new schools, so fewer will be built. In Germany the bulge in the middle of the pyramid means there are many middle-aged people. These are getting older so there will be a great demand for the kinds of services they will need in the future. The government must plan to provide them when needed.

ACTIVITY 5

Study Brazil's population pyramid. Then explain what you think the Brazilian government should do to cater for the future needs of (a) its young population; (b) its ageing population.

MIGRATION AND POPULATION STRUCTURE

Movement of people from one country to another is **international migration**. The migration from Ireland to Britain and the USA after the Famine is an example of international migration. People also migrate within countries from one region to another. The migration of people from the Irish counytryside to towns and cities is an example of this **inter-regional migration.** People also migrate within cities. There is a tendency for people to migrate from inner city areas to the suburbs.

Migration may be forced or voluntary. When people are compelled to migrate it is **forced migration**. In the 17th and 18th centuries African people were captured and brought to North and South America to work as slaves. These people had no choice. This forced migration was called the Slave Trade. The Irish plantations of the 16th and 17th centuries were also forced migrations. The land was confiscated and people were forced to move to other parts of Ireland.

When people choose to migrate it is a **voluntary migration**. Emigration from Ireland in the 20th century is an example of a voluntary migration because people made their own choice to migrate.

POPULATION STRUCTURE

MIGRATION AND AGE/SEX STRUCTURE

Migration affects the age/sex structure of a population. The slave traders only took young healthy adults from West Africa. They left the very young and the old behind with no young adults to look after them. The population of West Africa declined because of this. West Africa had been robbed of its wealth and food-producing age groups and only the dependent groups were left.

The shape of Ireland's population pyramid, figure 15.1, is partly due to migration. The narrowing of the pyramid in the 50 to 70 age groups indicates a decrease in numbers in these age groups. Emigration is one reason for this. The bulge in the 5 - 19 age group is due to the drop in emigration during the period 1960 to 1980. More people remained at home then, so the natural increase was not wiped out by emigration. The birth rate also increased as more young adults stayed at home, married and had children. In the late 1980s and early 1990s emigration increased. This partly explains the narrowing of the base of the pyramid. The decreasing birth rate also played a part.

ACTIVITY 7

1 The population pyramids for County Kerry and County Dublin are shown in figure 15.4. Co. Kerry has lost many people through emigration and Co. Dublin has gained people through immigration. Examine the pyramids carefully. Decide which of the pyramids represents the population of each of the counties. Use two pieces of evidence from the pyramid to support your choice in each case.

Fig 15.4A   Fig 15.4B

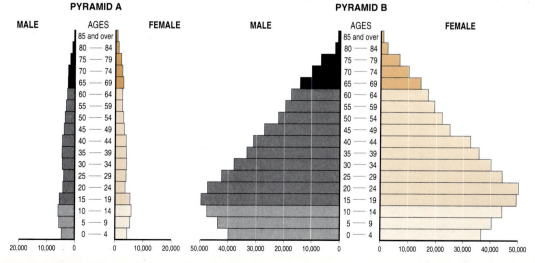

2. Explain the difference between forced and voluntary migration. Give examples to illustrate your explanation.
3. Using figure 15.1 explain how emigration affected the age/sex structure of the Irish population.

Pyramid A represents Kerry's population. This pyramid shows that Kerry has a larger number of old people than expected compared with the number of middle-aged people. Migration is the cause of this. The migrants are mostly young adults so the economically active group is smaller than it should be. As the young adults leave there are fewer marriages and fewer children are born, so the numbers in the young age groups decline. With its ageing population Kerry becomes a less attractive place for young people. Major push factors include the following: the lack of social life due to the age structure of the population; the poor soils in the extensive mountain areas which make it difficult to get a living from farming; the lack of adequate opportunities for work other than farming.

Pyramid B represents the population of County Dublin. It shows that County Dublin has many people in the young, economically active age groups. This is partly due to the immigration of young adults from rural areas such as Kerry and the West of Ireland. Pull factors in this immigration include the following: the opportunity to get a job ; the social life; the wide range of services available, such as schools, colleges, entertainment and sports facilities.

As people migrate within a city, the age/sex structure of the population varies from area to area. People tend to migrate out of the inner city to the suburbs. It is mostly young married adults who migrate outwards. This leads to a predominance of married people in the suburbs, with young unmarried adults and old people living nearer the city centre. Numbers of young children will be high in suburban areas; there will be few in the inner city.

ACTIVITY 7

The population pyramid in figure 15.5 represents the population in an area of a city. Examine it carefully, then do the following:
1. Describe the age/sex structure of the population.
2. Decide whether the pyramid represents the population in an inner city area or a suburban area. Using evidence from the pyramid explain your choice.
3. List the services needed in such an area.

POPULATION STRUCTURE

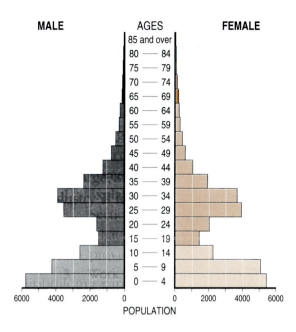

Fig 15.5

REVISION

Rewrite the following text into your copy using the words in the box.

> dependent population   international migration
> population pyramid   forced migration   economically active
> age/sex structure   voluntary migration   inter-regional migration

When a population is broken down into males and females in different age groups we can see the _____ _____ of the population. A graph called a _____ _____ is the most suitable graph for showing the breakdown of the population by age and sex. The _____ _____ are the age groups which rely on others for their survival. The wealth producing age groups are called the _____ _____ age groups. A migration of people from one country to another is called an _____ _____. An _____ _____ is a migration from one area of a country to another area within the country. When people have no choice, the migration is a _____ _____. A _____ _____ is when people choose to migrate.

POPULATION FIELDSTUDY

Title The Age/sex Structure of my Local Population
Aim The aim of this fieldstudy is to determine the age/sex structure of the local population and to compare it with the age/sex structure of the Irish population as shown in figure 15.1.
Equipment Clipboard

Procedure Decide on the location and size of the study area. It may be your parish, street, village or town. If done as a class project, a large area may be studied. Make out a record sheet like the one shown in figure 15.6 and get it copied as many times as you need. Get a letter from your teacher explaining that you are doing a fieldstudy on population in the area and asking for people's co-operation in the study. When a person answers the door to you show them the letter. If they agree to co-operate, explain exactly what you are doing and what information you need from them. Give them a record sheet and ask them to insert on it the number of males and females in each age group who reside in the house.

Analysis Back at school total the numbers of males and females in each age group and use these figures to construct a population pyramid for the study area. Study the pyramid carefully and see what it tells you about the population in the study area. Compare the pyramid for the local area with the pyramid for the population of Ireland in Figure 15.1.

RECORD SHEET

AGE GROUP	MALE	FEMALE
85 +		
80 — 85		
75 — 79		
70 — 74		
65 — 69		
60 — 64		
55 — 59		
50 — 54		
45 — 49		
40 — 44		
35 — 39		
30 — 34		
25 — 29		
20 — 24		
15 — 19		
10 — 14		
5 — 9		
0 — 4		

Date: _____
Location: _____

Fig 15.6

WRITTEN REPORT

Write a report on the fieldstudy under these headings:
Title
Aims
Fieldwork
Analysis of data
Results
Conclusions
Problems I Faced

16 Primary Industries

IN THIS CHAPTER YOU WILL LEARN

It is suggested that you revise Chapters 4 and 5 of Book One before you read Chapter 16.
- Renewable and non-renewable resources.
- The collecting, processing and distributing of water.
- Types of peat and peat harvesting techniques.
- Effects of mechanised harvesting on peat lands.
- Reasons why the seas around Ireland are suitable for fish growth.
- How over-exploitation has affected fish stocks.

A resource is something that is of use to us. Natural resources are things found in nature which are useful. Some resources are renewable, others are non-renewable. A **renewable resource** is one which can be renewed or replaced after it is used. Water and wood are renewable resources. For example, water is used for cleaning. After use the water is poured down a drain and flows to a river or the sea. There it enters the water cycle and becomes available again. So water can be used over and over because it is renewable.

Wood is also a renewable resource, but it is renewed differently to water. If we cut down trees and burn the wood for heat, the wood is destroyed. But, though we use up the burnt wood, we do not destroy the Earth's ability to produce wood. If we replace the wood by growing trees, then the supply of wood is renewed. Other important renewable resources include air, soil, fish, solar energy, wind and wave energy.

Non-renewable resources cannot be replaced once they are used. For example, if oil or natural gas are burned they are destroyed, but unlike wood and trees they cannot be replaced. They are non-renewable resources. Other non-renewable resources include coal, peat and minerals, for example iron and copper.

THE GEOGRAPHER'S WAY 2

ACTIVITY 1

1. Explain the terms resource, natural resource, renewable resource, non-renewable resource.
2. Examine the words in the box carefully then divide them into renewable and non-renewable resources.

| milk | sand | iron | rainforest | wheat |
| podzol | gold | turkey | salmon | lobsters |

3. List five renewable and five non-renewable resources found in your home.

PRIMARY INDUSTRIES

Primary Industries involve work which gathers natural resources of some kind. The four main primary industries are farming, fishing, forestry and mining. Since earliest times people have gathered resources provided by nature. They could not have survived without them. At first when people had little knowledge and skill, the resources they could make use of were very limited. Without a knowledge of metal working, they could not use metal to make tools and weapons. They did not know how to use the chemicals all around them to make everything from plastics to artificial fertilisers. As they learned more, the resources grew in number, because to be a resource, a thing must be of value. To be of value, you must know how to use it for some purpose. Bauxite is a good example of something occuring in nature which did not become a resource till recently. Bauxite is found in many places but it was of no use whatever till scientists learned to smelt it to make aluminium. Now, aluminium is one of our most valuable metals because it is hard and light. There would be no modern aircraft without it.

Water – a renewable resource

Water is a basic natural resource. All living things need it to survive. People need it for drinking, washing, cooking, manufacturing, transporting, irrigating, generating power and for recreation. Animals need drinking water and plants need water to absorb life-giving nutrients from the soil. Without water life, as we know it, would not exist. The collection and storage of water is a very important primary industry.

Collecting water Water must be obtained, collected and stored before it can be used. It is collected in a number of ways. Surface run-off collects naturally in lakes or it can be collected by damming a river and making an artificial lake or **reservoir**. Ground water collects and is stored underground. It is pumped to the surface for use. Sea water can be **desalinated,** that is it has the salt taken out of it. This is a very expensive process as it involves heating water to evaporate it thus separating it from the salt. Only very rich countries or countries with cheap power supplies can afford to desalinate sea water. In Ireland we use run-off and pumped ground water which we collect in lakes and reservoirs.

ACTIVITY 2

1. Describe three ways of gathering water.
2. Describe each of the photographs in figure 16.1. Explain how water is being obtained in both areas.

Fig 16.1A

Fig 16.1B

Dublin's Water Supply It is estimated that the average Irish person uses 275 litres of water each day. So Co.Dublin with a population of just over 1 million people requires 275 million litres of water per day. Dublin is lucky that the Dublin and Wicklow mountains are nearby as they are ideal for collecting water. Most of the mountain areas receive about 1200mm of rainfall. This is mainly relief rainfall and it falls throughout the year so there is no dry season. The rocks in these mountains are impermeable rocks such as granite and quartzite. These don't allow water to seep down through them and are ideal for collecting and storing water. The height of the collecting area allows the water to flow to Dublin under its own pressure.

ACTIVITY 3

1. Explain three reasons why the Wicklow Mountains are suitable for gathering water. Provide a labelled diagram to illustrate your answer.
2. Examine the map in figure 16.2 then answer the following:
   (a) Name three rivers from which Dublin gets its water.
   (b) Each of the three rivers has a reservoir on it. Name the reservoirs and the rivers on which they are located.
   (c) Why does most of Dublin's water supply come from areas south of the city?

Fig 16.2

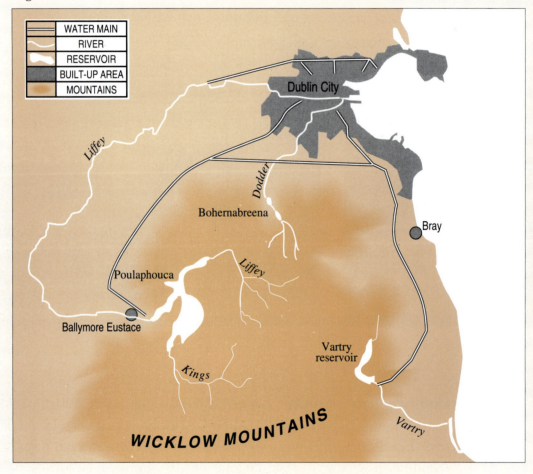

Processing the water When water is collected it has to be processed before it can be used by people and animals and by industry. Processing takes place in a **waterworks** and involves removing impurities suspended in it, killing bacteria and adding fluoride to protect our teeth. The flow chart in figure 16.3 represents 'the stages of processing'.

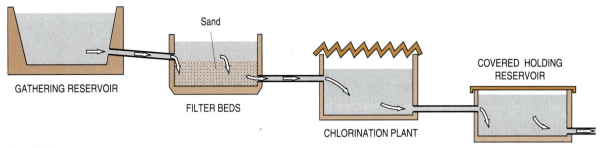

Fig 16.3

The first stage filters suspended particles from the water. The water from the Wicklow mountains tends to be brown because it carries small particles of peat and other impurities. These are trapped when the water is filtered through sand. When the water emerges from the filter beds it is clear. It may still contain bacteria so chlorine is added to disinfect it and kill any bacteria in it. Finally flouride is added to help prevent tooth decay. The water is now ready for consumption and is piped to holding reservoirs near the city until it is needed. A network of pipes called water mains is used to distribute the water through the city.

GROUND WATER

In Ireland 25% of our water supply comes from ground water. In rural areas ground water is used more than surface run-off. For example, in County Roscommon ground water makes up 80% of the water supply.

Many farmers get their water supply from springs or wells on their land. A reliable water supply is essential nowadays, so many farmers ensure their supply of ground water by drilling a deep well. This is often cheaper than linking into a surface water scheme. There are two reasons for this. Firstly, ground water is usually pure because it is filtered naturally as it seeps down through the regolith. Secondly, the water supply is on the farm and so the expense of laying pipes to a distant water main is avoided. So, for ground water, processing and distribution costs are usually lower than for surface run-off. Once the cost of drilling a well is covered the only running costs are disinfection and pumping.

Though the cost of a ground water supply is often cheaper, users have to be careful that the ground water does not become polluted. Water is **polluted** when it contains harmful substances. The main sources of groundwater pollution are sewage, chemicals such as artificial fertilisers, and silage effluent. **Effluents** are liquids which flow out of something. Where ground water is used for the water supply poisonous effluents from farms and factories must be strictly controlled to prevent pollution. Effluents can also pollute surface water in rivers and lakes.

ACTIVITY 4

1. The production of water is an example of a system with inputs, processes and outputs. Using the words below draw a flow chart to show the system of producing water.

   damming   drinking water   disinfecting   rainfall   filtering
   seepage   fluoride   piping   pumping   labour   chlorine

Fig 16.4A   Fig 16.4B

2. Examine the photographs in figure 16.4 then do the following:
   (a) Describe each of the photographs.
   (b) Decide whether each photograph shows collecting, processing or distribution of water. Explain your decision using evidence from the photograph.
3. Prepare a project on the water supply to your home. Find out information about the following:
   (a) The source of the supply; whether it comes from a surface or ground water source.
   (b) The processing it goes through; where this is done and what the processing stages are.
   (c) How it is distributed from the source to your home.

(d) Are there any problems with your supply ? For instance, is the supply unreliable; is the water discoloured; is the water pressure too low. Is anything being done to improve the service?

(e) Do you pay for your water supply? How much does it cost ? How is payment made?

You can get information about your water supply from your parents or guardians, or from the County Council or Corporation. The local library will probably have information about your water supply, as well as books, reports and newspaper articles .

PEAT

Mining is a primary industry which gathers rock, minerals and fuels from the crust of the Earth. Sometimes mining and quarrying are called **extractive** industries because they take material out of the crust. Quarrying of rock of different kinds is carried on in various places to supply building stone, sands and gravels and limestone to make cement. There are rich deposits of the 'base metal' ores, lead and zinc, in Ireland. One of the biggest base metal mines in Europe operates in Navan. Ireland is not rich in fuel resources like coal and oil, though there is a natural gas field off the coast near Kinsale, Co.Cork. Peat, or turf as it is often called, is Ireland's principal natural fuel resource. It is a good example of a non-renewable resource. After less than 50 years of commercial exploitation, we are already getting near the point when the resource will be exhausted.

Peat is composed of plant remains which have partly decayed. The partial decay is due to waterlogging which prevents bacteria completing the break down of the dead plants. Over time the plant material builds up layer on layer to form a thick mass which is compressed by its own weight. When cut out of the ground and dried, peat burns well. It gives about half the amount of heat that good quality coal gives.

Large areas of peat are called **bogs** or **peatlands**. There are two types of bog: blanket bog and raised bog. **Blanket bog** is a fairly thin carpet of peat up to 2 metres deep spread like a carpet on top of the ground. It occurs in areas of high rainfall where more than 1200mm of rain falls in a year. Such high rainfall is only common in mountain areas and in the lowlands of the West of Ireland, so most blanket bogs are found on hills and mountains and on western lowlands. **Raised bog** is

Fig 16.5

a much thicker deposit of peat, often 10 metres deep. These bogs formed in the large lakes left on the Central Lowlands after the Ice Age. These gradually became filled with peat. As the peat accumulated it formed a low dome-shaped deposit which rose a little higher than the surrounding lowland as shown in figure 16.5.

ACTIVITY 5

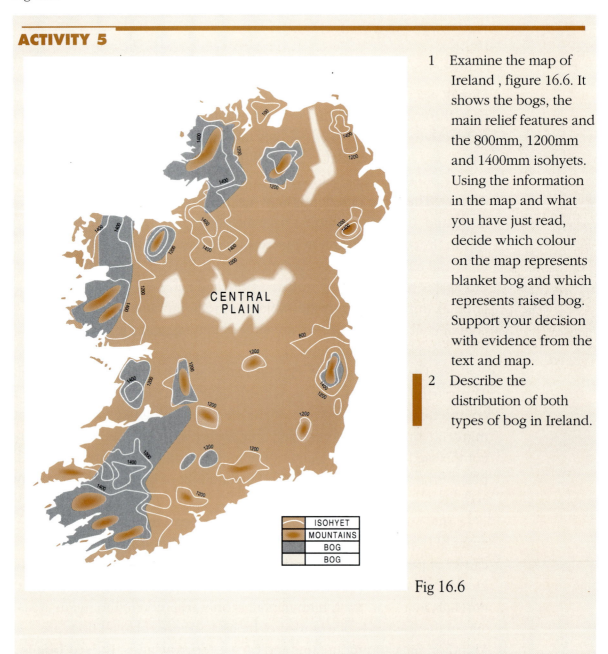

Fig 16.6

1. Examine the map of Ireland, figure 16.6. It shows the bogs, the main relief features and the 800mm, 1200mm and 1400mm isohyets. Using the information in the map and what you have just read, decide which colour on the map represents blanket bog and which represents raised bog. Support your decision with evidence from the text and map.

2. Describe the distribution of both types of bog in Ireland.

PRIMARY INDUSTRIES

Most Irish blanket bogs are located in the West of Ireland especially on the lowlands and mountains of counties Donegal, Mayo, Galway, Clare and Kerry where the rainfall exceeds 1200mm. They are also found in the mountainous parts of Central and Eastern Ireland where relief causes an annual rainfall over 1200mm. The raised bogs are found mostly in the Central Lowlands. It was here that large lakes formed after the melting of the ice at the end of the last Ice Age.

HARVESTING TURF

Hand-won turf Peat has been used as a fuel in Ireland for centuries. It was cut from the bog by hand using an implement called a **sleán**. Peat cut in this way is called **hand-won peat**. The photograph in figure 16.7 shows people harvesting peat by hand. It is a labour-intensive method of harvesting peat. One person cuts the peat into sods with the sleán and throws them up to people on the turf bank. They catch the sods and lay them out to dry. When the sods can be handled, they are stacked in small piles so that the wind will dry them out. When dry the cut peat is transported home and stored. The cutting is usually done in late spring and the harvest is brought home in late summer or autumn. The production of hand-won peat is a low technology activity.

Fig 16.7

In the past it was usually part of a subsistence system of farming. Farmers produced their own fuel and so did not have to buy in fuel. If they cut more than they needed, they sold it locally to bring in a small cash income. This type of peat harvesting did little damage to the environment but it was very hard work.

Machine-won turf During the Second World War Ireland was dependent on Britain for coal supplies because we have very little of this important natural fuel resource. The Irish government decided to develop peat as a fuel to be burned throughout Ireland for domestic and industrial use and in the generating of electricity. This would make us less dependent on imported fuels. The government formed Bord na Móna in 1946 to develop the harvesting of peat on a commercial scale. The Bord set about designing peat harvesting machinery using as much high technology as possible. The development proved very successful and Ireland is now among the world leaders in peat harvesting technology.

Most of the commercial exploitation of peat takes place on the raised bogs of the Central Lowlands. The peat harvesting machines are large and heavy and are best used on raised bog which is fairly flat and very extensive. Also the greater depth of peat makes long-term exploitation possible. The raised bogs produce four main products: sod peat, milled peat, peat briquettes and moss peat. Of these, milled peat is the most important.

Milled peat is produced by a machine which tears up the top centimetre of the bog into fine pieces. This is called **milled peat**. A milled peat harvester is shown in figure 16.8. If there is sun and wind, this will dry in three days. When it is dry it is piled into long heaps and stored under plastic sheets until needed. It is mainly used as a fuel in power stations to produce electricity. The ESB built peat-burning power stations close to the raised bogs to use the milled peat. The ESB is Bord na Móna's biggest customer. Milled peat is also used to make briquettes. Sod peat cut by machine is also produced as a fuel. Moss peat is used as a soil conditioner by gardeners and horticulturists. Bord Na Móna exports large quantities of this product.

ACTIVITY 6

1. Describe two ways of harvesting peat.
2. Examine the photograph, figure 16.8. Then do the following:
   (a) Describe the photograph.
   (b) Contrast this photograph with the photograph in figure 16.7 under the headings: bog type, environmental effects, technology.

Fig 16.8

The mechanisation of peat harvesting has had a number of effects, some good and some bad.

- Before the bogs could be exploited by machine they had to be drained. This allowed the bacteria which cause decay to become active again, decomposing the partly decayed plant remains in the bog. So peat formation stopped in many places affected by the drainage.
- The different kinds of wild life which lived in the bogs and depended on them, lost their habitat and so decreased in numbers.
- The rate at which the peat was used up increased rapidly. Over 90% of the Midland raised bogs have had their environments changed completely. It is estimated that only about 4% of these raised bogs are in good enough condition to be conserved. To **conserve** means to protect from being damaged. We have very nearly completely destroyed an important part of our natural ecological heritage. **Ecological** means "having to do with the habitat and environment of living animals and plants".
- Many people in the midlands of Ireland make their living with Bord na Móna harvesting and selling peat. The development of the bogs provided work in areas where jobs were very scarce.
- The use of peat to generate electricity meant that less coal and oil had to be imported. This kept money in Ireland and helped the economy. The peat fired power stations created jobs in areas of high unemployment.
- The land from which the peat is cut is actually improved by being drained and having the thick layer of peat removed. The land remaining becomes reclaimed land which can be used productively.

Cut-away bog   A **cut-away bog** is what is left after Bord na Móna has cut away as much peat as they can. In some cases there is little peat left, in others there is a couple of metres left.

In the 50 years since the creation of Bord na Móna technological developments have made possible the nearly complete destruction of our raised bogs. We are now studying the question of how best to use the cutaway bogs. These are some of the ideas being examined:.

- Plant forests on them.
- Sell the land to farmers for farming.
- Let them grow wild and become nature reserves.

ACTIVITY 7

1. Decide whether Ireland's peat is a renewable or non-renewable natural resource. Give reasons for your answer.
2. What type of activity is the production of peat ? Give reasons for your answer.
3. Explain four results of the mechanisation of peat harvesting.
4. Explain what a cutaway bog is.
5. Explain how the creation of cutaway bogs can lead to the reclamation of land.

FISHING

Fishing is a primary industry because it involves work which gathers valuable fish provided by nature. The most important kind of fishing in Ireland is its commercial sea fishing. This operates all around our coasts centring on five important fishing ports : Howth, Dunmore East, Castletown Berehaven, Galway and Killybegs. At certain times of the year one sea area may become more important than another because fish "shoal" at different times and places and the fishing fleets must follow them. The area of the Atlantic off Donegal is now the busiest fishing area with big catches of herring, mackerel and white fish. White fish include cod, haddock and hake. Flat fish come mainly from sea areas where the bottom is sandy.

The shellfish industry is also important. Lobsters and crabs are caught along many parts of the coast, particularly where it is rocky. Prawns and scallops are taken in the Irish Sea. Oysters and mussels are now raised mainly as farmed species with important fisheries along the west coast and in Wexford.

The farming of fish has become a major activity in recent years. Large quantities of salmon and sea trout are reared in the bays and estuaries along the western seaboard, notably in Counties Galway, Mayo and Donegal. The farming of fish is a primary industry, just as farming on land is.

Freshwater fishing is also an important primary industry. It is mainly carried out as a recreational activity rather than for commercial profit. Fishing for salmon and trout, called game fishing, brings many tourists to Ireland. **Coarse fishing**, that is fishing for other kinds of fish like pike, roach, tench and so on, is also becoming very popular. Ireland is one of the few places in Europe that can still offer the amateur fisherman plenty of sport.

PRIMARY INDUSTRIES

ACTIVITY 8

Fig 16.9

Unloading mussels, Wexford 1994

Examine the photograph in figure 16.9 then do the following:
(a) Where and how long ago was this photograph taken?
(b) Explain in detail how mussels are unloaded from boats and transported.
(c) There is evidence of at least three types of transport in this photograph. Find and give the location of this evidence.
(d) What does the presence of three transport types in such a small area suggest about the functions of this town?

    Fish are a renewable resource. If they are allowed to breed, they will renew themselves naturally. But if they are overfished or fished before they reach maturity, they cannot renew themselves. The sea areas to the west and south of Ireland have rich fishing grounds with plenty of fish. This is because the sea around Ireland is clean and provides good feeding for them. There are several reasons for this. Firstly, nutrients are washed into the sea by rivers. Secondly, the stormy conditions ensure wave action which dissolves oxygen in the water and mixes nutrients through it. Thirdly, the shallow sea around the coast allows sunlight to penetrate the water and provide energy for plankton to grow. **Plankton** is the name given to the tiny living things, both plant and animal, which live in sea water. Many different kinds of fish feed on plankton which forms the bottom of the 'food chain' in the sea. Where there is plenty of plankton, there is rich and varied fish life

Until the 1960s most of Ireland's fishing fleet was made up of small inshore boats. **Inshore boats** are small vessels which fish close to shore and do not venture out for longer than a day or two at most. During the 1960s larger boats were introduced and better fishing technology was developed. The larger vessels made it possible to fish further out in the Atlantic and to stay out longer. The new equipment made it easier to locate and catch fish. Donegal and the southern fishing ports benefitted most. The most profitable fishery during the late 60's and early 70's was the herring fishery off Waterford. This attracted boats from other parts of Ireland and from other European countries. Dunmore East was the centre of this thriving industry and it grew along with the herring trade. But the herring was overfished and catches declined. To save the herring from extinction a ban on herring fishing was imposed. Gradually the herring stocks renewed themselves naturally and catches are now large again.

Overfishing of various species has been a serious problem along the coast of Europe for many years, including the seas around Ireland. Russia, Poland, Rumania as well as all the Atlantic sea-board countries of Europe wish to win a harvest from the sea. Under such pressure, fish stocks must suffer.

To protect the threatened fish resources the European Union has a Common Fisheries Policy. This lays down the rules for fishing in all the member states. They control the following:
- the fishing seasons for different fish.
- the amount or **quota** of fish each member state can catch.
- the size of the mesh in the nets. The larger the mesh the greater the chance of young fish surviving.
- the sea areas each country's boats are allowed fish in.

The aim of these rules is to conserve the stocks of fish in the seas around Europe. Irish fishermen often feel that they are not benefiting from the Common Fisheries Policy as much as other countries. European boats are allowed fish off the coast of Ireland in waters Irish fishermen think are theirs. Many believe that foreign boats should be banned from fishing around the Irish coast.

PRIMARY INDUSTRIES

ACTIVITY 9

Fig 16.10

Dunmore East 1993

1. Why have the seas around Ireland good supplies of fish?
2. Explain how herring stocks around Ireland were nearly wiped out in the 1970's.
3. List three ways stocks of fish can be conserved.
4. Examine the photograph, figure 16.10, then do the following:
   (a) In what county was the photograph taken?
   (b) How long ago was it taken?
   (c) Name and locate three different land uses in the photograph.
   (d) List three services provided by Dunmore East for fishermen. Support your answer with evidence from the photograph.
5. With the help of an atlas find the names of the fishing ports shown in figure 16.11. Learn them.

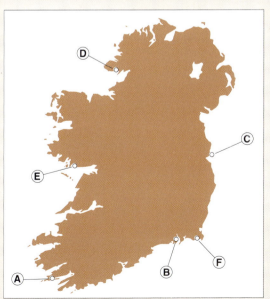

Fig 16.11

231

THE GEOGRAPHER'S WAY 2

REVISION

Rewrite the following text into your copy using words from the box to fill in the blank spaces.

> quota   game fishing   polluted   renewable resource
> cutaway bog   milled peat   blanket bog   reservoir   sleán
> non-renewable   inshore boats   desalinated   coarse fishing
> ecological   waterworks   conserve   effluents
> hand-won peat   extractive   raised bog

A resource which can be re-used is a _____ _____. A _____ resource cannot be reused. A _____ is an artificial lake created behind a dam. Sea water can be _____ that is it has the salt taken out of it. A _____ is where water is processed. When water contains substances which are harmful it is _____. Liquids flowing out of something are called _____ Industries which take material out of the crust are called _____ industries. A thin covering of peat spread across the surface of the land like a carpet is a _____ _____. A thick dome-shaped deposit of peat is called _____ _____. Peat is cut by hand with a _____. Peat cut in this way is called _____ _____. Peat torn into fine particles by a machine is called _____ _____. To _____ is to protect something from being damaged. When the peat in a bog has been cut it is called a _____ _____. _____ means having something to do with the habitat of living animals and plants. Fishing for salmon and trout is _____ _____. Fishing for pike, tench and roach is _____ _____. Fishing boats which fish close to the shore are called _____ _____. A _____ is a limit on the number of something.

17 Energy

IN THIS CHAPTER YOU WILL LEARN

- Primary and secondary sources of energy.
- Consumption and production of electricity.
- The greenhouse effect and global warming.
- Causes of acid rain and how it can be reduced.
- Effects of the oil industry on Saudi Arabia.

Energy is the power to do work. Very primitive people did all their work themselves. As time passed they gradually became aware that they could get natural resources such as animals, flowing water and wind to work for them. Sources of power provided in nature are called the **primary sources of power.** Today the main primary sources of power are wood, peat, coal, oil, natural gas, wind, waves, running water and the sun.

Knowledge and understanding of power increased with time and secondary sources of power were developed. **A secondary source of power** is produced by processing primary sources. For example, electricity is produced from primary power sources such as running water, coal, peat, oil etc. Electricity is a very flexible source of power. It can be used to power many things: trains, lights, machinery and so on. It is also clean to use and easy to distribute. These advantages make electricity the most important source of power in Ireland.

ACTIVITY 1

1. Explain the following terms: energy, a primary source of energy, a secondary source of energy.
2. Divide this list of energy sources into primary and secondary ones:

   | peat | wind | wood | rivers | waves | electricity |
   | oil | nuclear power | natural gas |

3. List the types of energy used in your home.
4. Examine the photograph in figure 17.1, then do the following:
   (a) List and give the location of the sources of energy shown in it.
   (b) Divide the sources of energy you mentioned in (a) into primary and secondary sources.

THE GEOGRAPHER'S WAY 2

Fig 17.1

USE OF ENERGY

The size of a person's income affects the amount of energy they use. If your income is high, you are likely to have a larger car and a house with much energy-using equipment such as washing machines, dish washers, irons, videos and televisions. You will use or **consume** energy at home and when travelling. Large amounts of energy will also have been used to produce the equipment you own. If you have a low income, you will own few machines and so will use little energy.

As incomes have risen in Ireland over the last thirty years the consumption of energy has risen. This increase is shown clearly by the increase in the amount of electricity being generated. The table in figure 17.2 shows the units of electricity generated each year since 1977.

ACTIVITY 2

YEAR	Million Units Generated	YEAR	Million Units Generated
1977	8,161	1986	11,465
1978	8,228	1987	12,491
1979	9,603	1988	12,563
1980	10,213	1989	13,187
1981	10,038	1990	13,895
1982	10,386	1991	14,635
1983	10,194	1992	15,471
1984	10,559	1993	15,779
1985	10,973	1994	16,420

Fig 17.2

Examine the table in figure 17.2 then do the following:

1. How many units of electricity were generated in each of the following years: 1980, 1986, 1990, 1994?
2. What was the increase in the number of units generated between 1977 and 1994?
3. Give the years when the number of generated units declined.

4. What was the percentage change in units generated between 1977 and 1994?
5. What type of graph would be most suitable to show the information in figure 17.2. Give reasons for your choice. Then graph the information.

THE GENERATION OF ELECTRICITY

To generate electricity copper wire must be made to spin around a magnet. As it does electricity is generated. This happens inside a machine called a **generator**. The power to spin the generator can come from a number of sources. The diagram shows how falling water is used to spin a generator. The dam holds back a reservoir of water and raises the water-level which gives the water more power when it falls. Water is made flow down through pipes called **penstocks** to the turbines. These spin as the water rushes through them. The spinning is transferred by a shaft to the generator where electricity is generated.

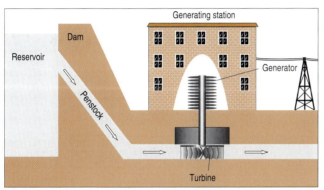

Fig 17.3

Electricity produced in this way is hydro-electricity. The map in figure 17.4 shows the locations and names of the HEP stations in Ireland.

ACTIVITY 3

Examine the map in figure 17.4 then do the following using an atlas. Match the letters in column X with the number of their pairs in column Y.

	X			Y			
A	Ardnacrusha	1	Erne	A	
B	Leixlip	2	Lee	B	
C	Inniscara	3	Liffey	C	
D	Kathleen's Falls	4	Liffey	D	
E	Golden Falls	5	Shannon	E	
F	Carrigadrohid	6	Liffey	F	
G	Poulaphouca	7	Lee	G	

Fig 17.4

Electricity is also produced in thermal power stations. **Thermal power stations** use heat to generate electricity. The word 'thermal' comes from the Greek word for heat. In these stations fuel such as peat, coal, oil or natural gas is burned to make steam. The steam drives the turbines which spin the generator to make electricity. Nuclear power stations work in a similar way. A nuclear reaction releases large amounts of heat which is used to make steam to turn turbines.

In recent years the sources of power used to generate our electricity have changed in importance. The composite graph in figure 17.5 shows these changes. The percentage of electricity generated from each of the sources is shown on the vertical axis. In 1974 64% of our electricity was generated from oil, 25% from peat, 10% from hydro and 1% from coal.

ACTIVITY 4

Examine the graph in figure 17.5 then do the following by ticking the correct answers to questions 1 to 10.

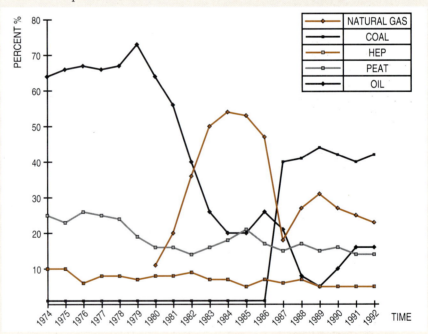

Fig 17.5

1. Coal was the least important source of electricity between:
   (a) 1990 and 1992 ❑   (b) 1986 and 1989 ❑
   (c) 1974 and 1986 ❑   (d) 1984 and 1987 ❑
2. The largest percentage of electricity generated from oil was:
   (a) 54% ❑   (b) 73% ❑
   (c) 44% ❑   (d) 26% ❑

3. The lowest percentage of electricity generated from oil was:
   (a) 1% ☐ (b) 20% ☐
   (c) 14% ☐ (d) 5% ☐
4. The most important source of electricity between 1983 and 1986 was:
   (a) natural gas ☐ (b) peat ☐
   (c) oil ☐ (d) HEP ☐
5. The most important source of electricity between 1987 and 1992 was
   (a) natural gas ☐ (b) oil ☐
   (c) peat ☐ (d) coal ☐
6. Oil and HEP produced the same percentage of electricity in
   (a) 1985 ☐ (b) 1987 ☐
   (c) 1989 ☐ (d) 1982 ☐
7. Which source of power never produced more than 10% of electricity?
   (a) oil ☐ (b) peat ☐
   (c) coal ☐ (d) HEP ☐
8. Which source of power increased from 1% of generated electricity to 40% in the space of one year?
   (a) oil ☐ (b) coal ☐
   (c) natural gas ☐ (d) peat ☐
9. Electricity was first produced from natural gas in:
   (a) 1980 ☐ (b) 1986 ☐
   (c) 1984 ☐ (d) 1979 ☐
10. The sources of electricity whose contribution to the generation of electricity has changed least are:
    (a) Natural gas and peat ☐ (b) HEP and peat ☐
    (c) oil and coal ☐ (d) coal and natural gas ☐

The graph in figure 17.5 shows that the sources of electricity changed in importance during the period. This happened for several reasons. During the 1970's oil was the most important source of electricity. It contributed over 60% of electricity in every year of the decade. In 1973/4 there was a serious oil crisis when the world oil supply became very uncertain. Oil producing countries such as Saudi Arabia and Iraq formed a group called the Organisation of Petroleum Exporting Countries (OPEC) to agree about the amount of oil they would produce and to fix its price. They thought the price of oil was too low and that if they didn't do something their oil would soon be exhausted and they would have received far too little for it. To prevent this happening OPEC countries raised the price of oil four times in a very short period. This sudden increase in oil prices had a serious effect on countries like

Ireland which relied on oil for so much of their energy. Very soon the price of electricity and oil products, such as petrol, rose. As a result many things increased in price because electricity and transport are used in the production and distribution of most goods. As prices increased people bought less, so factories closed and people lost their jobs. A period of economic decline set in. This is known as an **economic depression.**

The government and the ESB decided to change to a cheaper source of electricity than oil. This change could not be made overnight as it takes time and money to alter power stations from using one source of energy to another. It also takes time to plan and build new power stations. Fortunately for Ireland natural gas had been discovered off Kinsale, Co. Cork during the 1970's. The ESB decided to use this new resource to replace some of the oil being used because it was cheaper and oil-burning stations could be converted quickly to burn gas without too much expense. But the ESB knew that the gasfield would only last about 20 years so this was only a short-term solution. They had to plan to have a replacement for it. There are large supplies of coal available in the world and coal is quite cheap, so the ESB decided to build a very large coal-burning station at Moneypoint in Co. Clare. This station began generating electricity in 1986 and now produces over 40% of our electricity. Coal is likely to be our most important source of electricity for some time to come.

THE GREENHOUSE EFFECT

Oil, peat, coal and natural gas are fossil fuels. **Fossil fuels** form over millions of years from plants and animals which were trapped in sedimentary rocks as these were laid down. Fossil fuels store the sun's energy from the distant past because they were made from what were once living things. When burned they release this energy. They also release carbon dioxide and sulphur dioxide as well as other chemicals and pollutants such as smoke.

Carbon dioxide is released when anything burns. It is a **greenhouse gas**. A greenhouse gas in the atmosphere traps the long-wave radiation which is reflected by the Earth's surface. This causes the atmosphere to heat up. It is called a greenhouse gas, because it acts like glass in a greenhouse. Since the industrial revolution of the 18th century increasing amounts of fossil fuels, especially coal, have been burned.

This has made the amount of carbon dioxide in the air increase from 275 parts per million to 330 parts per million today. The result of this is that the atmosphere is getting warmer. This rise in temperature occurs in the atmosphere all round the Earth and so is called **global warming**. The increased amount of carbon dioxide is the main cause of global warming but there are other greenhouse gases such as methane and CFC's. Methane is produced by bacteria when decay occurs. Living creatures, rubbish dumps and swamps all produce methane naturally, so this gas is being added to the atmosphere all the time. CFC is a man-made gas used in aerosol cans and fridges. Its effect is so serious that its manufacture is being phased out.

Global warming can have some or all of the following effects:
1. A rise in sea-water temperature. This can cause sea-level to rise because the water in the sea expands with heating. Also the polar ice caps may melt releasing more water into the oceans.
2. A change in climate. Climate changes as temperatures rise. Some areas will get more rainfall and others will get less as the climatic zones shift.
3. A change in farming. Farming is affected by changing climate. Areas may become too hot or dry for the usual crops to grow.
4. A change in the natural environment as plants and animals adjust to the warmer conditions.

Solutions to global warming include the following:
1. The use of cleaner fuels. When burned, natural gas produces half the carbon dioxide made by other fossil fuels to generate the same amount of energy
2. Planting more trees. Trees take in carbon dioxide and give out oxygen.
3. Reducing the use of greenhouse gases like CFCs and developing replacements for them.
4. Improving our use of energy by wasting less. Better insulation to conserve heat and more efficient machines which use less energy will reduce energy needs and the burning of fuels. We can become more economical in our use of energy in the home. More use of public transport will also help.
5. Developing other forms of energy source which don't produce carbon dioxide. For example, wind, wave and solar power.

ACTIVITY 5

1. Describe and explain how the ESB changed the primary resources of energy it used for generating electricity between 1974 and 1992.
2. Explain what a fossil fuel is and give four examples.
3. Explain the greenhouse effect and how it causes global warming.
4. List and explain four effects of global warming.
5. List three things to do in your home to reduce global warming.
6. Was the ESB in the 1990s more or less likely to add to global warming than it was in the early 1980s? Explain your answer using evidence from the graph in figure 17.5.

ACID RAIN

When water vapour condenses in the atmosphere it usually has a pH value of 7. This means it is neutral. The gases carbon dioxide and sulphur dioxide released by burning fossil fuels mix with rainwater and make it acidic. This acid rainwater may have a pH value anywhere between 4 and 5.6. It will be as low as 4 in areas where a lot of fossil fuels, especially coal and oil, are being burned.

The effect of acid rain depends on the type of land it falls on. If the land is already acidic with granite rock, podzol soils and coniferous trees, the effect will be great. These are called 'acid sensitive areas'. An already acidic environment becomes much more acidic and water seeping into streams and lakes will be very acid. In parts of Norway and Sweden the water is so acid it cannot be given to babies. It can only be used for drinking when its acidity has been reduced by adding lime to it. **Lime** is a base and reduces acidity. Many Scandinavian rivers and lakes contain no fish as their waters have become too acidic. Tree and plant life is seriously affected by acid rain. The polluted atmosphere over Western Europe has seriously damaged German, French and Austrian forests. If acid rain falls on land rich in bases such as limestone, its effect is much less. The lime in the rock neutralises the acid.

The acid rain caused by burning fossil fuels can be reduced by the following:

1. Using natural gas, a low sulphur fuel, as much as possible.
2. Using coal with a low sulphur content.
3. When using high sulphur fuels, putting filters in chimneys to take out the sulphur dioxide gases.

ENERGY

ACTIVITY 6

Examine the map in figure 17.6 which shows the location of Moneypoint power station and the acid sensitive areas of Ireland. Do the following:

1. Using an atlas describe the location of Moneypoint.
2. Name three areas where Moneypoint is likely to cause increased acidification. Explain why this is so.
3. Suggest a location for a coal-fired power station which would cause the minimum acidification of Irish land. Give reasons for your choice.
4. Explain how acid rain can be reduced.

Fig 17.6

THE SEARCH FOR FUEL RESOURCES

You have already studied how Ireland's natural fuel resource of peat was developed in the 1940's and 1950's. In the 1960's a new phase of fuel resource exploitation began. Oil and natural gas were discovered beneath the North Sea. This discovery encouraged the exploration of the sea-bed around Ireland for oil and natural gas. The oil crisis in the early 1970's made it even more attractive to have our own sources of energy, particularly oil. This also stimulated the search for oil. One hundred and eighteen exploration wells have been drilled to search for oil and natural gas. Details of these wells are given in figures 17.7 and 17.8.

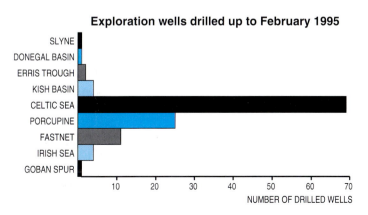

Fig 17.7

THE GEOGRAPHER'S WAY 2

ACTIVITY 7

Examine figures 17.7 and 17.8 then do the following:
1. In which sea area was the largest number of wells drilled?
2. Name the areas where only one well was drilled.
3. What was the total of wells drilled in the Fastnet and Porcupine sea areas?

Most drilling has concentrated in the Celtic Sea as this is the only area where an exploitable deposit has been discovered so far. In 1971 the Marathon Oil Company discovered natural gas about 30 miles off the Old Head of Kinsale. By 1973 the gas field was known to be large enough to be profitable. It began to produce natural gas in 1978. The gas was taken ashore by pipeline. A network of pipes brings Kinsale gas to our major towns and cities. The gas is used to generate electricity, industrial heating, to make fertilizers and for use in people's homes. A major advantage is that gas is the cleanest of the fossil fuels and does the least damage to the environment.

Fig 17.8

It is estimated that Kinsale gas will be exhausted by the end of the century. To prepare for this a pipeline has been laid across the Irish Sea to Britain. This will allow us to import gas when our own supply runs out. In the meantime exploration continues especially in the Celtic Sea and it is hoped that another deposit will be discovered before we have to start importing gas supplies.

ACTIVITY 8

Examine the graph in figure 17.9 which shows world energy use.
1. What type of graph is it?
2. Name sources of power which together contributed 12% to energy use.
3. What was the most used source of energy?
4. Rank the energy sources on the basis of how much they contributed to energy use. The highest percentage is ranked No.1.

ENERGY

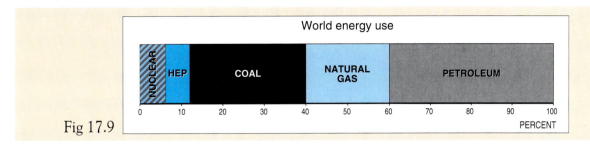

Fig 17.9

OIL

Oil, like coal and natural gas, is a non-renewable energy source. Once it is burned it is gone for good. Although oil became expensive during the 1970s and was replaced to some extent by other sources of energy, it is still the most used fuel resource in the world. Forty percent of the energy comes from oil. A lot of this is produced in the Middle-East which exports most of its production. The Middle-East is in Asia. It is located around the eastern shore of the Mediterranean Sea, the Red Sea and the Persian Gulf. The map in figure 17.10 shows the Middle East.

ACTIVITY 9

Fig 17.10

Examine the map in figure 17.10 then do the following:

1. Tick the corrrect box in each case.   **T F**
   (a) Oman has the largest area of oil fields. ❏ ❏
   (b) Iran borders Saudi Arabia.
   (c) The Persian Gulf lies to the west of Iran. ❏ ❏
   (d) The Red Sea has many oil fields on its shores. ❏ ❏
   (e) Saudi Arabia has the largest oil resources in the Middle-East. ❏ ❏
   (f) The oil fields in the Middle East occur both on land and sea. ❏ ❏

2. List the oil-producing countries of the Middle East.

3. Draw a sketch map of the Middle East and on it show: Arabian Sea, Persian Gulf, Red Sea, Mediterranean, Iran, Iraq, Saudi Arabia, United Arab Emirates, Kuwait, Riyadh, Baghdad, Tehran, three oil fields.

4. Describe the distribution of oil wells in the Middle East.

Outside North America and the CIS, the Middle East is the largest producer of oil. Within the Middle East the largest producer by far is Saudi Arabia. It is the third largest producer of oil in the world and is believed to have more oil reserves than any other country. An **oil reserve** is oil in the ground which has not been extracted. The Saudi Arabian oil is located along its Persian Gulf coast, on land and offshore under the sea. The oil is exported through the Persian Gulf by ship and overland by pipelines.

Before the oil industry became important Saudi Arabia was a country of desert herdsmen called Bedouin. These nomadic pastoralists herded sheep and goats and roamed constantly in search of pasture. The discovery of oil brought major changes. Their traditional wandering way of life declined. Instead towns and cities grew around the oil wells and refineries and a settled lifestyle became common. There were jobs in the oil industry and people immigrated to the oil fields in search of work. Many foreigners travelled to Saudi Arabia to look for work, creating tensions in a society not used to foreigners. Because the traditional agriculture declined, more and more food was imported. Today Saudi Arabia imports large quantities of Australian sheep, a product it was once self-sufficient in. The oil industry introduced western ways of life to Saudi Arabia. These differed from the strict Muslim customs of the Bedouin. Some people adopted western ways, leading to problems with those who didn't.

The most important result of oil development in Saudi Arabia is the amount of money it made for the country. The oil money was used to improve the life of the people by building hospitals, schools, universities, factories, power stations, roads and houses. Money was spent on agriculture to develop arable farming, especially of wheat and vegetables. Water wells were sunk and water provided for irrigation. The nomadic pastoralists and their traditional way of life were increasingly ignored.

Manufacturing industries were also developed. Cement factories were started early on to provide the raw material for the new building programmes. Fertilizer, chemical and plastics industries were set up as these use oil as a raw material. Desalination plants were built as there was plenty of cheap fuel to power them. Saudi Arabia became so rich after the oil crisis that uses for its money had to be found overseas. Money was invested in banks, property, industrial companies and land all over the world. These foreign investments produce a huge income for some Saudi Arabians.

ENERGY

The rapid development has not been problem free. The income from the oil industry is not spread equally among the population so poverty exists alongside great riches. Shanty towns have sprung up around the cities. These are the homes of poor migrants who have moved to urban centres in the hope of improving their lives. Conflicts about the ownership of the oil fields in the Middle-East have occurred. The most recent dispute started when Iraq claimed that Kuwait was an Iraqi province and invaded it. This led to the Gulf War. Many western powers became involved to protect oil supplies.

ACTIVITY 10

1   What are the advantages of the oil industry to Saudi Arabia?
2   Examine the photograph in figure 17.11.
    What evidence is there in the photograph that oil wealth has brought change to Saudi Arabia.

Fig 17.11

THE GEOGRAPHER'S WAY 2

REVISION

Rewrite the following text using words from the box to fill in the blank spaces

> acid rain   reserve   fossil fuels   energy   consume
> global warming   oil crisis   primary sources of energy
> greenhouse gas   generator   secondary source of energy
> OPEC   penstocks   economic depression

The power to do work is _____. Sources of energy provided by nature are called the _____ _____ _____ _____. When these sources are processed into electricity a _____ _____ _____ _____ is produced. To use something up is to _____ it. A machine for generating electricity is a _____. The pipes which take the water to the turbines in a hydro-power station are _____. In the early 1970s there was an _____ _____ when the price of oil rose four times. The Organization of Petroleum Exporting Countries or _____ as it is known was set up to protect the interests of the oil producers. When an economy is in decline with rising unemployment there is an _____ _____. Fuels made from dead plants and animals are _____ _____. A _____ _____ is one which traps the Earth's long wave radiation. The general rise in temperatures around the world is called _____ _____. If rain has acid dissolved in it is _____ _____. The _____ of a resource is the amount which is left waiting to be exploited by us.

18 Local Farm Study

IN THIS CHAPTER YOU WILL LEARN

- The importance of farming in Ireland.
- A typical Irish farm.
- Land use on an Irish farm.
- Farming as a system with imputs, processes and outputs.
- The likely future of farming in Ireland.
- How to approach a farm study.

Agriculture is Ireland's most important primary industry. It is also our most important economic activity. It employs directly 14% of working people. Many other jobs depend on agriculture. It produces raw materials for food manufacture in secondary industries: milk for creameries; livestock for meat factories; cereals for mills, breweries and distilleries; sugar beet for sugar manufacture. Agriculture produces 20% of the value of Irish exports. Many tertiary economic activities involve supplying the needs of agriculture: veterinary care, transport services, farm machinery sales and repair, the supply of fuel, fertilisers and feedstuffs.

Agriculture is almost always carried out on farms. Farms mainly produce food and the raw materials for food-processing industries. But they can also produce crops known as industrial raw materials. For instance flax and cotton are crops grown to provide fibres for textile industries. Wood is increasingly grown as a crop on Irish farms to provide timber and Christmas trees. Whatever they produce, farms can be thought of as systems with inputs, processes and outputs. A **system** is an organised way of doing something.

As Ireland's climate is very suitable for grass growing, most Irish farmers concentrate on pastoral farming. Their main concern is raising livestock of some kind: beef cattle, dairy cattle or sheep. But they often engage in some arable farming as well, growing crops for sale off the farm or to feed their stock. Therefore they are mixed farmers, even though their main interest is in pastoral farming. In eastern, south-eastern and southern counties where the climate is sunnier, there are farmers who concentrate on growing grain crops. These are arable farmers. Some farmers specialise in vegetable or fruit crops, producing maincrop potatoes, peas, carrots, onions, apples or strawberries. These are specialist farmers and market gardeners. In Ireland the mixed farm is typical, so we will examine a farm of this kind.

THE MURRAY FARM

The Murray farm is located in County Kilkenny in the South-east region. The farm is in one piece at a height of about 100 metres. The countryside in the area is quite hilly. Annual precipitation is 1000mm, falling throughout the year. Average January temperature is 5.5°C; average July temperature is 15.5°C. Over the year the average number of sunshine hours is 3.7 which is on the high side because the summers are usually fairly sunny The soils on the farm include browns earths, gleys and peaty soils.

ACTIVITY 1

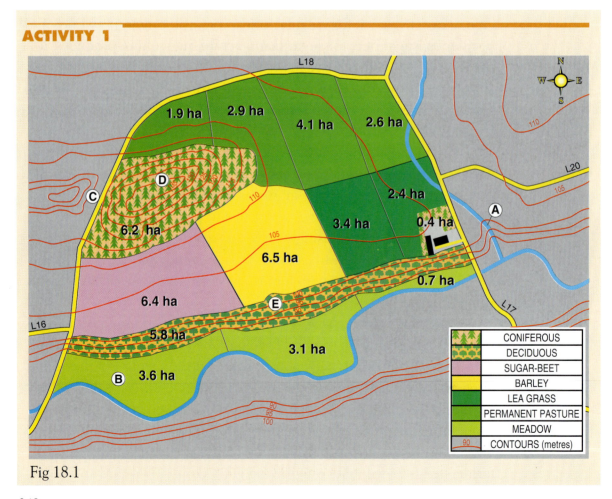

Fig 18.1

Figure 18.1 shows a map of the Murray farm. Examine it carefully.
1. Tick the correct answers.
   (a) The number of fields on the farm is
       (i) 13 ☐ (ii) 12 ☐ (iii) 14 ☐ (iv) 11 ☐
   (b) The highest point on the map is
       (i) 132m ☐ (ii) 112m ☐ (iii) 100m ☐ (iv) 110m ☐
   (c) The road bordering the north side of the farm is the:
       (i) L16 ☐ (ii) L17 ☐ (iii) L18 ☐ (iv) L20 ☐
   (d) The largest field is
       (i) 6.9 Ha ☐ (ii) 7.1 Ha ☐ (iii) 6.5 Ha ☐ (iv) 4.1 Ha ☐
   (e) The largest area of flat land on the farm is on the following side:
       (i) north ☐ (ii) west ☐ (iii) south ☐ (iv) east ☐
2. Match the letters on the map and shown in column X with the number of their pairs in column Y.

X	Y	
A	1 col
B	2 V-shaped valley
C	3 bluff-line
D	4 flood plain
E	5 ridge

A	
B	
C	
D	
E	

3. (a) Calculate the area under forestry.
   (b) Calculate the area under pasture.
   (c) Calculate the area under arable crops.
   (d) What percentage of the farm is used for each of the following: forestry, pasture, arable crops?
   (e) Draw a divided rectangle to show land use on the farm.

LAND USE ON THE MURRAY'S FARM

Grassland Grass is the most important crop on the farm. It is grown on 49.4% of the land. Land under grass consists of permanent pasture, meadows and lea. **Permanent pasture** is always grassland. The fields with permanent pasture have heavy gley soils unsuitable for tilling. Some permanent pasture is cut to provide silage as winter fodder. Silage is made by cutting grass and storing it in a way that preserves it. The **meadows** are also permanent grassland but are on the flood plain and liable to flooding, especially in winter months. They are used to provide good grazing in the late spring and summer. The flood water deposits alluvium which adds nutrients to the soil but the land must be dried out before animals graze it. **Lea grassland** is land used to grow a crop of grass in rotation with other crops.

Crop rotation is the growing of different crops on the same piece of land in different years. Crop rotation usually involves growing cereals, root crops such as sugar beet, potatoes or turnips, and grass in successive years. Farmers use two, three or four-year rotations depending on the climate and the soils on their farm. There are several reasons for crop rotation. One is to maintain soil fertility. Different crops take varying amounts and kinds of nutrients out of the soil. If one crop is always grown on the same land, the nutrients it needs will be used up so the crop cannot thrive. If a crop is grown in rotation with others, the land has a chance to recover and replace naturally the nutrients it has lost. Another reason for rotating crops is to prevent disease. Most crops are attacked by pests and diseases. If a crop is grown, year after year, in the same ground there can be a build-up of pests which may become severe enough to destroy the harvest. Rotation discourages the pests and diseases particular to a crop and helps keep the soil clean. Crop rotation is practised widely because it keeps soil fertile and disease free.

On the Murray farm barley, sugar beet and grass are grown in rotation. This reduces the amount of artificial fertilizers and insecticides they have to buy. The barley grown is fodder barley which is fed to the cattle on the farm in winter to supplement their diet. Sugar beet is grown as a cash crop. It is sold to the Irish Sugar Company which has a processing plant in Carlow town. Having a processing plant nearby to buy his crop is an advantage for a farmer. He knows he has a sale for his harvest and his transport costs will be low. Often the factory and the farmer work together under contract or agreement. In Ireland many crops are grown under contract to processors: vegetables, malting barley, sugar beet and potatoes are just a few.

The arable crops need fertile well-drained soils. Between the wooded hill and the bluff line there are well-drained brown earth soils. The land slopes gently towards the south which gives these fields a sunny aspect. This situation ensures that the soil will warm up quickly in spring so that growth can begin early. Barley and sugar beet both need sunny conditions to ripen so these fields are ideal for these crops.

LOCAL FARM STUDY

About 24% of the farm is used for forestry. There are two areas of woodland. The first is 6.2 hectares of coniferous trees on the hill in the north-west corner of the farm. This hill is an outcrop of granite. It was once covered with peat. The soil is poor and the slopes are too steep for farming. The government encourages farmers to use wasteland like this for planting trees. It pays about £1000 per hectare if conifer trees are planted. The Murrays decided to take up the government's offer. They think of this plantation of forest as their pension scheme. In thirty years the trees will be mature enough to cut and this should bring in a large sum of money at the time when they have to retire. The second area of woodland is mainly deciduous trees. This is located on the bluffline above the flood plain. The slopes here are too steep for agriculture. Over many years this land has been allowed to grow wild and deciduous trees have become established. This is the only part of the farm where anything like 'natural vegetation' is found.

The final land use on the farm is residential. The farmhouse and buildings are located on the L17 road in the south-eastern corner of the farm. The house has a sunny aspect and is sited well above the flood plain. Being on the road makes it very accessible, and it is easy to get to other parts of the farm by the L17 and the L18 roads. The trees around the house and farmyard have been planted to make a shelterbelt against the prevailing wind. It also gives the Murrays privacy.

ACTIVITY 2

1. Describe three kinds of grassland.
2. Explain crop rotation. Give reasons why rotation is used.
3. Using a sketch map, describe how the land is used on the Murray's farm.

The Murrays are dairy farmers. They have 36 dairy cows which are kept for the milk they produce. Each cow has a calf in spring. After calving the cow produces milk and goes on milking right through late spring and summer. There is plenty of grass at this time of year. This suits very well as cows produce a lot of milk if they have good grass. The cows go dry in the late autumn and winter. Mr Murray does all he can to improve the yield of his milking herd. The **milk yield** is the volume of milk produced over a period, usually a year. Nowadays the yield per cow and the quality of the milk are more important than the total quantity produced. If there is land to spare, the calves born in spring are reared until autumn when most are sold off. A few heifer calves may be kept to replace older cows whose milk yield is decreasing.

The Murrays are contracted to send all their milk to the creamery. There it is processed into many products: butter, cheese, cream, pasteurised milk, yoghurt. The farmer must take great care to ensure that milk is clean and chilled to keep it fresh. Every morning the milk is brought to the processing plant by the creamery's tanker lorry.

ACTIVITY 3

Examine the terms below carefully and divide them into inputs, processes and outputs:

medicine	milk	calves	ploughing	seed	barley
electricity	labour	soil	harvesting	vet	milking cows
weeding	fertilizer	water	cutting	silage	manure
climate	smells	repairing	fences	sugar	beet
	tractor	insecticide	machinery		

THE FARMING SYSTEM: INPUTS

The inputs on a farm can be divided into natural ones and those supplied by people. Climate, soil and relief are natural inputs. Climate determines the temperature, sunshine and rainfall. Soils provide the nutrients. Relief determines how high the land is, its aspect and how it drains and how sheltered it is.

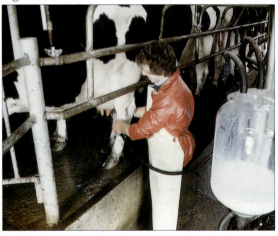

Fig 18.2

The inputs supplied by people include their labour, skill, knowledge and capital. On the Murray farm the mother and father work the farm and they are helped by their eldest son. They have invested capital in building a modern milking-parlour, a silage pit, cow sheds and new fencing. Recent expenditure on machinery has included a new tractor, a seed and fertilizer spreader, and modern ploughing equipment. **Capital** is the money used in the running of a business; farming is a business just like any other. A **milking parlour** is a special building for milking cows which ensures a high standard of cleanliness. The photograph in figure 18.2 shows a milking parlour.

LOCAL FARM STUDY

Another important input is the market. A farmer must be able to sell what he produces. In the case of the Murrays the Carlow sugar factory buys his sugar beet and the local creamery takes his milk.

ACTIVITY 4

1. Examine the photograph in figure 18.2 then do the following:
   (a) What is the person doing in the photograph?
   (b) Why is the walkway on which the person is standing below the level of the animal?
   (c) What advantages have the milking machine and the milking parlour over the older method of milking by hand?

THE FARMING SYSTEM: PROCESSES

The processes carried out on the farm change with the seasons but there are always urgent things to be attended to; a call to the 'vet' for a sick animal or to make an appointment for tests. Sometimes animals stray. A neighbour may send for help in a crisis. The day is rarely long enough on most farms.

Spring is a busy time. The ground for the arable crops has to be ploughed, prepared for planting and sown. Cows are calving and need a lot of attention and care. They are also beginning to produce milk so the time given to milking increases. As the ground dries out and grass growth improves cows are let out to graze.

In early summer the first cut of silage is taken and stored in the silage pit. Crops must be sprayed to protect them from diseases and insects. There is weeding and thinning of crops like beet. Milking and care of the dairy herd is now the major activity. Silage-cutting is done at intervals, depending on the weather and the rate of grass-growth. There is always plenty of work to do: looking after the young calves, mending fences, repairing machinery and so on.

In early autumn the barley crop is harvested. A contractor is hired to do this but the Murrays help in harvesting and make sure it is stored properly in the grain silo. The sugar beet has to be 'raised' and piled by the main road for collection by lorry. The calves are taken to market in Kilkenny. The milk yield gets less and less. The arable fields are ploughed, if the weather is dry enough, so that winter frost can break up the soil and cleanse it. Repair work to fences, drains, buildings and machinery continues.

By November the cattle are indoors. This makes more work because the animals have to be brought to the silage pit to eat, and they must be given 'rations' of barley and water when kept in. Cleaning manure out of the cowsheds and keeping the yard clean is a daily chore. The manure is kept for spreading on the land. By now the days are short so the outside work must be done quickly. This is the time of year for indoor repairs and maintenance.

ACTIVITY 5

1. Describe the processes carried out on an Irish mixed farm in spring and summer.
2. Examine the photograph in figure 18.3, then do the following:

Fig 18.3

(a) Describe what is happening in the photograph.
(b) List the inputs shown in it.
(c) Which season is shown in the photograph? Use evidence from the photograph to support your answer.

THE FARMING SYSTEM: OUTPUTS

The outputs of the Murray's farm include milk, calves, barley, sugar beet, silage and waste products. Some years the barley is consumed completely on the farm as fodder for the cows in winter. When this happens, it is not an output but is used within the system. If the harvest is good, there is a surplus, and the Murray's can sell this for cash. Then barley becomes one of the outputs of the farm. In the future timber will also be a product of the system when the conifers mature.

The waste products include slurry which is mainly water used to hose down the yard, silage effluent and smells. **Silage effluent** is the liquid which seeps out of a silage pit. Both slurry and silage effluent can be serious pollutants if they get into ground water or rivers. They are rich in chemical nutrients and may be poisonous. They can cause waterplants to grow rapidly. This growth uses up the oxygen dissolved in water and fish drown as a result. The rapid growth also chokes channels and streams slowing up the drainage of the land.

THE FUTURE FOR THE MURRAY FARM

Because too much milk was being produced in the European Union (EU), milk quotas were introduced. A **quota** regulates the quantity of a product which can be made or sold in a country. Each country can now produce only a certain amount of milk. The government shares out to farmers the EU quotas given to Ireland, so each farmer knows how much milk he or she is allowed sell. This is called the 'milk quota'. If the farmer produces more a penalty must be paid. This control of milk production has caused dairy farmers' incomes to fall as they may no longer sell as much as they wish. Because there is over-production, milk quotas are unlikely to be increased in the near future.

The milk quota has hit farmers like the Murrays hard because they are not allowed expand the dairying side of their business even though they are good at it. They are looking around for alternatives to milk. They are considering deer farming which is increasing in Ireland as there is no quota on venison (deer meat) production. They are also thinking of making the farm into a visitor centre where students can come and observe everyday life on a mixed farm. Mrs Murray is keen to diversify into running a 'bed and breakfast' guest house to cater for tourists. To **diversify** means to change to some new activity. In the future it is likely that Irish farmers will have to be prepared to change to new farming activities if they are to be prosperous.

ACTIVITY 6

1. (a) List some of the outputs on the Murray's farm.
   (b) Explain why waste disposal is a problem on many farms.
2. Consider some of the advantages and disadvantages of opening a farm to visitors. Explain your answer fully.
3. What do you think of the idea of opening a 'B & B' on the Murray's farm? In your answer refer to: accessibility; location; local interest; tourism; the effect on the running of the farm.

REVISION

Rewrite the following text into your copy and use the words in the box below to fill in the blank spaces:

silage effluent	diversify	lea grass	milk yield
permanent pasture	crop rotation	milking parlour
preserving	regulate	system	capital

Fields left constantly under grass are called _____ _____. Grass used in crop rotation is _____ _____. The growing of different crops in succession on the same piece of land is called _____ _____. The money used in the running of a business is called _____. The _____ _____ is the amount of milk produced in a year. The building where the milking is done is called a _____ _____. The juices which flow out of silage are called _____ _____. Silage-making is a method of _____ grass. A quota is used to _____ production of goods. In the future farmers must be ready to _____ their activities. An organised way of doing something is called a _____.

FARM STUDY

Visit a farm and interview the farmer. Prepare well so that you don't waste people's time. These suggestions will help you.

Aims – to find out about the type of farming carried on.
– to draw a diagram of the systems operating on the farm.
– to consider the future for the farm.

To achieve these aims you must prepare a worksheet including a questionnaire. A **questionnaire** is a list of questions designed to find out the information you want. The questions must be short, clear and to the point. An example of a worksheet with questionnaire follows.

FARM STUDY WORKSHEET

Name of Student _____ Date _____ Time _____
Location of farm: _____
Description of the relief of the farm: _____

QUESTIONNAIRE

How many people work on the farm _____?
What hours do they work _____?
What holidays do they get _____?
What are the soil types on the farm _____?
What fertilizers are used _____?
How many fields are there _____?

How many fields and roughly what area is used for each of the following crops?

Crop		Area	Number
permanent pasture			
meadow			
lea			
cereal crop:	barley		
	wheat		
	oats		
root crop:	sugar beet		
	fodder beet		
	turnips		
vegetable crop:	potatoes		
	other		

How many of each of the following animals are kept on the farm?

Animals	Number
dairy cows	
beef cattle	
calves	
young cattle	
sheep	
pigs	
poultry	
horses	
other	

What machines are owned and used on the farm? _____

What work is carried on in each season?

    spring _____

    summer _____

    autumn _____

    winter _____

What work is contracted out? _____

Where is the farm output sold?

    1 _____

    2 _____

    3 _____

What effect have government and EU measures had on the running of the farm? _____

What are the plans for the future development of the farm? _____

Draw a sketch map of the farm. On it show the following:
- the relief
- the fields and their crops. Give details of rotation.
- the roads and tracks
- the buildings

REPORT ON FARM STUDY

Using the following headings as a guide, write a report based on what you found out.

    Title

    Aims

    Fieldwork Activity

    Location map : land use map

    Flow charts showing inputs/processes/outputs of systems

    Work on the farm through the year

    Markets

    Future Developments

    Conclusions

19 The Location of Manufacturing Industry

IN THIS CHAPTER YOU WILL LEARN

- How entrepreneurs chose the location for an industry.
- The factors which influence the location of an industry.
- Case studies of heavy and light industry.
- Footloose industry and industrial inertia.
- The changing location of the British iron and steel industry.

Secondary industry changes raw materials of some kind into goods which can be used or consumed. It is also called manufacturing and is usually carried on in a factory. **Entrepreneurs** are people who risk setting up new industries. They invest their money and decide what to produce, how and where to produce it and how to sell it. An entrepreneur aims to make a profit by selling products for more than it costs to make them. Costs must be kept low to achieve this. An important element in keeping costs down is to have the factory located in its **least cost location**. Choosing a location for a factory is therefore one of the most important decisions an entrepreneur has to make. A number of factors must be taken into account when deciding this. These include some or all of the following:

* raw materials
* labour
* transport facilities
* markets
* services
* capital
* government or EU policy
* personal preference

Raw materials   Some manufacturing industries use heavy or bulky raw materials which are costly to transport. Often these materials lose weight and bulk in manufacture so it is cheaper to transport the final product than the raw material. In such cases the industry tends to be located close to the source of the raw materials. For example, to make one kilogram of butter about five kilograms of milk are used. It therefore makes sense to locate dairies close to the source of milk i.e. in dairy farming areas. Paper manufacturing industries usually locate near forests because the timber they require for raw material is much bulkier than the finished product.

Labour Labour means the workers employed in an industry. All industries need labour. Some are large employers, others are not. For instance, the low technology textile industries which produce clothes use many workers; the high technology chemical industries producing synthetic fabrics use little labour. Industries which are large employers are attracted to urban locations rather than rural ones because there is a better labour supply in towns and cities.

The level of education of the labour force is important. A well-educated labour force attracts industries which use high technology. Low technology industries which need a lot of labour usually require a poorly-educated workforce which is not highly paid. Many of the textile products bought in Ireland to-day are produced in the low-wage economies of South-east Asia such as Taiwan. The high standard of education in Ireland has made possible the rapid growth of the electronics industry here.

Transport Facilities Manufacturing industries need good access so that raw materials reach the factory efficiently and products are distributed quickly to market. Nodal points are the most accessible places and so are attractive locations for manufacturing industries. Dublin city, the major nodal centre in Ireland, is also linked to other countries through its deep-sea port and airport. This accessibility makes it an attractive location for manufacturing industry.

Markets The market is where the product is sold. It is probably the most important factor for any industry because without a market an industry cannot survive. Most industries try to locate where a market for their products is assured. Manufacturing is best developed in First World countries because here spending power is greatest. If the product is bulkier than the raw material, it is cheaper to locate the factory close to the market. For example, cars are bulky and more expensive to transport than the raw materials they are made from, so car industries are usually located close to markets. Perishable goods such as cakes and bread are made close to the market because they must be fresh when sold. Industries which make products for consumption in large quantities locate near cities where there is a large market. The concentration of industries around Paris is a good example of this.

Services Industries need services such as water, power supplies and telecommunications. If these are not available the industry has to pay to have them installed. This causes added cost. Manufacturers prefer to locate on **fully serviced sites.** These are sites which provide all the services industries need. Industrial zones near urban areas often have an industrial estate included in them. An **industrial estate** is an area planned and laid out to facilitate industrial development. It is usually located near an urban centre where suitable labour is available. It has a good road system connecting with the national road network and excellent services. It is built on flat land and has space for industries to expand. Sometimes the developer of the industrial estate builds 'advance' factories. These are attractive to entrepreneurs because the buildings are ready for use. This keeps costs down and means production can begin without delay.

Capital Capital is the money needed to start and run an industry. Most entrepreneurs borrow some or all of the capital they need. If there is a shortage of capital available for borrowing, entrepreneurs are discouraged from starting an industry. In Third World countries there is often a shortage of capital, so it is difficult to set up industries there. Only a small percentage of the world's industry is in the developing world.

Government or EU Policy Governments influence the location of industry. They build industrial estates, provide cheap loans, and develop training programmes to educate the workforce. They use the 'tax system' as an incentive for entrepreneurs. In Ireland manufacturing companies pay only 10% income tax on their profits whereas everybody else pays much higher rates. The EU also encourages industrial development by providing money to improve transport systems. The roads leading from Rosslare to Dublin, Belfast and Cork are being upgraded to improve Ireland's communications with countries abroad. Irish railways will also be improved with EU support.

The EU also makes funds available for education so that the Irish labour force can meet future demands for skills and knowledge.

Entrepreneur's Preference The entrepreneur may have a personal preference for a particular place even though it is not the 'least cost' location. Perhaps the preference is due to loyalty to a person's home area, or because it has a good golf course or school. Two of the biggest industries in France, Peugeot and Michelin, are located at Montbéliard and Clermont-Ferrand out of loyalty to the founders' home towns.

ACTIVITY 1

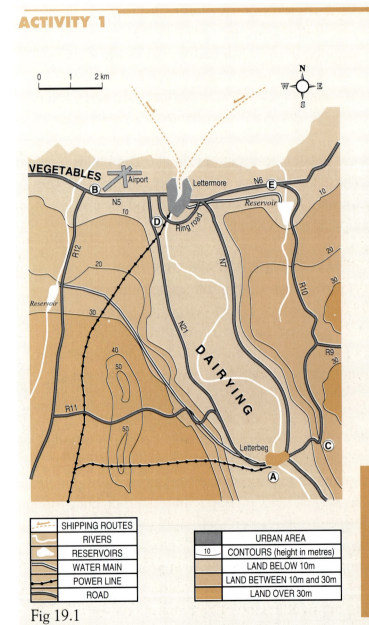

Fig 19.1

1. (a) List the factors which may influence the decision where to locate a factory.
   (b) Choose three of the factors you mentioned in (a) and explain them, giving an example in each case.
2. Which of the following industries do you think should be located close to its market?

   newspapers, fish processing, flour milling, oil refining, baking, TV set manufacture, paint-making, explosives

3. Examine the map in figure 19.1 then do the following:
   (a) Which of the A, B, C, D, E places is likely to be the most attractive location for a manufacturing industry? Explain your choice, giving four reasons.
   (b) At which of the places A, B, C, D, E on the map would you locate a dairy? Explain your choice giving four reasons.
   (c) At which of the places would you locate a car industry? Explain your choice giving four reasons.

THE LOCATION OF MANUFACTURING INDUSTRY

TYPES OF MANUFACTURING

There are many different kinds of industry. To simplify things industry is divided into heavy industry and light industry. **Heavy industry** involves the processing of large amounts of raw materials into big products such as ships, trains, bridges, electrical generators etc. **Light industry** involves the processing of small amounts of raw materials into products which are not large, such as TV-sets, textiles, bicycles, books, bread etc. Most industry is light industry.

CASE STUDY : HARLAND AND WOLFF A HEAVY INDUSTRY

Harland and Wolff shipbuilding yards in Belfast are an example of a heavy industry. The photograph in figure 19.2 shows the shipyard. It takes up most of the middleground of the photograph.

Fig 19.2

THE GEOGRAPHER'S WAY 2

ACTIVITY 2

1. What type of photograph is it?
2. What evidence is there that the docks and shipyards are built on reclaimed land?
3. What evidence is there that the cranes in the centre middleground are extremely large?
4. Give the location of a residential area in the photograph.
5. List three types of transport in the photograph.

Ships have been built in Belfast since 1800. During the 19th century the linen industry grew rapidly in the north of Ireland. Much of the linen was exported to Britain through the port of Belfast. As imports of coal and exports of linen increased more ships were needed. The shipbuilding industry developed to satisfy this demand. Belfast was a suitable location for a number of reasons.

* It is located at the head of a large bay called Belfast Lough. This shelters it from rough seas.
* The mud flats at the head of the bay were easily reclaimed and this provided a large, flat waterside site ideal for shipbuilding which requires a lot of land.
* Steel, coal and wood, the main raw materials, were not available locally. But they could be imported easily from the North of England, Scotland and Scandinavia.
* Shipbuilding needed a labour force of skilled workers. As Belfast was already an industrial city, it had such people.
* The abilities and hard work of the entrepreneurs Edward Harland and Gustav Wolff played an important part in making the company the largest shipbuilder in the world, with at one time 51,000 employees.

Harland and Wolf employs 1,700 at the moment. This number has decreased from the huge numbers that used to be employed. There are several reasons for this. Firstly, new technology has been introduced which reduces the need for labour. Secondly, Belfast specialised in building large passenger ships and the demand for these fell as air transport became cheaper and more available. Thirdly, countries such as Japan entered the shipbuilding market. Their new yards were more modern and efficient than Belfast's and could produce ships more cheaply. It

THE LOCATION OF MANUFACTURING INDUSTRY

is more difficult for the Belfast yards to compete and win orders against such competition.

Harland and Wolff diversified into producing bulk carriers, naval ships and ship repairs to enable it to compete.

ACTIVITY 3

1. Explain what is meant by heavy industry.
2. What factors influenced the location of the shipbuilding industry in Belfast?
3. Explain how changes in costs and markets have caused the decline of the Belfast shipbuilding industry.

WARNER LAMBERT: A CASE STUDY OF A LIGHT INDUSTRY

Warner Lambert is a large American multinational company which manufactures healthcare and consumer products. A **multinational company** is a company which operates in a number of countries. Warner Lambert operates in 130 countries, has 82 manufacturing plants and employs 34,000 people around the world. It manufactures many well known consumer products such as *Benylin, Listerine* and *Wilkinson Sword* razors.

Warner Lambert has manufactured healthcare and confectionery products in Dublin for over thirty years. The company has two plants at Dun Laoghaire in Dublin's south-eastern suburbs. One plant produces pharmaceuticals and the other chewing gum base. The pharmaceuticals produced are anti-clotting and debriding agents both of which are used in medicine. The clotting agent stops bleeding and the debriding agent kills severe infections. Both of these products are extracted from ox-blood, purified and freeze-dried in the pharmaceutical plant. The second plant produces chewing gum base which is the main raw material in chewing gums. The base is produced by the heating and blending of a variety of waxes and resins. The chewing gum base is exported to companies which process it into chewing gum. The main markets are in the USA and Japan. Warner Lambert is the second largest chewing gum producer in the world. Between its two plants Warner Lambert employs 240 people in Ireland. The fuel used in the factories is mainly natural gas.

Warner Lambert's Irish plants are good examples of light industry. They use fairly small amounts of raw materials and produce small, light goods which are inexpensive to transport.

THE GEOGRAPHER'S WAY 2

ACTIVITY 4

Fig 19.3

The photograph in figure 19.3 shows the location of Warner Lambert's two plants in Dun Laoghaire. Examine it carefully, then do the following:
1. What type of photograph is it?
2. Identify and give the location of four different land uses in the photograph.
3. Using evidence from the photograph give three advantages this location has for Warner Lambert Ireland Ltd.
4. Contrast the Warner Lambert's factories shown in figure 19.3 with the Harland and Wolff plant shown in figure 19.2 on page 263 under these headings: location, size, transport, activity.

WHY WARNER LAMBERT CHOSE IRELAND

Warner Lambert chose Ireland for a number of reasons.
- As many companies in the Warner Lambert group supply one another with partially-processed products, they need to be accessible to one another. Dublin is accessible through its sea port and airport. This made it an attractive location.

- Dublin had a large, well-educated labour force which reduced training costs.
- The government introduced a number of incentives for foreign industries to set up in Ireland. These included reduced taxes on profits and capital grants for buildings and equipment.
- The location was well-serviced with electricity, water, roads and telecommunications.

In the last year Warner Lambert have invested $17 million installing sterile manufacturing facilities in the Dun Laoghaire pharmaceutical plant. This investment is an indication of the confidence the company has in the future of its Irish manufacturing plants.

ACTIVITY 5

1. Draw a flow chart to show how Warner Lambert's manufacture of chewing gum base operates as a system with inputs, processes and outputs.
2. Explain four reasons why Warner Lambert located factories in Dublin.

FOOTLOOSE INDUSTRIES

Many modern manufacturing industries are 'footloose'. **Footloose industries** are ones which are not tied to a particular location. They could be located equally well in a number of places. The computer industry is a good example of a footloose industry. It is not tied to the source of its raw materials as these are few and inexpensive to transport. The computer industry does not have to be located close to the market because the finished product is easy to transport. The cost of transport adds only a small amount to the price of such an expensive product.

Two important locational factors for the computer industry are a suitable labour supply and accessibility. Computer manufacturers need a well-educated work force which it will be easy and quick to train. They also need to be accessible to sources of raw materials and world markets. Computer companies such as Apple in Cork and Hewlett Packard in Dublin could be located in many other cities around the world as they are footloose industries. They remain in Ireland because it is the 'least cost' location at present.

In the recent past one such industry, Digital, shifted its manufacturing base from Galway to Scotland because Scotland was believed to be the 'least cost' location for that company when it expanded.

As technology and transport systems improve, industries are going to become more footloose. This means they will come and go much more than they did in the past. Years ago an industry tended to stay and grow where it began. The advantage of the new mobility is that Ireland may be able to attract new industries from abroad. The disadvantage is that footloose industries can move away to other countries if they can become more competitive by doing so.

ACTIVITY 6

1. What is meant by a 'footloose' industry?
2. (a) Which of the following would you regard as footloose?
   camera making   paper making   cigarette manufacture
   watch making   washing machine manufacture
   (b) In each case explain your answer.
3. Explain why it is more important than ever to educate Irish students to the highest possible standard.
4. Explain the advantages and disadvantages of 'footloose' industries.

CHANGING LOCATION: THE BRITISH STEEL INDUSTRY

The 'least cost' location for an industry at present may not be the ideal location in the future. As time passes the factors influencing the location of an industry can change. The iron and steel industry in Britain is an example of an industry changing its location as factors changed.

Before the 18th century iron was smelted using charcoal made from wood. To **smelt** means to extract metal from its ore. The iron industry needed two raw materials: iron ore and timber. It was impossible to transport these raw materials any distance because the roads were bad, so large forests with supplies of iron ore nearby were the places where iron and steel were made. The Forest of Dean and The Weald were the main centres of the iron and steel industry at the end of the 17th century.

THE LOCATION OF MANUFACTURING INDUSTRY

In the early 18th century it was discovered that coke could be used to smelt iron more efficiently. Coke is a product made from coal. The iron industry soon shifted from forested areas to coalfields. Coalfields where deposits of iron ore were found in the rock between the layers of coal became very successful. These deposits were called 'black band' ores. The South Wales coal field, the 'Black Country' of Staffordshire and the Midlands coal fields now became the important iron and steel centres.

By the middle of the 19th century most of the 'black band' ores had been used up so the industry now began to rely on imported ore. At the same time improvements in technology reduced the amount of coke that had to be used in the smelting process. These two changes meant that coastal locations became more attractive as the costs of production there were lower than on the inland coalfields. The industry moved gradually to the coast.

Another discovery in the technology of steel production now allowed ores with a high phosphorous content to be smelted to make steel. This meant that the high phosphorous ores of Cleveland, Lincolnshire and Northamptonshire could be used. New steel works were built on these iron ore fields at Scunthorpe and Corby. Britain now had two kinds of steel centres: coastal locations in South Wales, Scotland and north-east England and inland steel towns located on the iron ore field of the East Midlands. This locational pattern continued for many years.

The economic depression after the oil crisis in the 1970s caused a sharp fall in the demand for manufactured goods. This led to a fall in the demand for steel. Too much steel was being produced all over the world and it became difficult to find markets for it. The British Steel Corporation which controlled the steel industry decided that the industry had to be rationalised if it was to survive. To **rationalise** an industry means to get it working as efficiently as possible by cutting costs. It was decided to concentrate steel production in a few very large steel works. Each steel works would specialise in a particular kind of steel production so that they would not be competing with each other. By 1995 only six major steel works remain in Britain. These are shown on the map in figure 19.4.

ACTIVITY 7

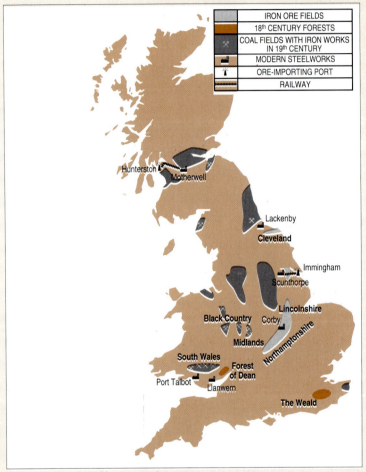

Fig 19.4

1. Examine the map in figure 19.4, then answer the following:
   (a) Name two areas which were thickly forested at the beginning of the 18th century.
   (b) Name three coal fields where there were many ironworks in the 19th century.
   (c) Name three modern steelworks. A steelworks is where steel is produced.
   (d) Through which ports do Motherwell and Scunthorpe get their imported iron ore?
2. Draw a sketch map of Britain. On it show the following:
   (a) Two important iron and steel producing areas at the beginning of the 18th century.
   (b) Three coalfields which were important locations for the iron and steel industry in the 19th century.
   (c) The names and locations of six modern steel plants.
3. Explain why location of the iron and steel industry in Britain changed a number of times between the 17th and 20th centuries.

INDUSTRIAL INERTIA

When the locational factors affecting industries change, individual companies or industries react in different ways. Some move to less costly locations or more suitable ones. Others consider moving too risky or too costly, so they remain where they are. The tendency to remain at a place even though it may no longer be the 'least cost' one is called **industrial inertia**. 'Inertia' means the tendency of something to stay where it is. Industrial inertia is particularly common in heavy industries. Some British steel firms affected by industrial inertia stayed where they were when they should have moved to more favourable locations. As a result their costs gradually increased compared with those of firms that had moved to better locations. Their prices became uncompetitive and they were eventually forced out of business.

REVISION

Rewrite the following text using the words from the box.

heavy industry	industrial inertia	smelt
fully serviced site	least cost location	footloose
entrepreneur	rationalise	light industry	industrial estate

An _____ is a person who takes the risk of setting up a company. A factory site with water, power, telecommunications and other services is a _____ _____ _____. An area developed specially for industry is an _____ _____. The cheapest location for an industry is called the _____ _____ _____. _____ _____ uses large amounts of raw materials in the production of large products such as ships. To _____ means to extract a metal from its ore. _____ _____ uses small amounts of raw materials to produce small goods such as radios. An industry which can locate anywhere is a _____ one. To _____ an industry means to trim it down and make it more efficient. _____ _____ is when an industry remains in the same location even when it would be more profitable for it to move to a new location.

20 Industrialisation

IN THIS CHAPTER YOU WILL LEARN

- The industrial revolution.
- The various levels of industrialisation.
- The role of women in the Irish economy.
- Benefits and diasadvantages of industrialisation.
- Examples of environmental effects of industrialisation.

The increase and spread of manufacture in an area is **industrialisation**. For thousands of years people have manufactured things. The ancient Chinese made fine textiles and pottery. In Roman times factories produced table-ware, pots and tiles which were exported all over Europe. The workers in these industries lived where they worked creating settlements not unlike factory towns.

Manufacturing activity tended to cluster in industrial settlements. Availability of raw materials, labour supply, transport facilities and nearby markets caused industries to group together. Other factors also caused clustering. People stayed in their industrial centre to keep their skills and knowledge secret to prevent competition. A local energy resource, fuel or a waterfall, tended to tie industry to a place. The steel industry in Britain shows how manufacturing concentrated in certain towns because local coal provided energy. As the numbers in an industry grew, other manufacturing and service activities came, thus increasing the population.

Modern industrialisation began in Britain about 250 years ago. What made it different to earlier industrial development was the speed and extent of its growth. Improved knowledge of science and mechanics made better machines possible. Steam was used to drive the new machinery. This brought a great change. Factories were built to house the machines and engines. In some places one powerful engine became the core of a manufacturing settlement with factories grouped around taking energy from the 'engine house'. In others each factory had its own engine to provide power.

INDUSTRIALISATION

Industrialisation brought about a revolution in society. People moved from the countryside to work in factories. Densely packed housing was built close by so workers could be on time. Strict discipline was introduced because expensive machines could not be allowed stand idle when people were late or absent. Workers became full-time employees doing specialised jobs. Hiring and firing was decided by markets. There was a new attitude to work and employment and the traditional pace of life quickened.

Industrialisation changed many towns. In some places factories started in market towns making manufacturing rather than trade their most important function. In others, new towns were built on coal fields, at ports or on sites which suited particular industries. At first many industrial centres were overcrowded and unplanned with wretched working and living conditions. But as time passed conditions improved due to worker pressure and the efforts of social reformers. Today the ugly face of industrialisation has almost gone from First World countries. This is not the case in the Third World.

LEVELS OF INDUSTRIALISATION

There are different stages of industrialisation. Some countries have been industrialised for a long time and manufacturing is well-developed there. These are the 'industrialised countries'. Others have become industrialised recently. These are the 'newly industrialised countries' where industry is getting on its feet. Some states are only emerging as industrialised countries. Here the process of industrialisation is starting. Many Third World countries have little industry. These are the 'least industrialised countries'. The map in figure 20.1 shows the different levels of industrialisation around the world.

The Industrialised Countries These include most of the countries of Europe, North America, New Zealand, Australia and Japan. They have been industrialised for many years and are wealthy. They own a large part of world manufacturing industry and control much of world trade. Seven of them, known as the 'G7' countries, account for half of all exports. The seven are: USA, Germany, Japan, France, U.K., Italy and Canada.

THE GEOGRAPHER'S WAY 2

ACTIVITY 1

Examine the map in figure 20.1, then do the following:
1. Name five industrialised countries.
2. Name five newly industrialised countries.
3. Decide whether each of the following statements is true or false. T F
   (a) Most industrialised countries are in the southern hemisphere. ☐ ☐
   (b) Australia is a newly industrialised country. ☐ ☐
   (c) Brazil is a newly industrialised country. ☐ ☐
   (d) Japan is an industrialised country. ☐ ☐
   (e) Africa is the least industrialised continent. ☐ ☐

Fig 20.1

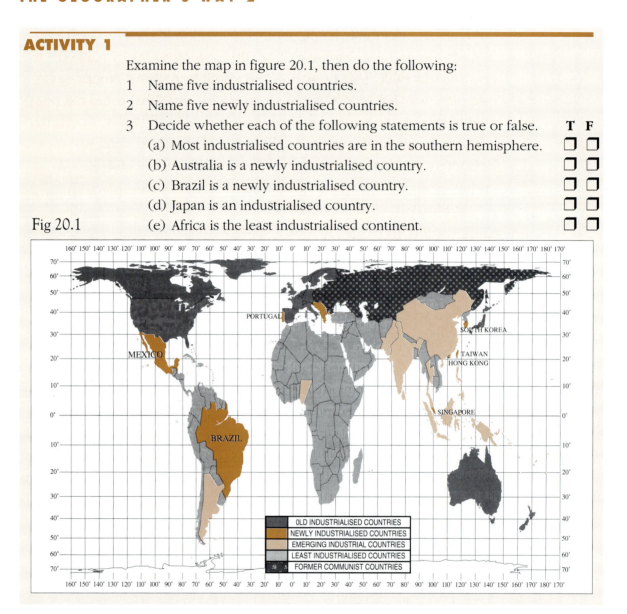

The Newly Industrialised Countries (NICs) These have industrialised during the last twenty years. Their industrialisation is **export led**. This means that they concentrate on making goods for export such as textiles which need a lot of labour. The long hours and low wages of the workforce in NICs keeps the price of manufactures low, making them competitive. As exports grow so does investment in new factories and processes, so the range of products made and exported increases. Many multinational firms open factories in NICs to take advantage of their skills and wage-rates. The Asiatic NIC countries Hong Kong, Taiwan, Singapore and South Korea account for 9 % of world exports.

Emerging Industrial Countries   These are industrialising rapidly. The development of their industry is also 'export led'. The level of investment in factories and machinery is not as high as in the NICs but very low wage-rates make them competitive. The emerging industrial nations are replacing the NICs as the 'least cost' location for industries which need cheap labour. Most are in Asia. Important ones include Malaysia, Indonesia, China and India. These are countries with high populations. When they become more developed, they will be powerful competitors on world markets.

The Least Industrialised Countries   Most of these are located in Africa. They have little industry and mainly produce primary products and raw materials for sale to industrialised countries. Metal ores, petroleum, timber and farm produce such as coffee, tea, cocoa and vegetable oils make up most of their exports. As primary products are cheap, these countries earn little by exporting. Therefore there is little capital for investment, so industrialisation cannot start. These are the poorest countries in the world.

Saudi Arabia and the other Oil States of the Middle East must be included with the 'least industrialised countries' though they are a special case. They have little industry which is not directly concerned with oil production. They are, however, very wealthy because of their income from petroleum exports.

The Former Communist States   These countries are at various stages of industrialisation. Under communism great stress was placed on heavy industry producing military and transport equipment. Less interest was taken in making consumer goods such as cars and domestic appliances. Much of their industry was old fashioned and inefficient, so it could not compete on world markets and did not progress. Many of these countries are now modernising their industries to supply their own people and world markets. Czechoslovakia, Poland and the former East Germany are rapidly re-industrialising with the help of technology and investment from the industrially-developed countries.

THE GEOGRAPHER'S WAY 2

ACTIVITY 2

1. (a) Explain each of the following terms:
     industrialised country
     newly industrialised country
     emerging industrial country
     least industrialised country

   (b) Name four countries which fall into each of the categories mentioned in (a) above.

2. Describe and explain the distribution of the NICs and the 'least industrialised countries'.

INDUSTRIAL WORKERS

Before industrialisation most people lived in the country. People were self-sufficient, making nearly all the things they needed. Manufacture was done in the home or the workshop. Women worked in the home and on the farm. In cottage industries like cloth-making women played a more industrial role, sharing with men the tasks of spinning, washing, dyeing and sewing. Men could work away from home but women rarely did unless they were 'in service'. Then they 'lived in' at their place of work.

Industrial manufacture brought great changes. Work moved out of the home to the factory. Industrialisation destroyed the cottage industries and forced people to move to factories to get employment. Men continued to do most of the heavy work but machine-minding and some processing was done by women. Light industries such as textiles, clothing, pottery, light metal goods and foodstuffs employed increasing numbers of women. Gradually they became an important part of the manufacturing workforce. Employing women kept costs down because women were always paid less than men. And women were more nimble-fingered than men when it came to operating intricate machines. The number of women in manufacturing rose steadily to peak during the World Wars when men left their jobs to join the forces.

Recently the numbers of women in manufacturing in developed countries has decreased. Wage equality between men and women has made female labour less competitive and the automation of machinery has reduced the need for industrial workers generally. Now women are being employed mainly in service industries which are expanding rapidly. Improved education allows women to choose better-paid, more interesting work. This is not the case in the newly industrialised

INDUSTRIALISATION

and emerging industrial countries: Here the poor wages paid to women and children keep industrial costs low, so large numbers continue to be employed in manufacturing.

THE ROLE OF WOMEN IN THE IRISH ECONOMY

In Ireland the role of women in society is also changing. These changes affect practically all aspects of life including the family, work and recreation. The photographs in figure 20.2 illustrate some of these changes. Examine them and decide what change you think each represents.

Fig 20.2A

Fig 20.2B

Fig 20.2C

One way to find out about changes in society is to study job information. We will examine employment statistics to find out about the changing role of women in Ireland. Figure 20.3 provides information about the participation of men and women in the labour market over a period of thirteen years. It shows that there is a definite trend towards change.

ACTIVITY 3

Percentage Male / Female in Irish Labour Force 1972-1992

	1979	1985	1992
Male	72%	69%	65%
Female	28%	31%	35%
Total	100%	100%	100%

Fig 20.3

Examine the table in figure 20.3 then answer these questions.
1. Which sex made up most of the labour force in 1985?
2. What percentage of the labour force was male in 1992?
3. What percentage of the labour force was female in 1979?
4. In which period did the largest increase in the female labour force occur?
5. Describe the change in the female labour force between 1979 and 1992.
6. What type of graph is most suitable to illustrate the information in the table? Give reasons for your choice.

The table shows that more women entered the labour force as time passed. In 1979 28% of the labour force were women. By 1992 the percentage had risen to 35%. The increase was due to a number of factors. These included: greater employment opportunities for women; a change in the attitude to women working outside the home; the improved knowledge and skills which women brought to the labour market.

The next table, figure 20.4, provides information about the sectors of the economy where women worked during the same period. This also shows a trend towards change. Examine the table and compare and contrast the statistics carefully. Look for trends shown by the figures and identify these.

INDUSTRIALISATION

ACTIVITY 4

Percentage Employment of Female Labour Force by Sector 1979–1992

	1979	1985	1992
Agricultural workers	6.2	5.4	2.8
Producers, makers and repairers	12.5	10.8	10.5
Labourers and unskilled workers	0.4	0.0	0.2
Labourers and unskilled workers	0.4	0.0	0.2
Transport & communication workers	3.2	3.0	2.5
Clerical workers	28.2	27.5	27.4
Commerce, insurance and finance	12.9	13.1	13.0
Service workers	14.8	15.3	16.3
Professional workers	20.6	23.5	24.6
Others	1.2	1.4	2.7

Fig 20.4

Answer the following questions.
1. What percentage of the female labour force was employed in agriculture in each of the years 1979, 1985 and 1992?
2. What was the least important sector for women's employment in 1992?
3. Rank the sectors according to their importance in the employment of women in 1992.
4. Which sectors grew in importance in the employment of women between 1979 and 1992?
5. Using what you have learned about the three kinds of industrial activity, calculate the percentage of women working in each in 1992. When you are doing this disregard the 'others' category.

Between 1979 and 1992 the female labour force in Ireland increased from 322,500 to 399,400. The number of women in agricultural work decreased by more than half to a low figure of less than 3%. Unskilled labouring work for women hardly exists any more. Female employment in the manufacturing sector has decreased but the downward trend is slow. The percentage in services increased from 76.5 % to 81.5% but the pattern is uneven. The number of women in transport services has decreased. So have the numbers in clerical work. Service workers have increased by 1.5% over the period. There has been a big change in professional employment with a continuing increase to nearly one quarter of the total female workforce.

THE GEOGRAPHER'S WAY 2

INDUSTRIALISATION: FOR AND AGAINST

Industrialisation is often accused of bringing disadvantages which injure society and damage the environment. The charges against it include pollution, environmental damage, migration causing rural depopulation, unhealthy living conditions, social upheaval and destruction of traditional ways of life and culture. With so much to complain about, it is easy to overlook the benefits that industrial development brings.

BENEFITS OF INDUSTRIALISATION

- Industrialisation creates wealth. This may be spread through the economy to the advantage of all or it may be kept by a few privileged people. Wealth can make more development possible by providing capital for investment.
- Industrialisation provides employment. Jobs in industry are usually better paid than in primary activities.
- Industries pay local and government taxes. These help to pay for the running of the country and improved services.
- Industries carry out research which adds to human knowledge and skills.
- Progress in medicine and health care would be impossible without industrialisation. Industries also produce many products which are labour-saving or improve the quality of life. This makes life better for many.
- Industry provides training and education for the workforce.
- Industry supports many cultural and sporting activities such as festivals and games.
- Industries often take an interest in the improvement of their locality. In Dublin the owners of the Guinness brewery laid out the park in St Stephen's Green and paid for the renovation of St Patrick's Cathedral.

In many cases the benefits of industrialisation have come through argument and conflict. The improvement in wages and working conditions since the start of industrialisation are mainly the result of workers organising themselves politically and in trade unions. Through their parties and unions they have forced governments to introduce laws to protect them. Such laws provide for a minimum wage, maximum working hours, entitlement to holidays and redundancy payments. Trade unions also negotiate with employers to improve conditions and negotiate changes. In the 1960s most people worked a 45 hour week. Today the average week worked is 40 hours.

ACTIVITY 5

1. List five of the more important ways you think people have benefited from industrialisation.
2. Explain how conflicts can develop between industrialists and employees. What is the function of trade unions in the relations between the industrialist and the workforce?

DISADVANTAGES OF INDUSTRIALISATION

Industrialisation has revolutionised society and people's way of life. These changes affect us in many different, often personal, ways. They sometimes seem to have brought more disadvantages than benefits when our world is compared with that of our ancestors. For instance,

- Living is more hurried, less free and much more complicated than it once was. Though we now have more control over our environment, life appears to be less secure and settled.
- The air we breathe, the water we swim in, the ground we walk on are less safe than they once were.
- The countryside and its wildlife has never been so threatened.
- War seems more terrible today than it ever was because it is backed by the industrial might of the Great Powers.

To study the disadvantages of industrialisation, we will take two concrete examples of damage caused by the industrial waste made by manufacturing industry. Industry creates large amounts of waste products. These can be gases, solid materials, or liquids. The first case concerns industrial waste emitted in the form of gas.

Acid Rain in Europe Waste gases play a big part in causing acid rain and global warming. Global warming may eventually have the more serious results. It could cause climate changes, serious flooding of coastlines, crop failures and famine. But as scientists are still in doubt about the extent of the changes it causes in the atmosphere and how quickly they are happening, we will not discuss this further. About the damage being done by acid rain, there is no doubt whatever. Trees are dying all over central and northern Europe due to it. Pollution by industrial gases is by far the biggest contributor to this disaster. Emission of gases, particularly sulphur dioxide (SO_2) and nitrous oxide (N_2O) by industry in Europe causes acid rain to form. The areas worst affected are the coniferous forests of central Europe and Scandinavia. Here relief rainfall over hills and mountains concentrates the effect of the acid precipitation. Run-off from these areas enters the rivers and lakes which become heavily polluted. In Germany, Austria and France forests have been badly affected. The acid rain releases aluminium from the soil as it seeps down through it. Aluminium in large quantities acts as a poison to plants and fish life. In Germany 68% of tree stocks have been damaged and only 32% remain healthy. In a country which has one third of its area forested this is a very serious problem. In Sweden 4,000 lakes are dead without any fish life. This problem is worst in Southern Sweden and Norway.

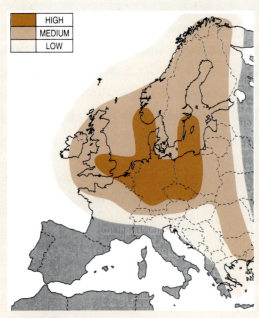

Fig 20.5

ACTIVITY 6

Examine the map in figure 20.5, then do the following exercise with the help of an atlas.

1. Name the countries with the most acid rainfall.
2. Which of the following statements best describes the distribution of acid rainfall in Europe?
   (a) Acid rainfall is worst in Scandinavia and decreases southwards from there.
   (b) Acid rainfall is worst on the periphery of Europe and decreases towards Europe's industrial core.
   (c) Acid rainfall badly affects all European countries, both those on the edge and those in the centre.
   (d) Acid rainfall is worst in the industrial core of Europe and decreases as one moves outwards.

INDUSTRIALISATION

3 The table in figure 20.6 shows the percentage share of world gas emissions for a number of countries.

Country	% World Gas Emissions	Country	% World Gas Emissions
Sweden	0.22	Denmark	0.18
Norway	0.21	Finland	0.18
France	1.54	Japan	4.68
USA	17.84	Luxembourg	0.03
Netherlands	0.52	Ireland	0.13
United Kingdom	2.21	Italy	1.60
Germany	4.44	Spain	0.93
Austria	0.22	Greece	0.29
Belgium	0.37	Portugal	0.21

Fig 20.6

(a) Which three countries have the highest emissions?
(b) Rank the European countries on the basis of their percentage of emissions. No.1 is the country which has the highest percentage.
(c) Which four countries have the lowest emissions?

It is clear from the table figure 20.6 that Norway and Sweden don't have large emissions of the gases which cause acid rain. It is estimated that these countries are responsible for only 17% of the gases which cause acid rainfall there. The rest of the polluting gases are blown to them by the prevailing winds from the core industrialised countries of Europe, especially the UK and Germany. Acid rainfall is therefore an international problem as the gases which cause it are carried from one country to another. If the problem is to be solved, there must be international agreements to reduce the emissions of the gases which cause it.

Germany was quick to react to the pollution problem. Filters were installed in the chimneys of power stations to extract the polluting gases. Between 1983 and 1993 emission of sulphur dioxide was reduced by 84%. Nitrous oxide emission was reduced by 74%. The cost of installing these filters was about £1.5 billion. To tackle the problem of acid rain countries must be willing to pay the price these precautions cost.

ACTIVITY 7

1 Describe how acid rain forms. (Refer to Book One p.159 if necessary.) Explain how it has affected German forests and Swedish lakes.
2 Explain how Germany is proving to be a 'good neighbour'. How is it tackling the problem of acid rain?
3 Why are international agreements needed to deal with acid rain?

Fig 20.7A

Fig 20.7B

4 Examine the cartoons in figure 20.7. They show how industrial pollution has affected agriculture and the quality of people's lives. Explain the message of each cartoon.

The Minimata Disaster Minimata is a town on the island of Kyushu in Japan (32°50'N 130°50'E). A big chemical manufacturer, the Chisse Company, was located there producing vinyl, a kind of plastic. In the early 1950s strange things began to happen. Birds dropped dead out of the sky. Dead fish floated on the surface of the sea nearby. Cats got fits and died. In 1953 a number of people in the area began suffering from a disease which affected their eyesight, hearing and ability to move. Most of the victims died or became completely paralysed. People naturally became very frightened and tried to find the cause of the strange sickness which affected both humans and animals.

After a number of years it was discovered that the disease was mercury poisoning. Mercury was getting into the human food chain through plankton which fish feed on. Although mercury was in the industrial effluent dumped into the sea by Chisse, the company denied it was responsible for the disease, even though mercury was known to be poisonous. It continued to dump the effluent and the mercury it contained until the the late 1960s.

Relatives of the victims campaigned for years to get Chisse to admit it was at fault but they had no success. They publicised the disaster around the world, making it clear that the disease was due to Chisse's pollution. Eventually they won a court case against Chisse in 1973, twenty years after the poisoning first happened. Over 100 people had died from poisoning and another 1000 victims had been affected. They were granted compensation of £3 million.

INDUSTRIALISATION

The Minimata disaster was just one of a number of tragedies which caused the Japanese government to introduce pollution controls for industry. The first law for environmental control was passed in 1967. In 1974 a pollution compensation law was introduced. Under the compensation law people affected by industrial pollution are entitled to compensation from the polluting manufacturer. Under this law Chisse has to pay the medical expenses of the Minimata victims as well as compensating them for their injuries and suffering.

ACTIVITY 8

1. Using a flow chart, explain how mercury got into the diet of the Minimata victims.
2. Explain why there was a conflict between the Chisse Company and the families of the victims. Tell how it was resolved.

REVISION

Rewrite the following text using the words in the box to fill in the blank spaces.

> least industrialised countries
> newly industrialised countries
> emerging industrial countries
> export-led
> industrialisation

The process of developing manufacturing industries is called _____. Developing industry by concentrating on producing goods for export is called _____ _____ growth. The _____ _____ _____ are those countries which industrialised rapidly over the last 20 years. The _____ _____ _____ are industrialising rapidly at present. The countries with very little industry are known as the _____ _____ _____.

21 Tourism

> **IN THIS CHAPTER YOU WILL LEARN**
>
> - Ireland's tourist attractions.
> - Tourist attractions in Co. Clare.
> - The development of karst landscape.
> - The Mullaghmore Visitor Centre; a conflict of interest.
> - Tourism in Ibiza.
> - The advantages and disadvantages of tourism.

Economic activities which provide services are tertiary industries. They include the work of doctors and lawyers, the sale and distribution of goods, banking, insurance, education and tourism. Service industries employ 60% of the workforce in Ireland and this percentage is rising. Tourism is growing more rapidly than any other economic activity. In Ireland it accounts for much of the increase in the tertiary sector. A **sector** is a part or division of something.

Tourism means travel for enjoyment, usually as part of a holiday. There are many reasons why tourism has grown quickly in recent years. In the First World, and elsewhere too, many people have a paid annual holiday. This gives time for travel. More people can afford to take holidays away from home. Travel facilities and services have improved; journeys are quicker and cheaper. Nowadays people are better educated. They want to know more about the world and see for themselves other lands, peoples and cultures. Television has stimulated interest in many different kinds of holiday, e.g. sport, education, sightseeing, 'activity' holidays.

TOURIST ATTRACTIONS: IRELAND

People are attracted to places which give them the kind of holiday they want while providing suitable services and facilities.

Accessibility   A place must be easy to get to. Ireland has good air links with North America, Britain and Europe; these are the areas most of our tourists come from. There are a number of ferry services to carry people, cars, buses, and caravans between Ireland, Britain and

TOURISM

mainland Europe. Within Ireland good road, rail and air networks allow tourists to travel easily. However, Ireland is an island. This has the disadvantage that there is no direct access to Ireland by road or rail. This makes travel to Ireland slower or more expensive than to many countries with land borders.

ACTIVITY 1

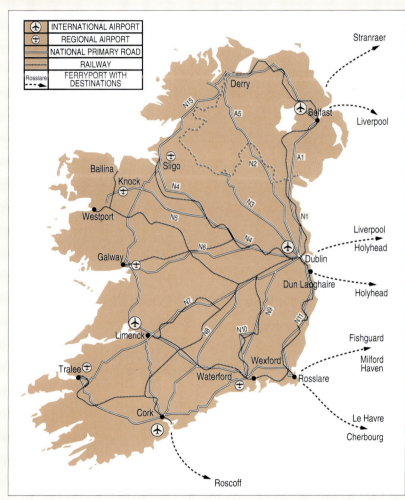

Fig 21.1

1. Examine the map in figure 21.1, then do the following.
   (a) List Ireland's international and regional airports.
   (b) List cities and big towns linked to Dublin by rail.
   (c) List the national primary roads which link Dublin to; Wexford, Galway, Belfast, Sligo, Limerick, Cork.
2. Using an atlas to help you, match the ports in column X with their country in column Y.

X	Y
A Roscoff	1 Scotland
B Stranraer	2 Wales
C Holyhead	3 France
D Le Havre	4 England
E Liverpool	5 France

A	
B	
C	
D	
E	

3. Explain why our island location is a disadvantage when developing tourism.

Accommodation There must be a variety of accommodation on offer to suit tourists. Wealthy tourists need luxury hotels while back-packers need hostels or campsites. Many tourists look for 'bed and breakfast' accommodation which suits a touring holiday. Guest houses often provide the good value and pleasant atmosphere which visitors look for. The amount and variety of accommodation available in Ireland has increased. The facilities are graded and supervised by Bord Failte, the organisation responsible for tourism in Ireland.

Scenery Tourists are attracted by fine scenery. Ireland has a variety of natural landscapes: the mountains and lakes of Kerry, Wicklow, and Donegal; the rugged Connemara landscape; the lakes and boglands of the Central Lowlands; the cliff scenery of the south and west coasts. Clean beaches and coasts appeal to foreigners whose own coastlines have been ruined by pollution and overcrowding. Ireland's Atlantic coastal waters are among the cleanest in Europe.

Sport and recreation Good sporting facilities attract tourists. Ireland has plenty to offer, being well known for horse racing, riding, freshwater fishing and golf. The sea, rivers and lakes provide opportunities for watersports: swimming, fishing, board sailing, surfing, boating and scuba-diving. The uncrowded hills and mountains are ideal for walking, hiking and trekking.

Culture Many tourists are attracted by this interest. Cities like Dublin, Cork, Galway and Belfast offer many cultural and entertainment centres, including theatres, cinemas, museums and art galleries. An increasing number of visitors come to Ireland attracted by our heritage. Our **heritage** means what we have inherited from the past. It includes antiquities from many periods, for example: the tombs at New Grange and Poulnabrone, monastic settlements, like Skellig Micheal and Clonmacnoise, many castles and mansions and Georgian Dublin. Heritage includes the distinctive way of life of people, their language, music and dance. Our heritage is a rich one and different from that of many of our visitors who find Irish culture fascinating. Our literature in English and Gaelic is known worldwide and brings many visitors to literary festivals.

TOURISM

ACTIVITY 2

Fig 21.2A

Fig 21.2B

Fig 21.2C

Fig 21.2D

Fig 21.2E

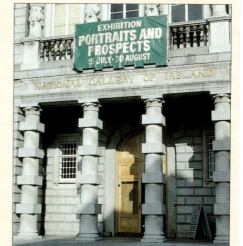
Fig 21.2F

1. Examine the photographs in figure 21.2, then decide which tourist attraction each shows.
2. Draw a sketch map of the OS map, figure 5.28 on page 84. On it show the coastline, land over 50m, four tourist attractions.
3. (a) List four tourist attractions found in your area.
   (b) Suggest how facilities in your area could be improved to attract more tourists.

289

THE GEOGRAPHER'S WAY 2

TOURISM : CONFLICTS OF INTEREST

Tourism can cause problems and conflicts of interest, and people can disagree strongly about how it should be managed. For instance bringing lots of people to see a place of interest can damage or destroy the very thing people come to see. Many features of the natural environment are very fragile and can be ruined by even slight disturbance of the conditions which make them possible. Improved roads, toilet facilities, information centres and cafés can intrude on the environment and change it. The growth in the number of visitors resulting from publicity and better facilities can cause overcrowding, noise and pollution. Careful planning and control are needed to conserve what is there and to prevent tasteless development while ensuring adequate access to the public. The debate about the building of the Mullaghmore Visitor Centre in the Burren illustrates how conflict and disagreement arise.

Case study: Tourism in County Clare

Study the map of County Clare, figure 21.3 making sure you know its location and principal physical and cultural features. The county has a very long coastline with the Atlantic to the west and the Shannon Estuary to the south. To the east there is part of Lough Derg. Therefore it was not a very accessible county until recently, when improved roads and a ferry-service across the Shannon made it easier to get to. It has an important tourist asset in the international airport at Shannon, the entry point for many visitors. The county has a rich heritage and many attractions. One of the most important of these is the Burren.

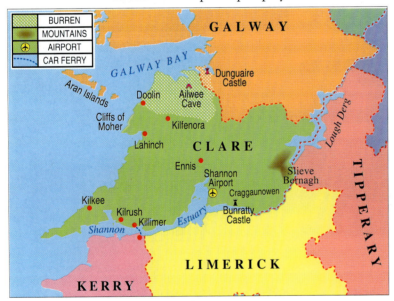

Fig 21.3

The Burren The Burren is a karst. A **karst** is a plateau of rugged, limestone countryside where there is little soil cover and little or no surface drainage. Karst develops when a limestone upland is chemically weathered by rainwater. In the Burren a thin covering of glacial deposits was left at the end of the Ice Age. Light soils developed on these deposits. As the climate warmed forests of hazel, yew and pine spread across the area. Stone Age people were attracted by the light fertile soils and began to clear the trees for pasture. Deforestation and overgrazing of the land over a long period left the soil unprotected by vegetation. It was gradually washed away. The limestone was now exposed to the full force of weathering and erosion. The diagram, figure 21.4, shows the features that resulted. They are typical of a karst area.

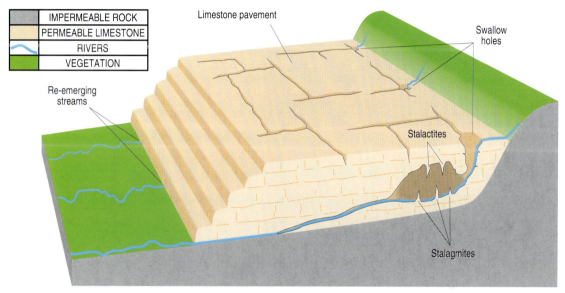

Fig 21.4

When the limestone was laid bare, rainwater entered its cracks and widened them by solution. A limestone pavement formed with clints and grikes. Water in the grikes seeped down into the rock dissolving as it went. Gradually a network of channels developed along the bedding planes and joints in the rock. In some places water flowing on the surface eventually dissolved a hole large enough for a stream to disappear down. Such a hole is called a **swallow hole**. As a stream flowed underground it enlarged its channel by solution and abrasion. Where the rock was weaker the passage widened to form a cave. Some caves can grow very large. There are many caves connected by passages beneath the surface of the Burren. The photograph in figure 21.5 shows a cave made by an underground river. Inside caves stalactites and stalagmites form. **Stalactites**

Fig 21.5

THE GEOGRAPHER'S WAY 2

Fig 21.6

Fig 21.7

are icicle-like deposits of calcium carbonate left by water dripping from the roof of a cave. They grow down from the ceiling and can grow into a pillar. **Stalagmites** are formed similarly but grow upwards from the point where the drips fall. Figure 21.6 shows a stalactite.

As a stream erodes its way down through the limestone it eventually reaches a layer of impermeable rock. Because it cannot pass through this, it flows along the top of the layer, coming out at the surface of the land as an **emerging stream.** The photograph, figure 21.7, shows the Oweentoberlea Stream emerging at Killeaney in the south of the Burren. It has travelled 11 km underground before reaching this point.

The Burren area has much to offer the tourist. An area of karst landscape as large as this is uncommon in northwest Europe, so many visitors come to see it. They find its harsh beauty very impressive. Its caves, such as Ailwee Caves, attract sightseers and 'cavers'. Many botanists come to study its rare plant life which includes alpine plants which have survived since the Ice Age. The area has been settled continuously since the Stone Age so there are many interesting antiquities. The coastline near the Burren is also beautiful with long beaches, sand dunes and the famous Cliffs of Moher.

As you would expect, more and better tourist facilities are needed for the growing number of visitors to the Burren. There has been much disagreement about how and where these should be provided. Many fear that the facilities, and even the visitors themselves, will intrude upon, and possibly destroy, the unique character of the area.

TOURISM

ACTIVITY 3

Fig 21.8A

Fig 21.8B

1. Using the map, figure 21.3, name five tourist attractions in Co. Clare.
2. Examine the photographs in figure 21.8 which show some of the attractions for tourists at the Ailwee Caves.
   (a) List some of the services provided for tourists at the Caves.
   (b) Explain why tourists find this an attractive place.
3. Using a diagram explain how karst features form.

The Office of Public Works (OPW) is the State body responsible for conserving Ireland's built and environmental heritage. The **OPW** looks after 35 visitor centres and has 40,000 hectares of land under its control, mostly in the National Parks. About 1.5 million people visit the centres and parks every year. A **National Park** is an area of environmental interest owned and maintained by the OPW for the enjoyment of everyone. There are two main aims. Firstly, to conserve important ecological environments in the Parks; secondly, to provide access to these interesting areas.

Over the last 20 years the OPW bought land in the south-east of the Burren around Mullaghmore. This area contained good examples of karst features, many different wild flowers and rare animals such as the pine marten. In 1991 these lands were opened to

Fig 21.9

THE GEOGRAPHER'S WAY 2

Fig 21.10

the public as the Burren National Park. The location of the national park is shown in figure 21.9. The OPW decided to build a visitor's centre in the park near Mullaghmore. The photograph, figure 21.10 shows Mullaghmore. The centre was to provide information about the area in a slide show and display. There was to be a nature-study room for students. Tea rooms and toilet facilities were included in the plans. The centre was designed to cater for 60,000 visitors each year.

Reaction to the plan was mixed. Some people agreed with it. Others objected to it strongly. The arguments for and against the plan are given below. At the time of writing the government has just decided not to go ahead with the visitor centre at Mullaghmore.

ARGUMENTS FOR THE VISITOR CENTRE AT MULLAGHMORE

1. It would attract more tourists. This would benefit the whole of Co. Clare by creating jobs.
2. Fifty people would be employed to build the centre. Twenty-five would be employed locally to run it during the summer season.
3. The local environment would be made accessible in a controlled way. The numbers visiting the centre would be limited.
4. Paths would be laid out for visitors to follow, thus avoiding damage to the fragile environment.
5. Sewage would be treated on the site, so there would be no pollution of the groundwater.
6. The centre would be built in an old quarry. The limestone pavement would not be disturbed.
7. The centre would achieve the aims of conserving the unique area while giving visitors access to it.
8. The centre must be located in the Park so that people can see directly the features referred to. If it was located outside the Park, some people would not take the trouble to drive to the Park to see it.

ARGUMENTS AGAINST THE VISITOR CENTRE AT MULLAGHMORE

1. The environment of the National Park is a very fragile one. The Burren could be seriously damaged if the Centre was built there.
2. The roads to the Centre are narrow and pass through hazel thicket. Road widening would involve destroying the hazels.
3. Increased traffic would lead to noise and air pollution.
4. People would stray from the paths and damage areas of great ecological importance.
5. The Visitor Centre will cost about £3.5 million to build. If this large sum was spent building the centre in a town like Kilinaboy or Corofin, it would have a long-term beneficial effect on the town.
6. Building the Centre outside the Park or on the edge of it would divert visitors from fragile areas within the Park.

ACTIVITY 4

1. Describe the aims and work of the OPW.
2. Draw a sketch map of the Burren. On it show the karst area, the Burren National Park, the proposed site of the visitor centre.
3. Examine the photograph of Mullaghmore in figure 21.10 then describe its landscape.
4. Select what you think are the four strongest arguments for or against the siting of the proposed centre at Mullaghmore. Give reasons for your choice.

CLIMATE AND TOURISM

Climate is an important factor in most tourist regions because people usually want fine weather during their holiday. The success of tourism in the southern European countries of France, Spain, Portugal, Italy and Greece owes much to their Mediterranean climate. The reliable hot weather of their summer months is ideal for tourists who want sun and outdoor activity.

In Ireland the frequent rainfall interferes with many outdoor pursuits. To overcome this disadvantage, all-weather facilities are becoming more common. People don't have to depend on fine weather to enjoy these. Visitor centres and attractions like Ailwee Caves are examples of all-weather facilities. Many other developments of this kind include 'Celtworld' and 'Splashworld' in Tramore, the Leisureland complex in Salthill, Co. Galway and Trabolgan in Co. Cork.

THE GEOGRAPHER'S WAY 2

CASE STUDY : TOURISM IN IBIZA

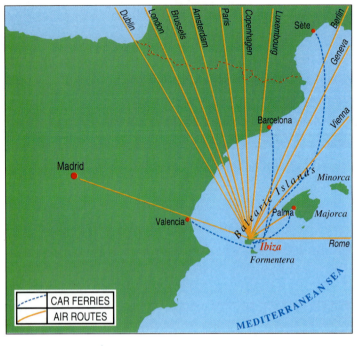

Ibiza is one of the Balearic Islands located off the eastern coast of Spain. It has a population of 60,000. There are three other islands in the group. They are shown in figure 21.11.

Fig 21.11

ACTIVITY 5

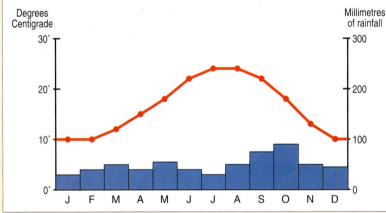

Examine the graph in figure 21.12 showing the average monthly temperature and rainfall for Ibiza. Then find out the following information:

Fig 21.12

1. (a) Which is the warmest month?
   (b) Work out the annual range of temperature.
   (c) How long is the growing season on the island?
   (d) Which is the wettest month?
   (e) Which is the driest month?

TOURISM

Fig 21.13A

Fig 21.13B

Fig 21.13C

Fig 21.13D

The climate statistics show that Ibiza has a hot dry summer. This is attractive for many in northern and western Europe who have a much cooler and wetter climate. The photographs in figure 21.13 show how sunny Ibiza is. But there are other attractions for tourists; the photographs in figure 21.13 show some. Identify what they are. It is clear that there is little need for all-weather facilities in places like Ibiza. Most activities, even cinema-going, are outdoor ones.

THE GEOGRAPHER'S WAY 2

ADVANTAGES OF TOURISM

Mass tourism means a tourist industry involving very large numbers of visitors. Ireland has about 5 million visitors a year and is not considered a mass tourist country. Spain and Italy each have mass tourist industries which bring in more than thirty million tourists per year. Ibiza attracts one million tourists a year. Mass tourism has brought enormous changes to places affected by it. Many of these have been good, involving the provision of better services like roads, telecommunications, water and power supplies, sewerage and so on. Ibiza is a good example of such progress.

Fig 21.14

Since the start of mass tourism in the 1960s Ibiza has changed rapidly. Farming, fishing and salt production were once the main activities. Cereal growing was important along with fig, almond and wine production. There was plenty of groundwater for irrigation during the hot dry summers. Fishing concentrated on sardines as the boats were mainly small inshore ones. Salt was obtained by evaporating seawater. The photograph in figure 21.14 shows the salt pans where the evaporation happens and how the salt is collected.

Since the 1960s these traditional industries have contributed much less to the wealth of the island. Tourism has taken their place as the largest source of income. Ibiza is now a much wealthier place with little or no unemployment, many small industries which manufacture products for visitors and a booming tertiary sector providing tourist services. The impact of tourist growth is greatest along the coast because most tourists wish to be beside the sea. Much of the building development involving hotels, apartment blocks and other facilities has been linear, following

Fig 21.15

298

TOURISM

the coast. The photograph in figure 21.15 shows the spread of high-rise blocks along the coast in the left middleground. Immediately inland from the high-rise blocks there is tilled land which is now geared to supply the increased demand for fresh food. Internal communications have also been improved, especially the trunk roads linking the main towns of San Antonia and Santa Eulalia with the capital Ibiza.

This growth in tourism was only possible with the development of good transport links with the rest of Europe. The vast majority of visitors come to Ibiza by plane, so the opening of an international airport with capacity to handle the largest jets was very important. The island is also linked to Spain, France and Majorca by car ferry services. These bring in only a small percentage of the total number of tourists.

ACTIVITY 6

1. Examine the map in figure 21.11, Page 296, then do the following.
   (a) List the countries linked to Ibiza by air routes.
   (b) List the ports in Spain and France linked to Ibiza by car ferry.
2. What attractions has Ibiza for tourists?
3. How has Ibiza benefited from tourism?
4. Examine the information in the table below, then do the following.
   (a) Work out the total number of tourists visiting Ibiza in 1993.
   (b) Rank the countries in order of the number of tourists. Number 1 is the country with the largest number of tourists going to Ibiza.

ORIGIN OF VISITORS TO IBIZA 1993

Country	No. of Tourists	Country	No. of Tourists
Spain	114,600	Luxembourg	3,000
Holland	20,000	Denmark	6,700
Britain	455,600	Belgium	27,300
Italy	88,700	Switzerland	1,700
Austria	14,700	France	35,800
Ireland	2,300	Others	6,000
Germany	264,000		

5. Imagine you live in Limerick and you wish to drive to Spain for a holiday. Using an atlas work out a convenient route to take.
   Write a description of the route mentioning the countries and the major towns and cities you would pass through on the journey.

THE GEOGRAPHER'S WAY 2

THE DISADVANTAGES OF TOURISM

The natural environment is often seriously damaged by tourist development. Building high-rise blocks along coasts takes from their natural beauty. Beaches become crowded and coastal roads are congested. This leads to noise and air pollution. Sewage and waste disposal can become serious problems because of the high population density.

Much money is spent providing services and facilities for tourists. Some people in Ibiza think a greater proportion of this investment money should be spent on improving agriculture and fishing and on providing better services for local people.

Fig 21.16

The traditional way of life on Ibiza was built around customs to do with farming and fishing. As fewer young people enter the traditional industries their customs are dying out. The photograph in figure 21.16 shows a traditional parade of horse-drawn carts through a tourist resort. Most of the carts carry older people because it is they who keep the traditions alive.

Another disadvantage of tourism is that much of the income goes to companies rather than private individuals. For example, airline, ferry, hotel and apartment-owning companies make most of the money. Many of these are foreign or international organisations with no roots in the countries where they operate. These companies provide employment but much of this is part-time during the peak tourist months. Many such jobs in tourism are insecure and low-paid.

ACTIVITY 7

1. Study the photograph of Ibiza town in figure 21.17, then do the following:
   (a) What type of rock are the cliffs made of?
   (b) Identify, name and locate three coastal features.
   (c) Describe the site of the houses. Why was this site chosen?
   (d) What evidence is there that the sea is polluted?
2. Study the photograph of Ibiza town in figure 21.18, then do the following:
   (a) Contrast the buildings in the foreground and middleground with those in the background.
   (b) What attractions does Ibiza town offer tourists?
   (c) What effects has mass tourism had on Ibiza town?

TOURISM

Fig 21.17

Fig 21.18

Dear Helen, Here we are in the middle of things, having a great time. We feel we are really getting to know this exotic country.

3 Examine the cartoon in figure 21.19, then do the following:
(a) Describe the buildings in the cartoon.
(b) Who are using up most resources, the tourists or the local people?
(c) How does the cartoonist view tourism and tourists?
(d) Do you agree or disagree with the cartoonist's view? Explain.

Fig 21.19

301

THE GEOGRAPHER'S WAY 2

REVISION

Rewrite the following text into your copy filling in the blank spaces using words from the box

> stalactite   karst landscape   National Park
> all weather tourist attraction   re-emerging rivers
> Office of Public Works   swallow hole   stalagmite
> caves   heritage

Our _____ is the buildings, language, literature, music and dance which survive from the past. A bare upland limestone landscape criss-crossed with grykes is a _____ _____. A hole in a limestone area down which a river disappears is a _____ _____. _____ develop where underground streams erode weaker rock. An icicle-like deposit of limestone hanging from the roof of a cave is a _____. A similar deposit which grows up from the floor is a _____. Rivers which appear at the surface having flowed underground are called _____ _____.
The state body charged with conserving Ireland's heritage is the _____ _____ _____ _____. A _____ _____ is an area of ecological importance under the control of the OPW. A tourist facility which can be used in any type of weather is called an _____ _____ _____ _____.

22 Inequality

IN THIS CHAPTER YOU WILL LEARN

- Local inequality in the inner city.
- Regional inequality in Ireland.
- National inequality in the European Union.
- The European Union Structural funds.
- Global inequality.

Resources, wealth, economic activity and opportunities for improvement are not spread equally among people or around the world. This lack of equality is known as **inequality**. This chapter deals with aspects of inequality at local, national and international levels.

LOCAL INEQUALITY: THE INNER CITY

The **inner city** is located in the transition zone on the edge of the CBD. It usually has a mixture of land uses including offices, small industries and houses. It is often a run-down, deprived area with old housing and many flats. There is little open space and recreational facilities for children and teenagers are few. Unemployment is high, so poverty is common. Social problems include ill-health and crime.

ACTIVITY 1

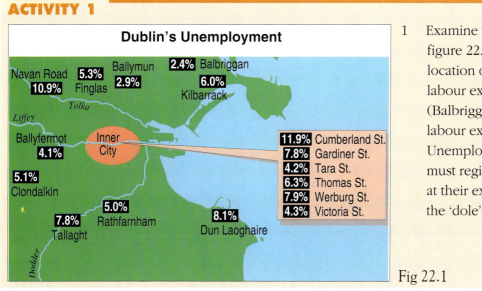

1. Examine the map in figure 22.1. It shows the location of Dublin's labour exchanges. (Balbriggan is a Dublin labour exchange.) Unemployed people must register each week at their exchange to get the 'dole'.

Fig 22.1

The map also shows the percentage of Dublin's unemployed who register at each exchange.

    (a) How many labour exchanges are there in Dublin?
    (b) What percentage of Dublin's unemployed register at the following labour exchanges: Finglas, Dun Laoghaire, Navan Road, Tara Street?
    (c) Which labour exchange has the largest percentage of Dublin's unemployed?
    (d) List the labour exchanges in the inner city. Calculate the total percentage of unemployed people which registers at them.
    (e) Write a paragraph about the distribution of unemployment in Dublin.

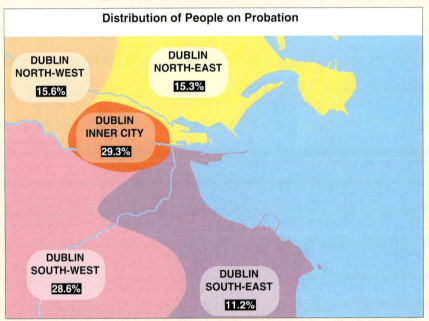

Fig 22.2

2   The map in figure 22.2 shows the percentage of people on probation in each of the five Dublin regions. People who have committed a crime may be put on probation rather than sent to prison. Examine the map carefully then do the following:

    (a) Name the regions shown on the map.
    (b) Rank the regions in order of the percentage of people they have on probation.

The maps in figures 22.1 and 22.2 show that there is great inequality even in a fairly small area. Figure 22.1 shows that over 40% of Dublin's unemployed register at exchanges in the inner city. Some of these people may live outside the inner city but the great majority don't. Unemployment is low in the wealthier suburbs to the south-east and north-east. Figure 22.2 shows that nearly 30% of all Dublin people on

INEQUALITY

probation are from the inner city. Only 15.3% and 11.2% of those on probation live in the suburbs of the south-east and north-east.

The planners in Local Government tackled the problem of inequality in a number of ways. The first was to develop the new towns mentioned already: Tallaght, Clondalkin, Lucan and Blanchardstown. These provided good housing and better facilities for people who were moved out from the inner city. Unfortunately sufficient jobs to end unemployment and poverty could not be provided. This meant that the social problems of the inner city were transferred to the new towns. The maps in figures 22.1 and 22.2 show that the new towns of Tallaght, Clondalkin and Blanchardstown (shown as the Navan Road) have nearly one quarter of Dublin's jobless and nearly one third of its crime. These figures are similar to the figures for the inner city.

The second way the planners tackled the problem was through urban renewal. **Urban renewal** means bringing new life to an old urban area by replacing old buildings and providing pleasant open spaces and playgrounds for children. It also means ensuring that there are jobs in the area to provide people with a livelihood.

Fig 22.3

Fig 22.4

The Liberties is an area of Dublin's inner city. It is going through the process of urban renewal at present. Many old houses and flats have been knocked down and replaced by houses like the ones shown in figure 22.3. The new housing is well-designed and built to a high standard. Open areas and small parks have been included, as well as small industrial estates like that shown in figure 22.4. Urban renewal has improved the living standards of the people of the Liberties and their environment. Just as important, the community spirit of the area which has developed over generations has not been destroyed by scattering people to the new towns. But the problem of high unemployment remains. Until this is ended it is unlikely that all the social problems affecting the people in this part of inner Dublin will be solved.

Statistics show that the likelihood of being employed or unemployed is closely linked to a person's level of education. The better the education a person has, the less likely they are to be unemployed. So, to improve people's chances of employment more money must be spent on education in the inner city. This means providing better schools, equipment and more teachers to overcome the disadvantages poverty causes. It also means helping students to continue their education by making sure it does not put a financial strain on their family.

Local community groups often play an important part in urban renewal. They know the needs of their areas and can act to see that they are met. Well-organised groups with clear demands can put pressure on the authorities to provide the resources for improvement.

ACTIVITY 2

1. Describe the social problems of people who live in inner city areas using statistics from figures 22.1 and 22.2.
2. Describe two solutions to the 'inner-city problem' tried by Dublin Corporation. Compare and contrast them. Which do you think is better? Explain your answer.
3. What part can improved facilities for education play in the development of the inner city?

INEQUALITY AT REGIONAL LEVEL

Inequality exists on different levels. There is the inequality which exists between countries. There are rich countries and poor ones. Within countries there are rich regions and poor regions. The name **regional dualism** is given to the situation where a wealthy region exists alongside a much poorer one. **Dualism** means that there are two different kinds of something together, in this case wealth and poverty.

Inequality exists in Ireland at a regional level. We can study this kind of inequality by examining our eight planning regions. The map in figure 22.5 shows these regions and the table in figure 22.6 gives statistics for them. Study the map carefully and identify the counties in each region using an atlas. Then examine the statistics making sure you know what each set of figures refers to. Activity 3 will help you do this.

Fig 22.5

INEQUALITY

	1990	1990	1981-90	1990	1990	1990	1990
	Population			Unemployed	Industry		
	in 1000's	Inhab./km²	Change (%)	%	%Agricult	%Manufacture	%Services
East	1330	190	3.2	16.0	4	27	69
South-West	534	44	1.7	15.1	19	27	54
South-East	382	41	2.1	15.8	23	31	46
North-East	198	50	2.6	16.5	18	36	46
Mid-West	308	39	0.0	14.4	23	29	48
Midlands	259	29	1.2	14.9	26	31	43
West	286	25	0.0	12.3	27	25	48
North-West & Donegal	207	25	–0.4	21.4	21	31	48

Fig 22.6

ACTIVITY 3

1. (a) List the counties in each planning region.
   (b) Name the planning regions each of the following cities is in: Cork, Galway, Waterford and Dublin.
2. Which planning region is the most densely populated and which are the least densely populated regions?
3. How many regions have a population density less than the average national density of 51 people per km²?
4. Which region had a population decrease between 1981 and 1990?
5. What percentage of the labour force is unemployed in the North-west and Donegal region?
6. Which region has the lowest level of unemployment? Suggest reasons why this is so.
7. Name the regions with more than a quarter of their workers employed in agriculture.
8. What type of economic activity is the most important employer of people in all the regions?

The eastern region is obviously very different from the other regions. It is the most populous with 1.33 million people. At 190 per km² the population density is nearly four times the density of the next most densely populated region, the North-east which has a density of 50 per km². The eastern region also has the most rapidly growing population; its population grew by 3.2% between 1981 and 1990. The population of the North-west and Donegal has opposite characteristics to those of the

Dublin region. It has a small population of 207,000 and a population density of only 25 people per km². Its population decreased by 0.4% between 1981 and 1990.

The economy of the eastern region is also quite different to the other regions. In the eastern region only 4% of the labour force is employed in agriculture and 69% have jobs in the service sector. In all other regions agriculture is a much more important employer usually accounting for around 20% of jobs. The service sector employs between 43% and 54% in the other regions; this is much less than in the eastern region. Manufacturing gives jobs to about 30% in all regions.

These figures show that the East is the most populous and economically developed region in Ireland. It has over one third of the population and it has many of the jobs and services which people want. These are strong pull factors which attract migrants from the other regions. Migration into Dublin is part of the reason for its growth in population.

NATIONAL INEQUALITY: EUROPEAN UNION HELP

Inequality in the European Union Inequality exists on a number of levels within the EU. Firstly, there is the inequality between countries. Secondly, within EU countries there are rich regions and poor regions. To decide which countries and regions are wealthy and which are poor, the EU uses the Gross Domestic Product.

The **Gross Domestic Product (GDP)** is the total amount of wealth produced in a country in a given period of time usually a year. This is used as a measure of the wealth of a country. It is often stated as a 'per head' (or 'per capita') figure, that is the figure for each person in the population. The 'per head' figure is calculated by dividing the total wealth produced by the number of people in the country. The EU considers that a country with a Gross Domestic Product (GDP) per head of less than 75% of the average in the EU is badly off and should be given most help. The regions with GDP's less than 75% of the EU average are called '**Objective 1 regions**'. The map in figure 22.7 shows the GDP per head. In this case the GDP of each region is stated as a percentage of the EU's average GDP, i.e. where it lies above or below 100% of the European average.

INEQUALITY

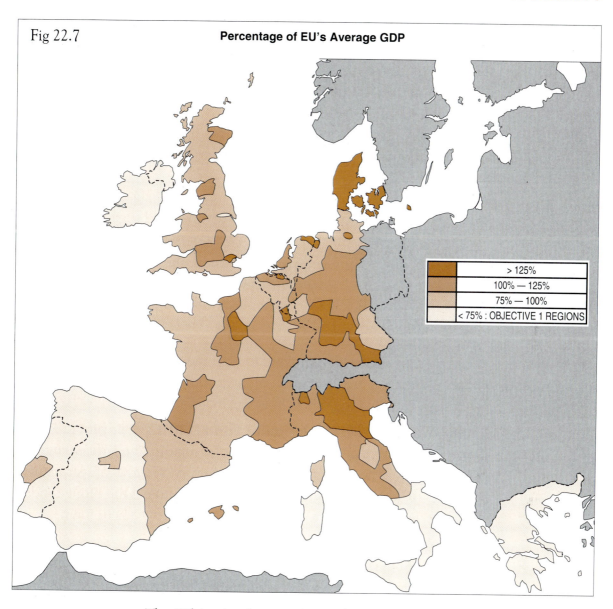

Fig 22.7 Percentage of EU's Average GDP

Legend:
- > 125%
- 100% — 125%
- 75% — 100%
- < 75% : OBJECTIVE 1 REGIONS

The 'Objective 1 countries and regions' are the poorest and least developed in the EU. They include all of Ireland, Greece, Portugal, Northern Ireland, and large parts of Spain and Southern Italy. Notice how these areas are on the periphery of the EU. They are the least accessible parts and so are not very attractive locations for manufacturing industries as they are far from markets. Agriculture plays a more important part in creating the wealth of the 'Objective 1 countries and regions' than it does in the wealthier developed areas. They have high unemployment levels and there are fewer job opportunities outside farming. Large towns are few and the range of services available is smaller than in the wealthier regions and countries.

ACTIVITY 4

1. What are 'Objective 1 regions'?
2. How do they differ from the other regions?
3. Name the countries which have all their regions classed as 'Objective 1 regions'.
4. Name the countries which have some of their regions classed as 'Objective 1 regions'.
5. Name five countries which have no 'Objective 1 regions'.
6. Which of the following statements best describes the distribution of 'Objective 1 regions' in the EU?
    (a) The 'Objective 1 regions' are all in the South and South-west of Europe.
    (b) The 'Objective 1 regions' are all located in the core of the EU.
    (c) The 'Objective 1 regions' are all located on the periphery of the EU.
    (d) The 'Objective 1 regions' are located in the North and East of the EU.

The Structural Funds

The European Union is committed to help the poorer regions of its member countries. Ireland is one of the poorer regions and so is helped by the EU. The EU provides help to Ireland in three ways.

European Regional Development Fund (ERDF) This provides money for improving the infrastructure of a region. The **infrastructure** is the network of services provided in a country. A good infrastructure is necessary to attract industries to an area. Four-fifths of the ERDF funds are spent on the 'Objective 1 countries and regions' to help them develop and make them attractive to investors.

European Social Fund (ESF) This fund was set up to help workers improve their skills and develop new ones. ESF provides funds for the education and re-education of workers. FÁS the body responsible for the training of workers in Ireland receives funds from the ESF. Schools doing the Transition Year get ESF funds to support the programme.

The Guidance Section of the CAP The **CAP** is the Common Agricultural Policy of the European Union which organises farming in the EU. The Guidance Section provides money for the improvement of agriculture.

The ERDF, ESF and Guidance Section Funds together are called the **Structural Funds**. Ireland receives large amounts of these funds. Between 1989 and 1993 this country received £3.3 billion from the Structural Fund. The map in figure 22.8 shows the amount of structural

INEQUALITY

funds per head spent in each region. Note how the regions used for structural funds are slightly different from the planning regions shown on page 306.

ACTIVITY 5

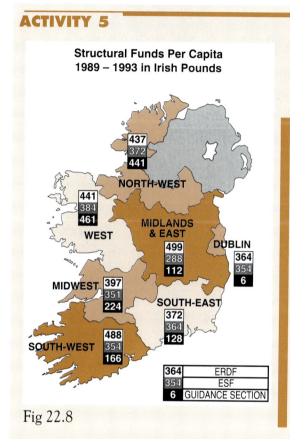

Fig 22.8

Examine the map in figure 22.8 then do the following.

1. Explain the terms ERDF, ESF, Guidance Section, Structural Funds.
2. What was the EU trying to achieve through providing structural funds?
3. Work out the total structural funds per head received by each region between 1989 and 1993.
4. Rank the regions in order of the amount of structural funds they received per head. The region receiving the greatest amount is ranked No.1.
5. What percentage of total structural funds was provided by each of the following between 1989 - 1993: ERDF, ESF and Guidance?
6. Find out if there is an EU funded project in your area? If there is, describe it, and explain the effects it will have on your area.

INEQUALITY AT A GLOBAL LEVEL

Inequality exists at a global level. This inequality is often illustrated by comparing statistics for Gross National Product (GNP) per head. **Gross National Product (GNP)** is the total amount of wealth produced inside and outside a country by its economic activities. Economic activity can create wealth outside a country by exporting goods or by having branches in other countries. GNP gives an idea of how wealthy or poor a county is. The map in figure 22.9 shows the distribution of different levels of GNP per head in the world.

THE GEOGRAPHER'S WAY 2

Fig 22.9

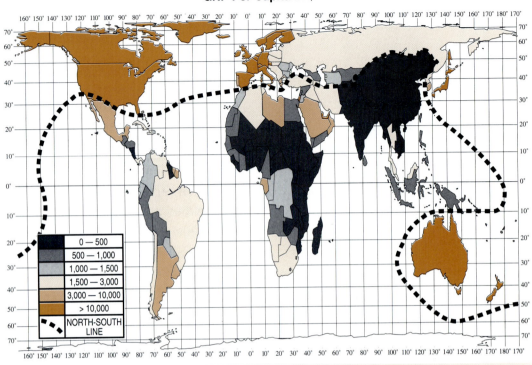

GNP Per Capita in $

ACTIVITY 6

Study the map in figure 22.9, then with the help of an atlas do the following:

1. Match the letters in column X with the numbers of their pairs in column Y.

X		Y	
A	Brazil	1	$10,000
B	Mali	2	$0-$500
C	Saudi Arabia	3	$1,500-$3,000
D	Indonesia	4	$1,000-$1,500
E	Turkmenistan	5	$3,000-$10,000
F	Ireland	6	$500-$1,000

A	
B	
C	
D	
E	
F	

2. At which level of GNP are each of the following countries?

   Argentina   Somalia   Mexico   India   Zaire
   Australia   USA   S. Africa   South Korea   Egypt

3. Which of the following statements are true? Tick the box.   T
   (a) The majority of the poorest countries are in South America. ☐
   (b) Asia is a very rich continent. ☐
   (c) The majority of rich countries lie between 30°N and 70°N. ☐
   (d) The southern hemisphere is much poorer than the northern one. ☐
   (e) The continents with the greatest ranges of GNP per head are Europe and North America. ☐

4. Write a description of the distribution of GNP per head in the world.

The map in figure 22.9 shows clearly the inequality in wealth around the world. Africa and Asia have the majority of poorer countries whereas Europe and North America have the majority of richer ones. Most South American countries are in the middle income group. The black dotted line on the map divides the richer parts of the world from the poorer parts. It is called the **North/South line**. The **North** includes the First World and Second World taken together. It is the richer area and includes North America, Europe, the CIS and Japan. The **South** consists of the poorer countries and includes South America, Africa and most of Southern and Eastern Asia. Australia and New Zealand are taken as part of the North because they are wealthy.

GNP figures give a good idea of the wealth of a country but they can be misleading because they are average figures. They may hide important facts. A high GNP figure may hide that wealth is unevenly spread. There may be a few very wealthy people and many poor people. To get a more complete view of the standard of life in a country we examine other important statistics such as the life expectancy, the infant mortality rate, the daily calorie intake, the percentage of the population living in urban areas and the number of daily newspapers bought per 100 of the population.

Life expectancy   This is the average number of years a new born baby can be expected to live. This is a good indicator of the wealth, standard of living and health care in a country. Life expectancy is low in poor areas and high in wealthy ones.

Infant mortality rate   This is the number of children who die in the first year of life. It is usually stated in terms of 'per thousand children born'. This is usually a good indicator of the standard of living in a country. If the standard of living is high, the infant mortality rate will be low as infants are well-fed and get good health care. This allows them to have a good chance of surviving their first year which is the riskiest. The opposite applies in poor countries.

Daily calorie intake   This is the average amount of calories consumed by each person per day. A **calorie** is a unit of measurement of energy which is applied to food. The **daily calorie requirement** of an average adult is 2400 calories. If a person gets much below this level of calories they are considered **undernourished**.

THE GEOGRAPHER'S WAY 2

Urban population as a % of total population This is often a good indicator of economic development because as development progresses the population becomes more urbanised.

Number of daily newspapers per 100 people This is a good indicator as it indicates that people's level of education is high if a large number of papers are bought. It also shows whether people have spare cash to buy newspapers.

ACTIVITY 8

Country	GNP per head in $	Life Expectancy	Infant Mortality	Daily Calorie Supply	% urban population	Daily newspapers per 100 people
Switzerland	36080	78	7	3565	63	46
United States	23240	77	8	3676	76	25
United Kingdom	17790	76	8	3181	89	40
Ireland	12210	75	8	3779	58	17
Saudi Arabia	7510	69	58	2930	78	4
Greece	7290	77	13	3793	64	14
Brazil	2770	66	57	2722	77	5
South Africa	2670	63	62	3104	50	4
Iran	2200	65	40	3300	58	3
Romania	1130	70	19	3252	55	NA
Indonesia	670	60	65	2708	32	2.8
China	470	69	27	2634	27	4.2
India	310	61	88	2196	26	3
Rwanda	250	46	112	1945	6	NA
Ethiopia	110	49	122	1750	13	0.1

Fig 22.10

The table in figure 20.10 gives the statistics mentioned above for a number of countries. Examine it, paying close attention to the heading on each column. When reading a table like this, it helps to lay a sheet of paper across it in line with the country you are studying at the time. Do the following:

1. (a) What is the difference in dollars between Ireland's GNP and Ethiopia's?
   (b) What is the range of GNP in dollars between the poorest and richest country on the table?
   (c) Approximately how many times is Switzerland more wealthy than Ireland?
   (d) What is the difference in life expectancy between Rwanda and Switzerland?
   (e) Name the countries where the infant mortality rate is greater than 50 per 1000.

(f) Name the countries where the daily calorie intake is less than the daily calorie requirement.
(g) Name the countries where less than 5 newspapers are bought per 100 people each day.
(h) Which is the most urbanised country in the table?
(i) Which is the least urbanised country?
(j) Which country with a GNP less than $3000 has a very high percentage of its people living in towns?

2   Contrast Ireland with Switzerland, China and Rwanda under the headings given in the table.
3   What do the statistics for Saudi Arabia tell us about the development of that country?

The table in figure 22.10 shows that the poorest countries have the worst standard of living. In Ethiopia life expectancy is low at 49 years, infant mortality is extremely high at 122 per thousand. These figures show that death rates are high both for babies and adults. The opposite is true in Switzerland which is very rich with a GNP per head of $36,080. It has a very high life expectancy at 78 years and a very low infant mortality rate of 7 per 1000 births. All of the statistics confirm that Ethiopia is a very poor country and Switzerland is a rich one.

In the middle of the table there are some statistics which illustrate how misleading GNP figures can be. China has a very low GNP per head of $470 but its infant mortality rate of 27 per 1000 is much lower than many countries which have higher GNPs per head including Indonesia, Iran, South Africa, Brazil and Saudi Arabia. This shows that China has a good health-care system and mothers and infants are well-nourished. Saudi Arabia has a fairly high GNP per head of $7510 but it has a high infant mortality rate of 58. This is much higher than many poorer countries including Greece, Iran, Romania and China. The number of papers bought is also very low at 4 per 100 people. These figures suggest that the standards of living and education in Saudi Arabia are not as high as you would believe by looking only at the GNP figure. The reason is that Saudi Arabia has become rich only in the last twenty years. It takes time to build education and health care systems.

THE GEOGRAPHER'S WAY 2

ACTIVITY 9

Annual marathon!
Are you kidding —
These folks are answering a newspaper ad
— for a job!

The cartoons in figure 22.11 show three different types of inequality.
1 Identify the type of inequality in each case.
2 Describe how the cartoonist conveys the message in each case.
3 Which cartoon do you think gets its message across most effectively?

Fig 22.11

REVISION

INEQUALITY

Rewrite the following text into your copy using the words in the box to fill in the blank spaces.

> daily calorie requirement   infrastructure   inner city
> South   Guidance Section   infant mortality rate
> Gross Domestic Product   undernourished   North
> urban renewal   life expectancy   calorie   inequality
> 'Objective 1 regions'   North/South line   Structural Funds
> European Social Fund   daily calorie intake   regional dualism
> European Regional Development Fund

The absence of equality is _____. The _____ _____ is a deprived area close to the centre of a city. Tearing down old houses and buildings in urban areas and replacing them with modern housing and facilities is called _____ _____. _____ _____ exists when there is great inequality between regions. The EU set up the _____ _____ _____ _____ to help improve the _____ of disadvantaged regions of the EU. The EU set up the _____ _____ _____ to improve the skills of workers and to retrain them. The _____ _____ was set up to improve agriculture within the EU. The combined name for the funds set up to improve the poor regions is the _____ _____. The amount of wealth produced in a country in a year is the _____ _____ _____ . The regions with GDP of less than 75% of the EU average GDP are called _____ _____ _____ . The _____ includes the First and Second worlds. The ———— is the Third World. The line dividing wealthy regions of the world from the poorer regions is called the _____ _____ _____. The number of years a new born baby can expect to live is the _____ _____. The _____ _____ _____ is the number of new born babies which die per thousand of those born. The unit of measurement used to measure the amount of energy in foods is a _____. The amount of food we consume per day is measured as our _____ _____ _____. The amount of food on average adult needs in a day is the _____ _____ _____. If you get less food than the minimum you need you are _____.

317

23 Inequality and Development 1

IN THIS CHAPTER YOU WILL LEARN

- Economic development. Differing rates of development.
- How to use pie-charts.
- Historical forces in development: Colonialism and Plantations.
- Brazil's economic development: 'Boom and Bust', 'Economic Miracle'.
- Sao Paulo, a city of the South.

In underdeveloped economies wealth is mainly created through primary activity. Farming and fishing are the wealth creators. Forestry and mining, if they exist, are limited to extractive work. Their products, timber and ore, are usually shipped abroad without processing. **Economic development** begins with the introduction of manufacturing and service activities. As development progresses these become more important, gradually replacing primary activities as the main source of wealth. Industrialisation is closely linked to economic development, bringing many changes. Economic activity becomes organised with banking, insurance and trading companies. Transport systems are improved. Development makes people change where they live and alters lifestyles. More people live in towns and wealth increases.

The economically **developed countries** are the First World industrialised ones. The **rapidly developing countries** are the NICs and emerging industrial countries. The **slowly developing countries** are those which are least industrialised.

The proportion of a country's labour force employed in the economic sectors, primary, secondary and tertiary is called the **economic structure** of the country. The economic structure can tell the stage of development that a country has reached. It can also indicate how quickly development is happening. Developed economies have a large tertiary sector, usually greater than 60%, a secondary sector of about 30% and a primary sector which is less than 10%. The slowly developing economy has a very large primary sector and small secondary and tertiary sectors. Countries with rapidly developing economies have economic structures which lie between these two extremes.

Pie-charts A pie-chart is often used to illustrate economic structure. A pie-chart is a circle divided into segments. The circle represents 100% and the segments represent the percentages of the parts which together make up the 100%. Study a pie-chart in the following way:
- Note the title.
- Find the percentage of each segment. This is usually stated. If it is not, you can estimate it. A quarter circle represents 25%, a half represents 50% and so on. To be more accurate, work out the percentage by finding the number of degrees in the segment using a protractor, then divide the result by 3·6. This gives the exact percentage.
- Check by adding the percentages. They should total 100%.

ACTIVITY 1

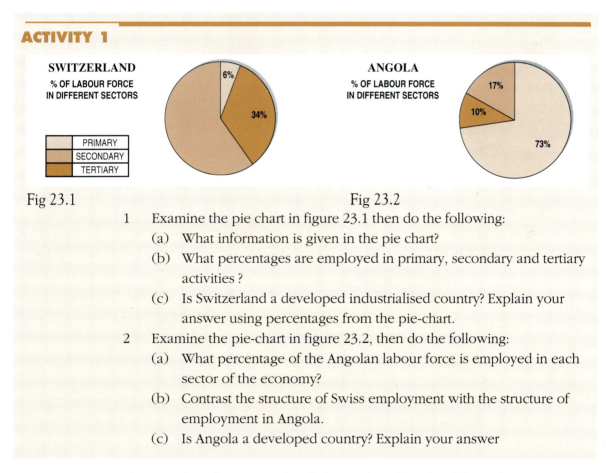

Fig 23.1 Fig 23.2

1. Examine the pie chart in figure 23.1 then do the following:
   (a) What information is given in the pie chart?
   (b) What percentages are employed in primary, secondary and tertiary activities?
   (c) Is Switzerland a developed industrialised country? Explain your answer using percentages from the pie-chart.
2. Examine the pie-chart in figure 23.2, then do the following:
   (a) What percentage of the Angolan labour force is employed in each sector of the economy?
   (b) Contrast the structure of Swiss employment with the structure of employment in Angola.
   (c) Is Angola a developed country? Explain your answer

The pie chart for Switzerland shows that 6% of its labour force is in primary industry, 34% in manufacturing and 60% in services. These figures indicate that Switzerland has a developed economy. The primary sector is very small. With 34% in manufacturing Switzerland fits the developed pattern. The large service sector also indicates economic development. People in developed countries use more services, for example education, health care, entertainment and transport etc.

The pie-chart in figure 23.2 representing Angola's work force shows a different type of economy. Primary activity employs 73%, 10% are in manufacturing and 17% in service activities. Such a large percentage in the primary sector shows that it is not an industrialised country but a slowly developing one.

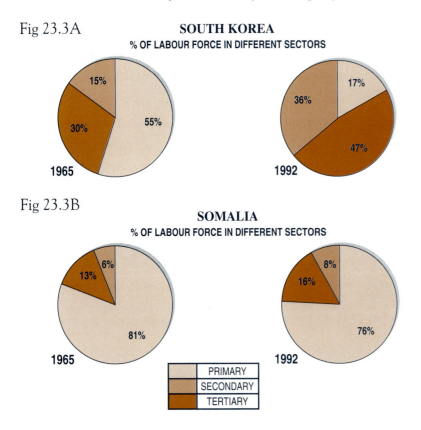

Fig 23.3A SOUTH KOREA % OF LABOUR FORCE IN DIFFERENT SECTORS

Fig 23.3B SOMALIA % OF LABOUR FORCE IN DIFFERENT SECTORS

The rate of economic development may be quick or slow. Comparison of the pie charts in figure 23.3 shows how the changes in the economic structures of Korea and Somalia differed in the period between 1965 and 1992. Refer to them as you read on. In 1965 55% of the South Korean labour force were in primary activities; by 1992 this sector had dropped to 17% a decrease of over two-thirds. In the same period employment in manufacturing more than doubled from 15% to 36%. Employment in services also increased from 30% to 47%. These changes show that South Korea industrialised rapidly, so it is considered a quickly developing country. Figure 23.3 B shows that Somalia's economy changed little during these years. In 1965 81% of the Somali labour force were employed in primary activities and this dropped by only about 5% in 27 years. Employment in manufacturing increased by 2% and service employment by 3%; these are very small increases. The Somali economy industrialised only slightly over the period so it is considered a slowly-developing economy.

INEQUALITY AND DEVELOPMENT 1

ACTIVITY 2

Examine the statistics in the table in figure 23.4, then using an atlas do the following:

EMPLOYMENT BY SECTOR 1965 - 1992

COUNTRY	PRIMARY 1965 %	PRIMARY 1992 %	SECONDARY 1965 %	SECONDARY 1992 %	TERTIARY 1965 %	TERTIARY 1992 %
Afghanistan	69	61	11	14	20	25
Brazil	49	25	20	27	31	48
Rwanda	95	90	2	2	3	8
Malaysia	58	26	13	28	29	46
Egypt	55	42	15	21	30	37
Tanzania	91	85	3	5	6	10

Fig 23.4

1. (a) In which continent is each of the countries located?
   (b) Which country showed the most rapid decrease in primary sector employment?
   (c) Which country showed no increase in manufacturing employment? Which country showed the slowest increase?
2. Which countries are quickly developing ones? Give reasons for your answer.
3. Which countries are slowly developing? Give reasons for your answer.

VARIATIONS IN ECONOMIC DEVELOPMENT

There are many reasons why some countries developed quickly and others slowly. We will study four of these:
- Colonies and Colonialism
- Plantation Economies
- International Trade
- Government Policy

COLONIES AND COLONIALISM

Throughout history powerful states have conquered weaker ones to exploit them. The powerful state takes over a weaker one and settles armed colonists there to control it. Transport networks are created to facilitate the extraction and shipment of resources to the **homeland**. The wealth of the conquered territory is systematically exploited for the benefit of the homeland and the colony becomes a market for exports from the homeland. This process is called **colonialism**; the conquered country becomes a **colony**. The colony is created to serve the interests of the homeland and is prevented from competing with it. Along with many African, Asian and South American countries, Ireland underwent colonialism. After the Tudor conquest it became an English colony.

Ireland – a colonial example You already know how the plantations in 16th and 17th century Ireland caused great changes in population and urban settlement. The results of these are still with us today. Colonial economic laws were also imposed which affected the development of the Irish economy for centuries. 'Penal laws' were passed which restricted the rights of Catholics and others to own land, organise education, live in towns and take part in politics. Other laws controlled Irish manufacturing so that it couldn't compete with English industry. At the time when English manufacturing was developing at the start of the Industrial Revolution, Ireland was forced to remain a producer of primary products for the English market. It supplied cheap food and was obliged to buy the manufactured goods it needed from Britain. Only in one important sector was industry allowed to prosper. There was an important linen industry in Ireland and as England was not a linen producer, the Irish industry was not considered a threat. So it was allowed to prosper. By these laws English colonial policy held back the development of the Irish economy making it almost entirely dependent on Britain. In 1921 when Ireland became independent, 98% of Irish exports went to Britain and 78% of Irish imports came from there. Today Britain is still our main trading partner but the balance has changed greatly: only 29% of Irish exports go to Britain and 38% of imports come from there.

ACTIVITY 3

1. (a) What is colonialism?
   (b) What steps were usually involved in colonising an area?
2. Examine the cartoon strip in figure 23.5, then answer the following questions.
   (a) Who do the people in the cartoon represent?
   (b) What is the message of this cartoon strip?
   (c) Could this cartoon represent Ireland's experience of colonialism? Explain your answer
3. Explain how colonialism affected Ireland.

INEQUALITY AND DEVELOPMENT 1

Fig 23.5

PLANTATION ECONOMIES - COFFEE

Coffee is a good example of how a valuable crop grown in one country is exploited largely for the benefit of another. Instead of the profits staying in the country where the crop was grown, they are sent abroad. This drains the wealth of a country and slows its economic development.

Coffee is a tropical crop. It was first cultivated in Ethiopia and Arabia. Introduced into Europe in the 17th century it became extremely popular. In the 19th century coffee 'plantations' were started to grow coffee for sale in Europe and North America. The name **plantation** is given to a large farm, usually in the tropics, which specialises in the production of a cash-crop such as coffee, cotton or tea. The coffee plantations were mainly in Third World countries but were owned by Europeans so most of the profits returned to Europe.

The coffee bean is the stone of a cherry-like fruit which grows on the coffee bush. The beans are extracted from the fruit, dried, sorted and packed in the growing countries. They are then shipped to the developed countries where they are processed and packed for sale as beans, ground coffee or 'instant coffee'. It is estimated that less than 20% of the price of coffee goes to the country that grew it; the rest is kept by processors and traders in the First World.

Why don't the coffee producers process the coffee to keep the profits where the crop is grown? Third World countries find it difficult to sell the processed product because the developed countries put high import taxes on processed imports. This makes processed coffee from the Third World uncompetitive. So the Third World countries remain producers of cheap coffee beans while others sell the processed coffee expensively.

323

THE GEOGRAPHER'S WAY 2

ACTIVITY 4

Coffee Producing Countries

PRODUCERS	1000'S of Bags	all exports % of value
Costa Rica	2680	22
Ethiopia	3000	70
Madagascar	1000	22
Brazil	28000	5
El Salvador	2500	40
Zaire	1640	10
Colombia	14500	28
Uganda	3000	96
Kenya	1600	23

Fig 23.6

Examine the table in figure 23.6. Then do the following:

1. Using an atlas, locate each country in the table in Figure 23.6. State in which continent each is located.
2. Rank the countries in order of the amount of coffee they produce. Number 1 is the country which produces most.
3. Rank the countries in order of the contribution coffee makes to the value of total exports. The country where the contribution is highest is ranked No.1.
4. Compare the importance of coffee experts to the economies of Brazil and Uganda.

Contrasts in Coffee Brazil is the largest coffee grower in the world, producing 33% of world supply. All the African countries together produce only 20% of world output. Frosts destroyed much of the 1994 crop in Brazil. This will cause a sharp drop in export earnings for Brazil, showing how vulnerable a country can be which depends on agricultural exports. But coffee nowadays represents only 5% of Brazil's total exports, so its economy will not be too hard hit. But the failure will cause price changes on world markets. Because it is so large a producer the Brazilian shortage will force up coffee prices. Other producers like Uganda will benefit from this for one year but if the Brazilian crop is better next year, then prices will fall again.

Fluctuating prices make it difficult to plan development. Uganda grows 3,000,000 bags of coffee ranking third in the world. It depends almost entirely on coffee for its export earnings, so coffee is very important to the economy. As its production is only about 10% of Brazilian output, it has little say in setting world prices. Like most

INEQUALITY AND DEVELOPMENT 1

slowly developing countries Uganda has to import manufactured goods such as medicines and fuels which are essential. With the rise and fall of coffee prices, there is great uncertainty about what imports Uganda can afford. Until the recent frosts in Brazil, the world price of coffee has been falling so Uganda has been unable to afford its needs. In this way international trade in coffee hinders progress in Uganda by contributing to its poverty. The rise in coffee prices due to the crop failure in Brazil will only help Uganda for a year or two.

Income from export sales is important for economic development. The NIC's are proof of this. Their rapid industrialisation has been based on growing export sales. Income from exports provides money for investment and further growth. The majority of Third World countries like Uganda earn little from exports and so are starved of the money needed for economic development. Uncertainty in world prices makes matters worse. If the profits from plantation crops are also sent abroad, then there is little hope of economic development left.

ACTIVITY 5

Fig 23.7

Examine the cartoon in figure 23.7 then do the following:
1. Which group represents the North? Explain your choice.
2. Why are the two groups of people sitting at a table?
3. What do the + and − signs, and flashes of lightning mean?
4. Explain how this cartoon represents what is happening in the coffee industry.

INTERNATIONAL TRADE

During the 18th and 19th centuries Europeans started plantations in many Third World countries. Coffee was only one plantation crop. Others included sugar-cane, tea, cotton and rubber. The pattern of trade established then has continued to the present. The Third World countries sell cheap primary products, mainly raw materials, to the First World; the developed countries sell expensive manufactured goods back to them. This pattern of trade keeps Third World countries poor and First World countries rich.

THE GEOGRAPHER'S WAY 2

The map of the world in figure 23.8 shows the share of world exports for most trading countries. The countries are represented by rectangular shapes. The larger the shape the greater the percentage of world exports the country has. Germany has a much larger share of world exports than Brazil. Ireland has about the same percentage of exports as Brazil. The North has the largest share by far of world exports.

ACTIVITY 6

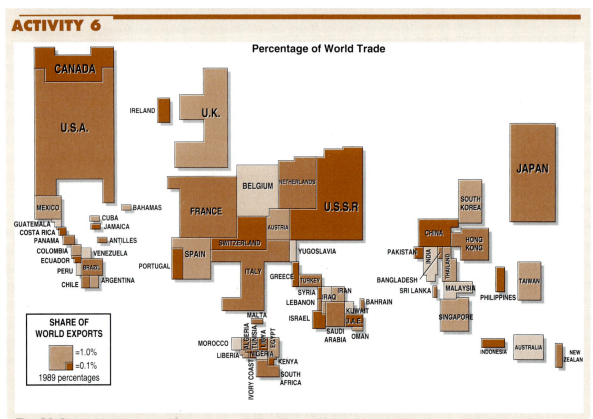

Fig 23.8

Examine the map in figure 23.8 then answer the following:
1. Which country has the largest percentage of world exports?
2. Which continent has the largest share of world exports?
3. Which continents have very small shares of world exports?
4. Does the size of Hong Kong's share of world exports surprise you? Explain.
5. Which of these statements best describes the distribution of world exports?
    (a) The Second and Third Worlds' share of exports together equal the First World's share.
    (b) The North and South have equal shares of world exports.
    (c) The North has the largest share by far of world exports.
    (d) The South has the largest share of the world exports.
6. Is the method used in this map to show world exports effective? Discuss.

INEQUALITY AND DEVELOPMENT 1

BRAZIL – BOOM AND BUST

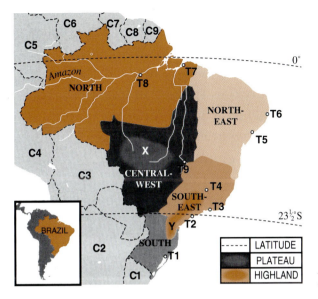

Brazil is the fifth largest country in the world. It is rich in natural resources with large reserves of wood, oil and minerals. It also has a large amount of fertile land. Brazil has developed very rapidly recently but many of its people are very poor despite its natural wealth. Before we examine this contradiction, study the map of Brazil in figure 23.9.

Fig 23.9

ACTIVITY 7

Examine the map, then find out the following using an atlas.
1. In which continent is Brazil located?
2. On which ocean does it lie?
3. Name the countries C1 – C9 which border Brazil.
4. Name the towns marked T1 – T9.
5. Name two important lines of latitude which pass through Brazil. What information about Brazil does this give you?
6. Name the plateau at X and the Highlands at Y.

South America was settled over 3,000 years ago by Indian tribes which migrated there from Asia coming through North America. Spanish and Portuguese explorers landed in South America at the end of the 15th century. They defeated the Indian peoples and took over the best land. The first Europeans to reach what is now Brazil were a Portuguese group led by Pedro Alvares Cabral. They landed in 1500 and settled in the North-East as this was closest to Portugal. A Portuguese colony was founded and this exploited the territory for its wealth and primary products. Many colonists became farmers; others gradually penetrated the vast interior over several centuries.

Sugar-cane plantations were started in the North-East as the first major colonial development. Slaves were imported from Africa to work on these. The sugar was sent to Europe for processing. Eventually competition from other South American producers caused the Brazilian sugar industry to collapse. Then the colonists moved to the Brazilian Highlands where there were deposits of gold and diamonds. This encouraged further immigration from Europe. When the surface deposits were exhausted the miners and prospectors left. Then in the late 19th century came the rubber boom. The rubber tree was the only known source of rubber and it only grew in the Amazon rainforest. The discovery of the pneumatic tyre for vehicles caused a huge demand for rubber and prices rocketed. The rubber industry 'boomed', centring on the city of Manaus deep in the Amazon rain forest. After a number of hectic years the boom ended when rubber tree seeds were smuggled to England. These were used to start rubber plantations in tropical British colonies like Malaya. Here rubber could be produced more cheaply. The Brazilian rubber industry could not compete so it collapsed.

After 1850 coffee growing became an important activity in South-East Brazil, especially in the state of Sao Paulo. Brazil soon became the world's largest producer, harvesting more coffee than all the other coffee-producing countries. But the price of coffee was uncertain and this became a serious problem as coffee increased to become Brazil's most important export. The financial uncertainty affected Brazil's economic development just as it does in Uganda today.

GOVERNMENT POLICY

This long history of 'boom and bust' left Brazil a slowly developing economy despite its natural riches. Then, in the 1960's economists suggested that the best way to develop a country was through industrialisation. They argued that this would create jobs, incomes would rise and wealth would trickle down to everybody even to the poorest. The Brazilian Government decided to follow this path to development. But it hadn't capital to invest in manufacturing so it had to attract foreign investment and borrow from rich countries with funds to lend. The policy of industrialisation was so successful it became known as the "Brazilian miracle". In 1950 only 14% of the labour force were employed in manufacturing. By 1992 the percentage employed in manufacturing had risen to 25%. Many foreign companies invested in Brazil including Shell, Volkswagen, Nestlé, IBM and Philips. Many Brazilians also started industries. The rapid industrialisation had a

INEQUALITY AND DEVELOPMENT 1

number of effects. The following figures show that the standard of living improved rapidly during the Brazilian Miracle.

- GDP per capita rose from $1406 in 1960 to $5202 in 1991.
- Life expectancy rose from 55 years in 1960 to 66 years in 1992.
- Adult literacy rose from 66% in 1970 to 82% in 1992.
- Infant mortality decreased from 116 per 1,000 in 1960 to 57 per 1000 in 1992.
- The percentage of the population living in urban areas increased from 45% in 1960 to 77% in 1992.

But when examining statistics you must take care. The figures are national averages and can mislead. They hide the fact that most of the industrialisation took place in the South-east region between the cities of Rio De Janeiro, Sao Paulo and Belo Horizonte. This is the core region and has 70% of the employment in manufacturing. Other regions are much less industrialised especially the peripheral regions in the north.

ACTIVITY 8

1. List the products for which Brazil was known between 1500 and 1900. Is there anything they have in common?
2. What was the Brazilian miracle and what were its effects on the Brazilian economy?
3. Study the pie chart in figure 23.10 then do the following:
   (a) Which region has the largest percentage of industrial employment?
   (b) Which region has the lowest percentage of industrial employment?
   (c) What is the total percentage of industrial employment in the North and North-East regions?
   (d) Which are the peripheral regions? Say why you chose these.

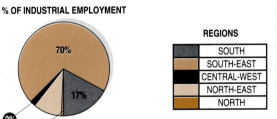

Fig 23.10

An economic miracle burdened with debt The industrialisation of Brazil has made the inequality between its regions greater. It has also left Brazil with an enormous national debt of $116 billion because much of the industrialisation was financed by loans from countries in the North. Paying off these debts and the interest on them is very difficult. Though more wealth is being created in Brazil, much of it leaves the country in the form of interest payments. Money has to be taken from other areas to pay off the debt. This slows down development in these important sectors. For example, less money is spent on education and health. This means that there will be fewer services for people especially the poor.

Most Third World countries have borrowed from First World countries to finance their needs. As a result they have large debt and interest repayments to make. These divert money from development projects and keep them poor. This problem is known as the **Burden of Debt**.

ACTIVITY 9

Examine the cartoon in figure 23.11 then answer the following:
1 What is the message in the cartoon?
2 Could this cartoon represent a Brazilian scene? Explain your answer.

Fig 23.11

SAO PAULO: A CITY OF THE SOUTH

Sao Paulo is Brazil's principal industrial city. At the heart of the coffee-growing region, it developed as its service centre. Manufacturing was begun in order to supply the needs of the coffee industry, and industrialisation continued slowly until the 1960's. Development speeded up when the government adopted the policy of rapid industrialisation. Industry was encouraged to come to Sao Paulo and it did. Today Sao Paulo's numerous manufacturing firms produce over half of Brazil's output of manufactured goods. Manufactured goods include motor vehicles, steel, textiles, shoes, pharmaceuticals and cement. Incomes in Sao Paulo are much higher than the national average.

The population of Sao Paulo has grown very rapidly due to the immigration of young people from the poorer parts of Brazil especially the North-East. The population was 600,000 in 1935. It increased to 4.5 million by 1960, and to 8.1 million in 1970. In 1991 it exceeded 16 million and is expected to reach 20 million by 2000. Such growth has had results which make it a very different city to those in developed countries. For instance, functional zones hardly exist in the way they do

INEQUALITY AND DEVELOPMENT 1

in First World cities. Other differences include:

1. First World cities do not experience such rapid growth.
2. The rapid growth rate makes planning difficult so there is much unplanned building especially of shanty towns called **favelas**.
3. The range of inequality is greater than in First World cities. Immigrants often arrive penniless after their journey to the city. Others who own or manage industries are very rich.
4. The inequality and the difficulty of planning such a rapidly growing city is reflected in the structure of the city. The favelas, which are residential areas, are mixed in with industrial zones because these are often the only places where there is unused land. Other favelas are located beside expensive housing or office blocks because there happened to be waste land there which the *favelados* could occupy. The favelados are the people who live in the favelas.
5. The favelas often don't have any proper infrastructure of roads, sewerage, water or electricity supply.

Fig 23.12 The photograph in figure 23.12 shows San Paulo. Examine it carefully. It illustrates clearly the sharp contrasts that exist in land use in San Paulo. In the foreground and right middleground there is a motorway with housing right next to it. There is a favela in the left and centre middleground. The poor quality of the dwellings is seen in the left foreground. The favela borders a zone of high-rise office and apartment blocks which are in stark contrast to it. Such contrasts between high

and low quality accomodation and living conditions are common in Third World cities.

Fig 23.13

The photograph in figure 23.13 shows housing in a favela. Notice the building materials. Dwellings in the favelas are built from any material available; it may be old boxes or tin drums which have been flattened. The dwellings rarely have a water supply or sanitation. The local authority may provide a stand pipe which people must go to for water. Sewage may be disposed of in pits. In such conditions disease spreads rapidly and infant mortality rates are high. As time passes a group of favelados may persuade the authorities to improve the infrastructure in their favela through community action. But this is a long and difficult process requiring great patience. But it can be successful.

Many Third World cities are growing rapidly like Sao Paulo and experiencing similar difficulties coping with this rapid growth. It is agreed by most that in the future the most pressing problem in the Third World will be urban inequality similar to that which is happening in Sao Paulo.

INEQUALITY AND DEVELOPMENT 1

ACTIVITY 10

Fig 23.14

1. Describe the growth of Sao Paulo.
2. How does Sao Paulo differ from First World cities?
3. Compare Sao Paulo with any other city you have studied.
4. Examine the cartoon in Figure 23.14 then answer the following:
   (a) Who are the men sitting around the table? Be specific.
   (b) What is the message in the cartoon?
   (c) What do the expressions on the men's faces tell you about their feelings on what has happened?

REVISION

Rewrite the following text into your copy using the words in the box to fill in the blank spaces.

burden of debt	rapidly developing	colony
economic structure	favela	economic development
plantation	developed countries	colonialism
	slowly developing	pie chart

_____ _____ begins with the introduction of manufacturing. The First World countries are also called the _____ _____. The NIC's and emerging industrial countries are the _____ _____ countries. The least industrialised countries are the _____ _____ countries. The _____ _____ of a country is the percentage of its labour force employed in primary, secondary and tertiary industries. A circle divided into segments each of which represents a percentage of the whole is a _____ _____. _____ was when stronger states conquered weaker ones and then exploited them. The conquered and exploited country was called a _____. A large farm producing one cash crop usually in the tropics was a _____. The _____ _____ is the strain put on the country by the loan and interest payments it has to make. A _____ is the name given to a shanty town in Brazil.

24 Inequality and Development 2

IN THIS CHAPTER YOU WILL LEARN

- Ethiopia: A case study of underdevelopment.
- Population, climate and war as factors in underdevelopment.
- The status of women in the developing world. Chinese case study.
- The role of aid. Irish Overseas Development Aid.
- Resolving inequality: a discussion.

So far you have learned how historical forces, the unfairness of international trade and national debt cause poverty and prevent development. Now we examine other factors which have the same result. These include population growth, climate, war and money spent on arms. We will make Ethiopia a case study as it has been seriously affected by these factors.

ETHIOPIA

Ethiopia is a big country, more than 17 times larger than Ireland. It is located in the Horn of Africa. The map in figure 24.1 shows its location.

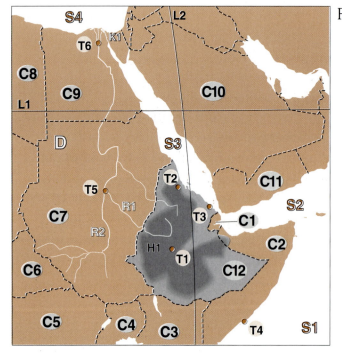

Fig 24.1

INEQUALITY AND DEVELOPMENT 2

ACTIVITY 1

Study the map in figure 24.1. With an atlas identify the following:
1. The countries marked C1 to C11.
2. The sea areas marked S1 to S4.
3. The rivers R1 and R2.
4. The towns T1 to T6.
5. The highland marked H1.
6. The line of latitude L1 and the line of longitude L2.
7. The canal marked K1.
8. The desert at D.

Ethiopia is one of the poorest, least developed, countries in the world. Its GNP per head is only $110. Farming employs 88% of the labour force. The standard of living is very low. Life expectancy is 49 years and infant mortality is 122 per 1000 births. The average daily calorie intake is 1750 calories which is well below the 2,400 calories required daily to keep people healthy.

Population In poor agricultural countries like Ethiopia people tend to have large families. This is because children are thought of as a benefit and not as a burden. There are no pension or health care programmes in poor countries so people depend on their family in time of need.
- Children provide labour and help on the farm.
- With high infant mortality rates people need to have a larger number of children to be sure that some survive.
- Children look after parents when they are old or sick.

Ethiopia has a population of 55 million with an annual growth rate of 3%. If this continues, the population will double in 20 years. Such a growth rate is happening because of a falling death rate and a continuing high birth rate. This rate of population increase will put a severe strain on resources just to keep people alive. There will be little to spare for development.

The situation is even worse. Because the increasing population needs more food and fuel, more land must be farmed. This is obtained by cutting down forest and by using steeper slopes than were used before. The increased demand for wood as fuel causes deforestation. Deforestation robs the soil of its protective cover of vegetation. It can then be eroded by being blown or washed away. Deforestation also causes the land to lose moisture so the climate becomes drier. In 1880 about 44% of Ethiopia was forested. The forested area is now only 4%. This huge reduction in forest is mainly the result of the increasing need for food and fuel. Another result of deforestation and farming steep slopes is serious soil erosion. It is estimated that soil forms 15% of the volume of rivers flowing from Ethiopia. Once soil is eroded it takes hundreds of years to replace it naturally.

Climate   The climate in Ethiopia appears to have changed. This may have happened because of deforestation. When trees are cut there is more run-off to rivers and the sea. Less water gets into the ground and less evaporates back into the atmosphere so the climate becomes drier. In the 1970s and 1980s Ethiopia suffered severe droughts especially in the north close to the Sahara Desert. Some scientists think these droughts are proof that the Earth's climate is changing due to the increase in the emission of greenhouse gases. Others argue that the cause of climate change is more local, caused by people deforesting the land. Some argue that in the absence of long term statistics it is impossible to be sure that the changes are permanent and not just part of some climate cycle. Most people would agree though that the desertification affecting Ethiopia has been helped by human interference in the environment.

Severe droughts between 1982 and 1985 greatly reduced the food supply in northern Ethiopia. About 1 million poor people died during the worst of the drought. Whatever chance the poor have of surviving one drought by selling possessions to buy food, they have little chance of surviving a series of droughts. To blame the Ethiopian famine disaster on the drought is too simple. Poverty was its main cause. Droughts are not confined to Third World countries. They happen in many areas. For instance, there have been severe droughts in the United States in recent years but they have not caused famine because most people have some wealth which they can fall back on. The government, too, is wealthy enough to give grants of money and assistance to help overcome people's problems.

ACTIVITY 2

1. Explain how the population of Ethiopia is likely to change over the next twenty years.
2. What is deforestation? What caused it in Ethiopia?
3. What are the effects of deforestation on the environment?

INEQUALITY AND DEVELOPMENT 2

WAR AND GLOBAL CONFLICT

Ethiopia is one of the most war-torn countries in the world. It has a strategic location at the mouth of the Red Sea controlling entry to the Suez Canal. As a result the superpowers, the USA and Russia, took a keen interest in it. Each wished to have influence in the Horn of Africa so that the other would not be able to control it. Control would permit the disruption of world trade as so much passes through the canal on its way to or from Europe. The superpowers interfered by supplying countries in the area with weapons and aid. Ethiopia was supported by Russia and so received little aid from the USA or Europe. Unfortunately for Ethiopia, Russia's aid mainly took the form of weapons and military advisers. Ethiopia ran up large debts as it armed to defend itself from the threat of invasion. In 1978 Ethiopia was invaded by Somalia and had to fight a war to drive the invaders out.

Ethiopia also had internal problems. Within its borders there were rebel groups prepared to fight for their independence. The largest groups were in the provinces of Tigre and Eritrea. Civil war eventually broke out and was made more serious because of the armaments already in the country due to the international situation. The fighting disrupted development work and diverted money from it. It also damaged the infrastructure, such as roads, and interfered with food production. It did much to keep Ethiopia very poor.

ACTIVITY 3

1. Explain three reasons why Ethiopia is so war-torn.
2. Examine the table in 24.2 then do the following:

	Military Expenditure as % of GDP	Number of Servicemen per teacher	per doctor
Ireland	1.4	0.3	0.9
Brazil	1.7	0.2	2.0
Ethiopia	13.5	4.8	548.0
Saudi Arabia	14.0	0.4	4.0
United Kingdom	4.2	1.5	9.2

Fig 24.2

(a) Rank the countries in order of the percentage of GDP they spend on their military. Number 1 is the country which spends the highest percentage.
(b) Which European country in the table has the largest number of soldiers per doctor? Suggest a reason for this.
(c) Which Third World country has the largest number of soldiers per doctor? Suggest two reasons for this.
3. Using the statistics in figures 24.2 and 24.3 suggest how Ethiopia's military expenditure affects the standard of living.

Although Ethiopia's level of development is low, progress has been made over the last thirty years as the statistics in figure 24.3 show. Examine them carefully before you read on.

	1960	1991
Life Expectancy at birth	36	49
Infant Mortality per 1000 births	175	122
GDP per capita	$262	$370

Fig 24.3

You can see that over the thirty year period life expectancy improved and infant mortality fell. Both these changes show that there was progress. GDP per capita also rose from $262 to $370 indicating an increase in income. But there is still a long way to go before Ethiopians have a satisfactory standard of living.

THE MOST UNEQUAL OF ALL: THE STATUS OF WOMEN IN THE DEVELOPING WORLD

In the developed world women have not yet achieved equal status with men. In developing countries the situation is worse. The information in the table in figure 24.4 illustrates how the status of women in Sweden, a wealthy developed country, contrasts with their status in Bangladesh, a poor developing country.

SWEDEN	BANGLADESH
Female life expectancy 78 yrs.	Female life expectancy 49.
One in 167 girls dies before the age of five.	One in 5 girls dies before the age of five.
Women bear 1 to 2 children on average.	Women bear 5 to 6 children on average.
Nearly all school-aged girls in school.	One in three school-aged girls are in school.
About half the secondary school teachers are women.	One in ten secondary school teachers are women.
60% of women are in paid labour force.	6.6% of women are in paid labour force.
2 out of 5 women are professionals.	3 out of 1,000 women are professionals.
Women live on average 7 years longer than men.	Women live on average 2 years less than men.
In 1988 women held 113 seats in the 349 seat parliament.	In 1988 women held 4 seats in the 302 seat parliament.

Fig 24.4

INEQUALITY AND DEVELOPMENT 2

ACTIVITY 4

1. Form groups of three or four in class. Discuss in your group some of the differences you would experience as a Swedish woman and as a Bangladeshi woman.
2. Imagine that you are a woman in Sweden or Bangladesh. Using the information in figure 24.4 and your discussion in class to help you, write a description of your life. In it refer to your family, work and recreation.

The life of most women in developing countries is hard but it is changing. In many places women have organised themselves into groups to help one another and to improve their situation. Study the photograph in figure 24.5. What evidence is there in it that women in developing countries are improving their quality of life?

Fig 24.5

WOMEN IN CHINA

Until China became a communist country in 1949 women were very inferior and had few rights. They couldn't take part in politics or education. They weren't allowed own property or land. After 1949 their situation improved quickly. In 1953 men and women were given the right to vote and stand for election. Before 1949, 90% of Chinese women were illiterate. In 1952 a campaign was launched to end illiteracy. Before 1949 women were forbidden to work outside the home. Today women make up 44% of the labour force and 72% of women over 15 are in the labour force. Although the principal of equal pay for equal work is agreed by the government, it has not been achieved yet. In manufacturing the average wage for women is about three-quarters the average wage for men. In agriculture it is a little higher at 81%.

Since the 1970s China has become more open to the outside world. It has developed its export industries and is a rapidly industrialising country. In this women have played a major role and as in Europe they have been particularly successful as entrepreneurs. Important Chinese exports are tea and textiles such as silk and knitwear. These are the big earners of foreign money. The vast majority of the workers in these industries are women. Women are often the entrepreneurs who started them.

ACTIVITY 5

1. Describe how the status of Chinese women has changed since 1949.
2. Compare the role of Chinese women in their society with the role of Irish women in ours. Use statistics where possible. (When answering, revise pages 277/279)

AID AND INEQUALITY

Many believe that giving money and resources will reduce the inequality between the North and South. Such giving is called **aid**. Aid takes many forms. It can involve the transfer of food, money, and equipment of all kinds. Skilled workers like nurses, doctors, engineers, even lawyers may go to where aid is needed. Volunteer workers may give their services to help. Some aid is given quite freely, without any conditions attached at all. Other aid may be tied to strict conditions about how it is to be used and what the recipient has to do to receive it.

When there is a crisis, such as a famine or flood, supplies of food, medicines and tents may be needed to save life. This kind of aid is called **emergency aid**. An example was the aid sent to Rwanda and its neighbours during the civil war of 1994. There is **development aid**. This is help given to improve agriculture, industry, infrastructure or services in an area. It may supply technology and skills, or provide all that is needed for a major project of irrigation, power generation or manufacture. The Aswan Dam project on the Nile provided by Russia to Egypt is an example of this kind of development aid. The structural funds Ireland gets from the EU may be considered to be development aid.

Those who give aid are called **donors**. The people who receive it are **recipients.** A donor may be a government or an international organisation like the United Nations or the EU. A donor may also be a **non-governmental organisation** such as Trócaire, Oxfam or Concern. These are called **NGO**s for short. An NGO is usually a charity which raises money to help development in the Third World.

INEQUALITY AND DEVELOPMENT 2

Aid – For and Against People have different views about aid. In particular there is disagreement about its usefulness as a way to reduce global inequality. A number of different opinions about aid are given below. Study them and then discuss them in class. Decide which of the opinions support aid as a positive force for development and which argue that aid is a negative force.

A. Giving aid makes donors feel superior to recipients.
B. Emergency aid saves people from dying in times of crisis.
C. Aid gives people in the North a chance to show concern for and solidarity with poorer people in the South.
D. Aid takes from the rich and gives to the poor. This helps to narrow the wealth gap between North and South.
E. Aid makes the South depend more on the North than on itself.
F. Aid from government to government often fails to reach the poorest people in a country.
G. Aid distracts attention from important issues such as unfair international trade and debt.
H. Aid often has conditions attached to it such as the recipient country having to buy goods from the donor country or employ its experts.
I. Aid makes the knowledge and skills of the North available to the South.
J. Aid helps prevent improvement by keeping the South dependent on the North.
K. Aid to governments helps them to provide the infrastructure needed for development.
L. Aid builds links between countries which helps them understand one another better.

ACTIVITY 6

1. What is aid? Use examples in your explanation.
2. What are the differences between each of these pairs?
   emergency aid / development aid   aid donor / aid recipient
3. Write three paragraphs about the advantages and disadvantages of aid.

IRISH AID

Ireland is both a donor and a recipient of aid. Ireland donates aid to the South and receives it from the EU. Irish aid for the Third World comes from two sources: the government and the NGOs. The aid from the government is called **Official Development Assistance** or **ODA** for short. ODA consists of emergency aid, development aid and money spent on educating Irish people about development issues. In 1993 ODA spending amounted to £55 million. NGOs such as Trócaire also send aid to the South but their total aid is much smaller than the ODA total. Because they have less money and because they believe to do so is more effective, the NGOs tend to assist small inexpensive projects which aim to improve the lives of the very poor, while ODA aid can assist bigger projects such as providing irrigation schemes.

The 'Aid League' The United Nations has asked the developed nations to donate 0.7% of their GNP to development assistance. The graph in figure 24.6 shows the percentage of GNP donated by a number of countries.

ACTIVITY 7

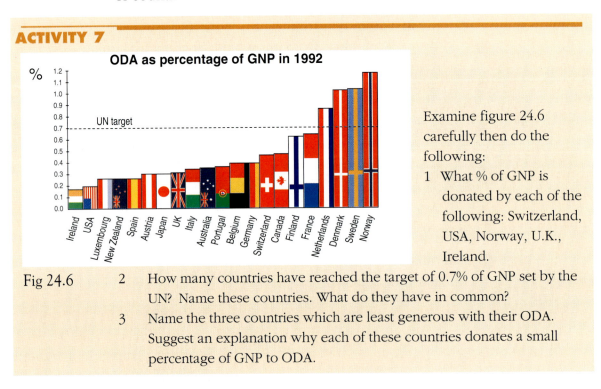

Fig 24.6

Examine figure 24.6 carefully then do the following:

1. What % of GNP is donated by each of the following: Switzerland, USA, Norway, U.K., Ireland.
2. How many countries have reached the target of 0.7% of GNP set by the UN? Name these countries. What do they have in common?
3. Name the three countries which are least generous with their ODA. Suggest an explanation why each of these countries donates a small percentage of GNP to ODA.

Ireland's ODA was 0.25% of GNP in 1994. The government has committed itself to increase Official Development Assistance to 0.4% by 1997. This is a large increase in such a short time but it will still leave us far behind the Scandinavian countries which all exceed the UN target. It is also intended as part of the government plan to increase the number of Irish people working in the Third World from 450 in 1992 to 2000 by 1997. About half of Ireland's ODA goes to large international institutions

INEQUALITY AND DEVELOPMENT 2

such as the EU and the United Nations which combine it with the contributions of other member countries to fund large projects in the South. The other half of Ireland's ODA goes mainly to six countries in Africa. These are called priority countries as they are the ones to get assistance first. The map in figure 24.7 shows the location of the priority countries for Irish Aid. It also gives information about the country and the types of project being assisted.

ACTIVITY 8

1. Study the map in figure 24.7. Then write a description of each of the priority countries and the aid it receives.
2. Using the information in figure 24.7 and the opinions about aid on page 341, discuss this statement with another student.
   'Irish aid is of little use to the priority countries.'
   Prepare together three arguments for or against it.
3. Does Ireland benefit from the ODA it donates to other countries? Explain your answer.

A major fear in Third World countries at present is that aid may be switched from them to the new states in Eastern Europe and the CIS. This is a very real fear as the EU and the USA are committed to providing aid to these states. This could mean less aid for the Third World. Any reduction in aid would severely hurt the most underdeveloped countries such as Ethiopia, Rwanda and Tanzania.

RESOLVING GLOBAL INEQUALITY

There is little agreement on how inequality in the world should be tackled. The opinions of people in the North on this issue are often very different to those of people in the South. A number of different opinions are given in below. Study each one carefully.

A "Global inequality will never be solved by emergency aid as this only tackles the effects of inequality not its causes. Dealing with the causes needs support for long-term development, the cost of which needs the backing of many governments."

THE GEOGRAPHER'S WAY 2

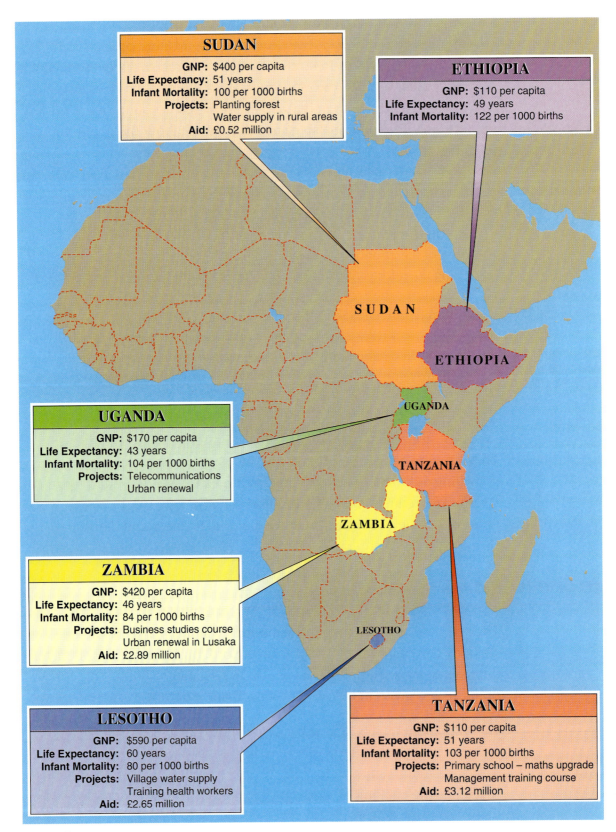

Fig 24.7

B "The road to equality lies through industrialisation. The South should develop manufacturing industries producing products for export. The exports will earn money which can be invested in new firms. Incomes in manufacturing are higher than in agriculture. As people spend these higher incomes the benefits of industrialisation trickle down to the poorest so everybody benefits from industrialisation."

C "The arms-producing countries in the North should stop selling arms to the South. The United Nations should do their best to solve disputes between countries peacefully. This would mean less spent on arms and armies and more spent on education, health and developing agriculture."

D "Before economic development is attempted everybody's basic human need for food, water and shelter should be met. This means investing in food crops and providing clean water and proper housing. Only when these basic needs have been satisfied can real development take place."

E "People in the North should educate themselves about the real causes of inequality such as colonialism, unfair international trade, the burden of debt, politics and war. When they understand the contribution the North makes to global inequality, then they will be better able to decide what they can do to reduce it."

F "People in the South have too many children and this causes poverty. The North should finance family planning education to reduce the birth rate in the South. Controlling population growth would reduce poverty and pressure on resources."

G "There are plenty of resources in the world to feed everybody and give people a reasonable standard of living. The problem is that most of the resources are controlled by the North and it is unwilling to share them fairly with the South."

THE GEOGRAPHER'S WAY 2

ACTIVITY 9

1. Decide which of these opinions about resolving inequality are likely to be expressed by people in the South. Explain your decision.
2. Choose the four opinions which you think are most likely, if implemented, to reduce global inequality.
3. Make out three arguments for and three arguments against the following statement:

    'The North is mainly to blame for global inequality.'

    Then debate the statement with other members of your class.

Fig 24.8

In the North people often think of poverty in the South as being caused from inside the area itself. For example, they quote over-population, ignorance, poor government, natural disasters such as drought and floods, as the causes of underdevelopment. In the South people look much more to external causes such as debt, trade and the legacy of colonialism.

The cartoon in figure 24.8 shows a view of the North from the South. What is its message? Is it justified?

INEQUALITY AND DEVELOPMENT 2

REVISION

Rewrite the following text into your copy using the words in the box to fill in the blank spaces.

NGO's	emergency aid	donors	development aid
recipients	ODA	non-governmental organisations	
aid	official development assistance		

Money and resources given to other countries to help them is called _____. Food, medicines and tents sent to another country when they have a crisis is called _____ _____. Money and expertise given to set up irrigation schemes or improve agriculture is called _____ _____. The _____ are the people who give aid. The _____ are the people who receive aid. Agencies such as Trócaire, Oxfam and concern are called _____ _____ or for short _____. The aid given by governments is called _____ _____ _____ or _____ for short.

25 Map and Photograph Section

In this section you extend the study of aerial photographs and OS maps and apply ideas you have learned when using them. You begin with a study of Bray using an aerial photograph and an OS map.

A STUDY OF BRAY

The aerial photograph in figure 25.1 is a vertical one. Certain features have been drawn in to help you interpret it: the railway station, the golf course and the R766 road. There is also a compass arrow to show 'north'. These can be used to locate features. For example, locate point A on the photograph by saying 'It is north of the railway station and east of the golf course.'

ACTIVITY 1

Photograph study

Examine the photograph in figure 25.1 then do the following:

1. Match the letters on the photograph with the features listed below:

Feature	Letter
bridge	
park	
harbour	
beach	
playing pitch	

2. Draw a sketch map of the photograph. Show on it:
   coastline, harbour, railway line, R766 road.

3. You want to open an amusement arcade in Bray. What location would you choose? Mark your chosen location on the sketch map with the letter D. Explain why you chose this location.

4. Using two pieces of evidence from the photograph, explain how people have changed this coastline.

5. Locate two pieces of evidence that the season is summer.

6. Find the letters X,Y,Z on the photograph. The land use at each location is different. Giving a reason for your choice in each case, decide which of the following land uses is found at each location:
   residential   educational   commercial

MAP AND PHOTOGRAPH SECTION

7 There is a small industrial estate at M. What are the advantages and disadvantages of this location for manufacturing industry?

Fig 25.1

THE GEOGRAPHER'S WAY 2

Map Study   Study figure 25.2 and answer the following questions.

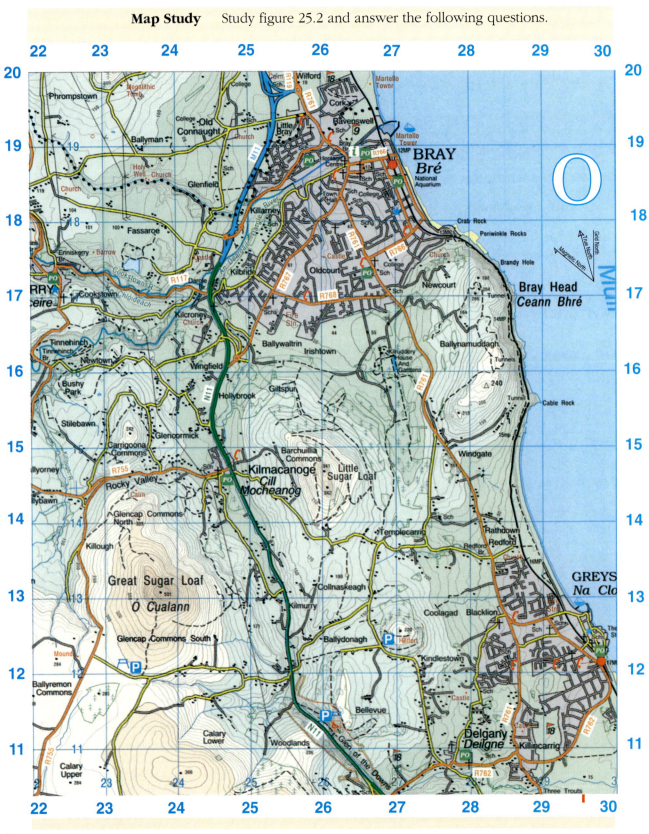

Fig 25.2

8 What is the scale of the map?
9 Match the grid references in column X with the number of its matching feature in column Y

X		Y	
A	0 238 131	1	post office
B	0 266 173	2	castle
C	0 243 175	3	cliff
D	0 243 172	4	confluence
E	0 289 156	5	summit of Great Sugar Loaf

A	
B	
C	
D	
E	

10 Give grid references for each of the following points:
Bray railway station   Bray fire station
Junction of the N11 and R117   Summit of the Little Sugar Loaf
Bray 9-hole golf course

11 Draw a sketch map of the Bray map and on it show:
land over 100m   national primary and regional roads
two named rivers   Bray urban area
a beach

12 List and give grid references for five tourist attractions.
13 What is the total length of dual carriageway on the map?
14 Identify the river features at each of the following locations. Then match the features in column X with the number of its grid references in column Y.

X		Y
A	V-shaped valley	0 228 126
B	flood Plain	0 251 179
C	bluffline	0 223 163
D	meander	0 225 164
E	interlocking spurs	0 240 118

A	
B	
C	
D	
E	

15 Give location references for the following features (a) on the photograph: (b) on the OS map:
railway bridge; The National Aquarium; level crossing on the R766.

BRAY

Bray is located on the coastal plain which lies between the Wicklow Mountains and the sea. To the south of the town there is a ridge of upland running from SW to NE.

Bray began as a Norman settlement. The Normans chose this location for strategic reasons. The coastal plain had fertile land which they wanted to control and farm. It was also on the natural routeway from Dublin, the centre of Norman power in Ireland, to other important Norman towns such as Wexford. This routeway survives as the R119 and R761 regional roads. Notice how this route enters Bray from the coastal plain to the north, crosses the river at the lowest bridging point and takes advantage of the col at Windgate (0 276 150) between Bray Head and the Little Sugar Loaf. Much later a new inland route was built to take advantage of the lower ground between the Little Sugar Loaf and the Great Sugar Loaf and the Glen of the Downs. This route is now the main route followed by the N11 from Dublin to Wexford.

The crossing point on the Dargle was the most strategic point on the old routeway. If the Normans didn't control this they couldn't move their troops north and south and so couldn't control the area. It was for this reason that they settled here, building a castle to protect the crossing point. The river also provided power for a water mill and a supply of fish. The site the Normans chose was on top of the bluff line overlooking the crossing point and the flood plain close to where the heritage centre and Bray Bridge are today. The Norman core of Bray can still be

traced as there are the remains of a castle, mill and church in a small cluster beside the bridge. The church in the photograph in figure 25.3 marks the location of the original Norman settlement.

The coming of the railway Bray remained a small market town and grew little until the railway was built. In 1854 Bray was linked to Dublin by rail. This link still plays an important part in the town's development. The coming of the railway caused Bray to start growing. The land between the main street R761 and the coast was developed as a residential area. Tourist facilities such as hotels, guest houses and baths were constructed and the promenade was built and laid out as a park known as The Esplanade. A sea wall, a mile long, was built to protect the Esplanade and to provide a comfortable walkway for visitors. This is known as The Promenade. Bray became an ideal base from which to tour the Wicklow Mountains. It also began to develop as a dormitory town for Dublin.

Changing functions Bray continued as a busy tourist resort until the 1960's when cheap holidays abroad created strong competition. But its gradual decline as a resort was balanced by growth as a dormitory town. The mile posts (MP) on the railway line show that it is 12 miles (19.2km) south of Dublin. This is a short journey especially since the introduction of the Dart electric service in 1984. The Dart journey to Dublin provides comfortable stress-free travel taking only half an hour. It allows people to live in pleasant surroundings close to mountains and sea and yet be able to work in Dublin. As Bray grew, many housing estates were built, especially to the south and south-west of the town, with new residential areas at Old Court, Ballywaltrim and on Killarney Road.

Bray already had a few industries. The number of these increased, to include high-technology ones, such as printing and Dell Computers. The industrial zone lies on the southern edge of the town along the Boghall Road R768. This location is suitable as there is flat land for building factories. There is local labour and the communications links with Dublin and Rosslare by road and rail are good. A new road is being built to the south of the R768 to feed traffic from the south of Bray onto the N11 dual carriageway at Wingfield (0 246 161).

Communications in the Bray area have improved with the opening of the Bray bypass in 1992, the motorway section of the N11. Before this the N11 passed through Little Bray to the north of the Dargle. This created severe traffic congestion and increased journey time between Dublin and Rosslare. The EU provided the funds for this improvement of the communications infrastructure. This project is part of the scheme to make Ireland, Belfast and the capital more accessible to Europe via Rosslare.

ACTIVITY 2

1. Using evidence from the map explain why the Normans chose Bray as a location for a settlement.
2. Fill in the following on the sketch map you drew of the map in figure 25.2. See Activity 1.11, page 351.
   the Norman core
   a nineteenth century residential zone
   a recently-built residential zone
   the main commercial zone
   an industrial zone
3. Fill in the following on the sketch map you drew of the aerial photograph in figure 25.1. See Activity 1.2, page 348.
   the esplanade
   a nineteenth century residential zone
   the Norman core
   a commercial zone
4. Three different views of Bray are given in this section: a vertical aerial photograph, an OS map and a ground level photograph. Compare and contrast the usefulness of each. If you were asked to provide information about Bray to an engineer, a map maker and a travel agent which view would you give each of them?
5. With the help of a sketch map explain the development of Bray from Norman settlement to modern dormitory town.

A STUDY OF CARRICK-ON-SUIR

Bray was founded as a defensive settlement and only developed when it acquired other functions. Carrick-on-Suir's beginnings are the same as Bray's but its development is due largely to it being a nodal point in a fertile agricultural region. It grew as a market town where local farmers sold their produce and bought supplies of tools, seeds, fertilisers and the consumer goods they needed.

ACTIVITY 3

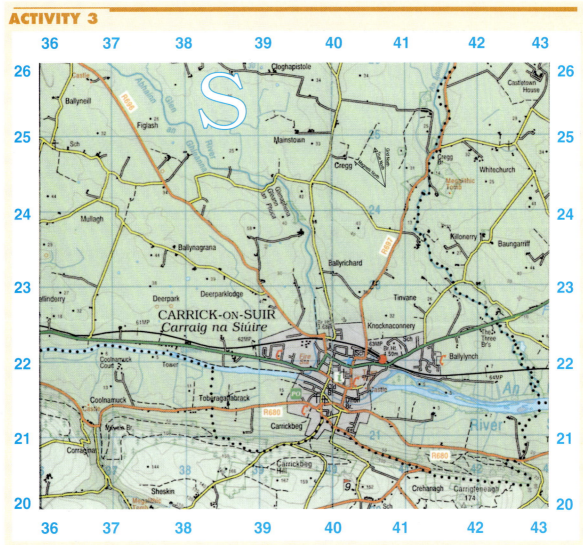

Fig 25.4

Study the map of Carrick-on-Suir, figure 25.4. Then do the following:

1. What river is the town on?
2. What does the Irish word 'carraig' mean? This word gives a clue to the origin of the town. What is the clue?
3. What evidence is there that Carrick-on-Suir was a Norman town?
4. Give all the reasons you can why the Normans considered Carrick-on-Suir a good location for a settlement.
5. Is the river at Carrick-on-Suir tidal? Give the evidence.
6. Is the pattern of rural settlement in the north of the map mainly linear, dispersed or nucleated? What does this suggest about the size of farms in the area?
7. What evidence is there that Carrick-on-Suir is an important nodal point. How would this have influenced the development of the town?
8. Describe the distribution of forestry on the map. Give two reasons for this distribution.

THE GEOGRAPHER'S WAY 2

A STUDY OF TRAMORE

Tramore which is the Irish for 'big strand' is similar to Bray in that it developed as a resort town in the nineteenth century when it was linked to Waterford city by railway. It also developed recently as a dormitory town for the growing industrial city of Waterford.

ACTIVITY 4

Fig 25.5

MAP AND PHOTOGRAPH SECTION

1. Study the aerial photograph of Tramore in figure 25.5 then:
   (a) Match the letters on the map with the features below:

Feature	Letter on photograph
beach	
race course	
pleasure lake	
golf course	
church	

   (b) Draw a sketch map of the photograph. On it show: the beach, the R675 and R682 roads, a farmed area, amusements, a modern housing estate, two caravan parks, a golf course.

2. What is the view in the photograph of Tramore figure 25.5? How should references to features in the photograph be given?

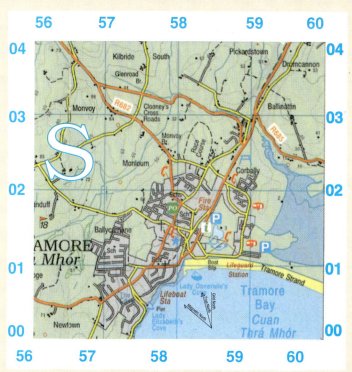

Fig 25.6

3. Examine the map of the Tramore area in figure 25.6 then do the following:
   (a) List the tourist attractions at each of the following points on the map:

   S 590 013   S 598 008
   S 585 016   S 582 025
   S 561 015

   (b) Draw a sketch map of the Tramore area. On it show: the coastline, the regional road network, the built-up area, a recreation area
   (c) On your sketch map mark in the area shown on the photograph.

4. Most of the new residential settlement has developed to the south and west of the town avoiding the east. Using evidence from the map suggest reasons for this.

5. If you were going to open an all-weather sports facility, where would you locate it? Identify the location with a grid reference. Give three reasons for your choice.

THE GEOGRAPHER'S WAY 2

A STUDY OF BLESSINGTON

Blessington is an estate village in West Wicklow built by the local landlord in the eighteenth century. It is situated close to the shore of the Poulaphouca reservoir. Recently it has become popular with commuters who wish to live in an unpolluted countryside and are able to afford the cost of commuting to Dublin.

ACTIVITY 5

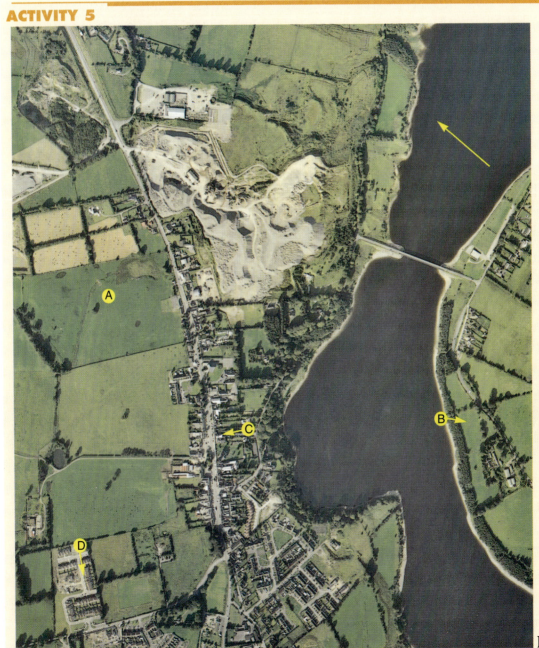

Fig 25.7

MAP AND PHOTOGRAPH SECTION

1. Examine the aerial photograph in figure 25.7 then do the following:
   (a) Name the land uses at points on the photograph A, B, C, D.
   (b) Identify and give the location of the primary industries for which there is evidence on the photograph.
   (c) What kinds of farming are there in the Blessington area? Support your answer with evidence from the photograph.
   (d) Blessington was planned and built by the local landlord. Search carefully for evidence of this in the photograph.
   (e) Suggest why woodland is found mainly on the edge of the reservoir.

Fig 25.8

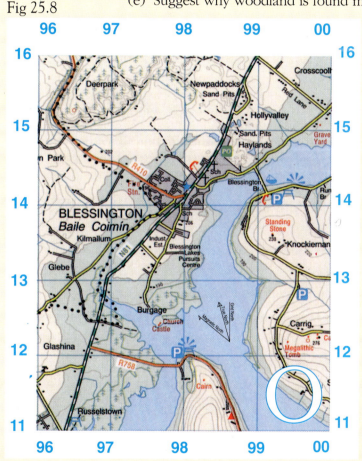

2. Examine the map of Blessington in figure 25.8 then do the following:
   (a) Draw a sketch map of Blessington. On it show: the reservoir, the national secondary and regional roads, the built-up area, land over 200 metres, a forest.
   (b) What evidence is there on the map to suggest that Blessington is a nodal point?
   (c) Describe the routeway of the R410 road, and explain how it is influenced by relief.
   (d) Give a grid reference for Blessington's industrial estate. List the advantages and disadvantages of this location for manufacturing.
   (e) On your sketch map mark in the area shown in the aerial photograph.

SCALE

The OS maps you have used so far have all had the same scale, except the map of Maynooth. The **scale** of a map is the amount by which all the measurements on it have been reduced. On the OS maps you have studied the amount of reduction is 50,000 times. The scale is stated as a ratio 1: 50,000. This means one unit of measurement on the map represents 50,000 units of measurement on the ground. In other words

1 centimetre on the map represents 50,0000 centimetres on the ground. Because 50,000 centimetres is 500 metres or half a kilometre, 2 centimetres on the map represent one kilometre on the ground. These are useful facts to remember about the 1:50,000 map:
- 1 centimetre represents half a kilometre
- 2 centimetres represent one kilometre

If you look up the scale ratios on your atlas maps, you will find that the ratios are about 1:70,000,000 on maps of the world which spread across two pages. This means that all the measurements have been reduced by about 70 million times. This amount of reduction means it is impossible to give any detail. As the amount of reduction increases the amount of detail decreases.

The 1:50,000 OS maps which you have been using represent the natural and cultural landscape in good detail. When you know how to interpret them you can identify natural and cultural features quite easily. These maps are at an ideal scale for studying landscapes which is why geographers use them so much.

Other OS Maps The OS produces maps at other scales. They publish a map of the Aran Islands at a scale of 1:25,000. This allows more detail to be shown and makes the map easier to read. The OS also produces maps at a scale of 1:1,000. This means every measurement is reduced only 1,000 times. As the reduction is so small on these maps the amount of detail given is very great. These are known as **large scale maps**. They are only published for the major towns. They include the large amount of detailed information needed by engineers, builders, lawyers and planners working in such a congested environment. We will study an example of each of these maps.

INISHMORE: OS MAPS 1:25,000 SCALE

The Aran Islands are three limestone plateaus which jut out of the Atlantic at the mouth of Galway Bay. The landscape is like the Burren with limestone pavements and no surface drainage. It is a difficult environment in which to make a living because there is little soil. Most of the soil there had to be gathered from the grikes and carefully placed on layers of sand and seaweed carried from the shore. Most fields in Aran were made in this way. Nowadays many people have turned to fishing and tourism as easier ways to make a living.

MAP AND PHOTOGRAPH SECTION

ACTIVITY 6

1. Examine the aerial photograph in figure 25.10 which shows part of Inishmore, the largest of the Aran Islands.

   (a) Match the letters with the features listed below:

Feature	Letter on Photograph
island	
shallow water	
sand spit	
lagoon	
headland	
sea stack	
limestone pavement	
flat rocks	
beach	
wave-cut platform	
airstrip	

   (b) Draw a sketch map of the photograph. On it show: the coastline, limestone pavement, an area of fields, sand dunes, a line of settlement.

   (c) Suggest a reason why there are features of coastal erosion on the south side of the island and features of coastal deposition on the north side.

   (d) Suggest reasons why the fields and settlements are mainly on the north side of the island.

2. Locate the following in the photograph without making reference to letters printed on it: a pier, a village, a boat.

Measuring distance and area

The map in figure 25.11 is a 1:25,000 map of the area shown in the photograph. At this scale 1 centimetre on the map represents 25,000 centimetres on the ground. As 25,000 centimetres is a quarter of a kilometre, 4 centimetres on the map represent 1 kilometre.

As the scale of this map is larger, each grid box is also larger. It can be divided as shown in figure 25.9. The scale line on this kind of map is also different to that used on the 1:50,000 maps, so examine it carefully.

To get your grid references accurately, copy the grid in figure 25.9 onto a sheet of tracing paper and use it as shown on page 227 of Book One.

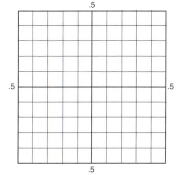

Fig 25.9

THE GEOGRAPHER'S WAY 2

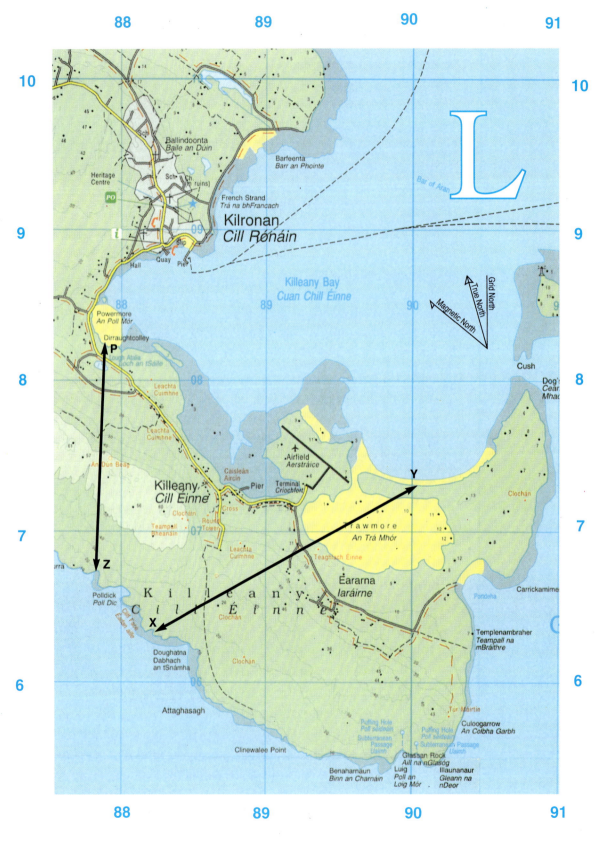

Fig 25.10

MAP AND PHOTOGRAPH SECTION

Fig 25.11

THE GEOGRAPHER'S WAY 2

ACTIVITY 7

1. Using the method suggested give grid references from the map of Inishmore figure 25.11 for:

   the lighthouse on Straw Island

   An Dún Beag

   the Garda Station in Kilronan

2. (a) Measure the length of the airstrip in kilometres.

   (b) Measure the length of the third class road shown on the map.

3. What is the height of An Dún Beag?

4. Locate the highest point on the map, using a grid reference. Give its height.

5. What is the area in km² of the land shown on the map? To revise the measurement of area on OS maps, see Book One pages 232 and 233.

HOW TO DRAW A CROSS-SECTION

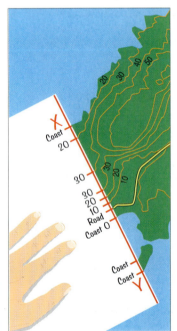

Fig 25.12

A cross-section gives an elevation view of the landscape between two points. It shows the height of the land and gives a good idea of its landforms and slopes. To revise cross sections, see pages 198/199 and page 221 in Book One. Drawing a cross-section converts the plan view along a line drawn across the landscape into the elevation view along that line. It is a very useful skill to know how to do. An example of how to draw a cross-section is given for the red line drawn between the points X and Y on the map of Inishmore. Follow these steps:

- Lay a straight edge of paper along the cross-section line. Mark the ends of the section line clearly as shown in figure 25.12.
- Put a tick on the edge of the sheet at each point a contour crosses it. Also mark any feature it crosses. In this case the road and coastlines are marked.
- Note the height of each contour which crosses the edge of the sheet as shown in the diagram.
- Transfer the line to a sheet of graph paper as shown in figure 25.13, plotting in the marks of contours and features.
- Draw in a vertical scale line. In this case let 2mm represent 10 metres in height. Don't make the vertical scale too large or the landscape will look unnatural. You now have the horizontal and vertical axes for a line graph.

MAP AND PHOTOGRAPH SECTION

- Plot the points as you would for any line or trend graph. A glance at the profile of the River Liffey on page 36 will help you to understand what you are doing. Mark in the features you noted on the line you have graphed.
- Annotate the cross section as shown.

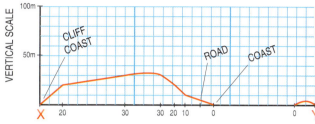

Fig 25.13

The cross-section in figure 25.13 gives an elevation view of Inishmore between X and Y. The south-western side of the island at X has a steep cliff coastline where erosion is eating into the limestone. The land rises gently to a summit between 30 and 40 metres. It then slopes steeply down to a narrow coastal plain. The road follows this plain as this is the location of most of the houses and fields. The houses and fields are located on this side of the island as it is sheltered from the prevailing south-west wind. From the coastal plain the cross-section runs across Tramore where there is a lagoon. The lagoon is formed behind the sand spit located at Y.

ACTIVITY 8

1. Draw a cross-section along the line ZP on the map in figure 25.11.
2. Describe the distribution of settlement on the map of Inishmore.
3. What has this part of Inishmore to offer the tourist?
4. Identify at least two antiquities on the map, figure 25.11.
5. Compare and contrast the north and south coasts of Inishmore.

TOWN PLANS

The largest scale OS maps are the 1:1,000 town plans. Measurements on these maps have only been reduced a thousand times. This means that 1 centimetre on the map represents 1,000 centimetres or 10 metres on the ground. As the reduction is small, much more detail can be given. These maps show a much smaller area of ground than the 1:25,000 and 1:50,000 OS maps.

The map in figure 25.14 is taken from a 1:1,000 town plan. Examine it carefully paying particular attention to the legend. The shaded features on the map represent buildings.

ABBREVIATIONS

Boundary Stone	BS	Hydrant	H
Chimney	Chy	Lamp Standard	LS
Electricity Station	ES	Manhole(s)	Mh(s)
Flagstaff	FS	Mile Post & Mooring Post	MP
Foot Bridge	FB	Pump	P
Footpath	FP	Sluice	Sl
Fountain	Fn	Spring	Sp
Garda Siochana Station	GS Sta	Telephone Kiosk	TK
Letter Box	LB	Transformer	T
Level Crossing	LC	Trough	Tr
Low Water Mark	LWM	Water Tap	WT
High Water Mark	HWM	Weigh Bridge	WB

SYMBOLS

Antiquities........(Site of)	✛
Archway	⌧
Bench Mark	↑
Surface Level	+
Glass House	◇
Electricity Pole or Pylon	•—
Control Point	⊙

Fig 25.14

MAP AND PHOTOGRAPH SECTION

ACTIVITY 9

Examine the map in figure 25.14 then do the following:

1. What do the following abbreviations on a 1:1,000 map mean?
   Mh   LS   TK   H   GS   FP   ES

2. Height is shown on these maps by spot heights which include bench marks and surface levels. Bench marks give the height to two places of decimals. Bench marks are shown on the map by the symbol (↑) and a corresponding mark can be found carved on walls and gateposts in the landscape. They were put there to help builders and map makers to get the altitude of places accurately. Surface levels appear on maps only. They are shown by the symbol (+).

   If a person walked northwards along York Road, would they be walking uphill or downhill? By how many metres would the height have changed?

3. Contrast the houses in Barrett Street with the houses in the south-west corner of the map.

4. Identify three different types of land use on this map.

5. Does the area on the map belong to any of the following functional zones? Give reasons for your answer.
   CBD, transition zone, residential zone, industrial zone

The area is in the zone of transition close to the CBD. In the north of the map the housing is old and the houses have no front or back gardens. Factories are squeezed in between the houses in small cramped sites. This is the pattern to be expected in a zone of transition. It is likely that the area will go through a process of renewal as the older houses are replaced by new ones and the factories move to less cramped sites in the suburbs.

The 1:1,000 map is ideal for doing urban fieldwork. Plotting the land use along a street in the CBD of your town or city makes a simple, interesting field study. By doing this you may be able to define the boundary of the CBD or confirm whether an area is in fact the CBD.

Index

abrasion, 35, 51, 69
accessibility, 149, 175, 286
acid rain, 281-83, 240-241
administrative centre, 146
age/sex structure, 207-211
agents of erosion, 22
aid, 340, 341, 342
air pressure maps, 111-113
air pressure, 100
air-mass, 107-108, 122-124
alluvium, 196
alps, 55
anticyclone, 'high' pressure, 101
arêtes, 52-53
backwash, 76
bar, 79-80
bay, bay head beaches, 67, 68, 71, 76
birth rate, 181
blowholes, 73-74
bluffs, 40, 42, 145
bogbursts, 28
bogs, 223
boreal climate, 125-127, 137
boreal forest, 136
Brazil, 118, 182, 189, 200, 210, 211, 314, 323-325, 327-333
breakers, 67, 69, 76
bridging points, 146, 153
brown earth zonal soil, 136
Burden of Debt, 330
Burren, The, 290-295
capital, 252, 261
cash crop farmers, 134
census, 179
central business district (CBD), 170, 176
climate, 115-129, 131, 140, 295-301, 336
climometer, 31
coastal defences, 81-83
coastal deposition, 76-80
coastal features, 72, 84-85
coastal transportation, 76
coastal types, 67-68
cold front, 108-109, 122-124

colony, colonialism, 200, 321-322
Common Agricultural Policy (CAP), 310
communications, 65, 174, 175
commuters, 162, 166, 353, 356
composite climate graph, 116
constructive waves, 76
convection rainfall, 117
convection, convection currents, 117
cool temperate oceanic climate, 120-122
corries, 52-53
crop rotation, 250
cultivated vegetation, 130
culture, 288
cumulo-nimbus, 109
cut-away bog, 227
daily calorie intake/ requirements, 313
day and night, 94-95
death rate, 181
deltas, 42
denudation, 22
dependent population, 208
deposition, 22, 39-42, 59-64, 76-80
depression, 'low' pressure, 100-101
desertification, 205, 335-336
destructive waves, 76
developed countries, 191, 318
Developing World, 191
development aid, 340
diversify, 255
doldrums, 103-104
donors, 340
dormitory town, 162, 353, 356
drumlins, 61, 62
Earth forces, internal/ external, 5, 22
Earth's axis, 94

Earth's core, 6
Earth's crust, oceanic/ continental, 6, 7
Earth's orbit, 95-98
earthquake, 11
ecological, 227
economic depression, 238
economic development, 318
economic power, 204
economic structure, 318
economically active, 209
economy, 164
effluents, 221
Emerging Industrial Countries, 275
emerging stream, 292
emigration, 185-189
energy, energy resources, 233-246, 234, 236-238
entrepot, 156
entrepreneurs, 259
equatorial climate, 117-119, 131-133
erosion, 22, 35, 52-58, 69-75, 80-83
eskers, 61, 63
Ethiopia, 334-338
European Regional Development Fund (ERDF), 310
European Social Fund (ESF), 310
export led growth, 274
extractive industry, 223
faults, 9
fetch, 67
First World, 191
fishing, 228-231
flood plain, 39-40, 42, 45
fold mountains, 11, 17
fossil fuels, 238
friction, 23
front, 103, 108-110, 122-124
frontal depression, 122-124
fuel resources, 238, 241-242, 243-245

functional zones, 169-173, 176
gap sites, 146
Georgian Dublin, 165-166
geothermal, 10
geysers, 10
glaciated valleys, 54-56
glaciation, lowland, 49, 57-63
glaciation, mountain, 49, 52-57
glaciers, 49-54
global warming, 239-240
gorge, 38, 155
gravity, 23
greenfield site, 149
greenhouse gas, 238-240
Gross domestic Product, (GDP), 308
Gross National Product, (GNP), 311
groynes, 78, 83
Guidance Section of the CAP, 310
hanging valleys, 55
headlands, 67
hectopascals (millibars), 100
heritage, 288
horse latitudes, 103-104
hot desert climate, 119
human response, 136
humidity, 105-106
hunters and gatherers, 133
hydro-electric power (HEP), 46, 64, 235
hygrometer, 106
hypothesis, 13
ice action, 48-66
ice advance, 50
ice sheets, 49
immigration, 187
industrial estate, 261
industrial inertia, 270
industrial zones, 173, 176
industrialisation, 272-285
industry, heavy, 176, 263-265